CliffsTestPrep®

CSET®: Mathematics

by

Enrique Ortiz, Ed.D.
and
Janet B. Andreasen, Ph.D.

Wiley Publishing, Inc.

About the Authors

Enrique Ortiz is an associate professor at the University of Central Florida, Department of Teaching and Learning Principles. Since 1987, he has been very active in the mathematics education profession.

Janet B. Andreasen is an assistant professor in mathematics education at the University of Central Florida. She has taught high school mathematics and college-level mathematics education courses for 8 years.

Publisher's Acknowledgments

Editorial

Acquisitions Editor: Greg Tubach

Project Editor: Suzanne Snyder

Copy Editor: Kelly Henthorne

Technical Editor: Tom Page

Production

Proofreader: Broccoli Information Management

Wiley Publishing, Inc. Composition Services

CliffsTestPrep® CSET®: Mathematics

Published by:
Wiley Publishing, Inc.
111 River Street
Hoboken, NJ 07030-5774
www.wiley.com

Copyright © 2007 Wiley, Hoboken, NJ

Published by Wiley, Hoboken, NJ
Published simultaneously in Canada

Library of Congress Cataloging-in-Publication Data

Ortíz, Enrique.
  CliffsTestPrep CSET : mathematics / by Enrique Ortiz and Janet B. Andreasen.
   p. cm.
  ISBN-13: 978-0-470-13197-8
  ISBN-10: 0-470-13197-7
 1. Mathematics—California—Examinations, questions, etc.—Study guides. 2. Mathematics—Study and teaching—Standards—California. 3. Teaching—California—Examinations—Study guides. 4. Teachers—Certification—Standards—California—Study guides. 5. CSET: Multiple Subjects—Study guides.
I. Andreasen, Janet B. II. Title.
  QA43.O483 2007
  510.76—dc22
                        2007029909
Printed in the United States of America

10 9 8 7 6 5 4 3 2 1

WILEY

Table of Contents

PART II: CSET PRACTICE TESTS

PART III: STUDY AIDS

Introduction

The California Subject Examinations for Teachers (CSET) utilized by the California Department of Education (CDE) is a key element of California's statewide teacher certification program. Besides being a tool to assess and evaluate a beginning teacher's content background, it is one of three ways to meet the state of California's requirements for teacher certification.

This introductory chapter of *CliffsTestPrep CSET: Mathematics* gives you more details about the CSET: Mathematics, as well as provides materials that help get you ready to take this test. The following sections involve expanded details related to the CSET in general followed by sections concerning the CSET: Mathematics in particular. They include:

- Requirements for Teacher Certification in California
- The Goals and Scope of the CSET
- Administration of the CSET
- Important Considerations for this TestPrep Book
- Content Specifications in CSET: Mathematics
- Types of Items
- Scoring Information
- Using the Calculator You're Given
- Test-Taking Strategies

Requirements for Teacher Certification in California

According to the CDE's general information about the CSET program, California has three types of teacher certification credentials:

- Single Subject Teaching Credential
- Multiple Subject Teaching Credential
- Educational Specialist Instruction Credential

A Single Subject Teaching Credential gives you the authority to teach a specific subject in a departmentalized and specialized subject system from Kindergarten to Grade 12, although this type of teaching credential is mostly used in middle (Grades 6 to 8) and secondary schools (Grades 9 to 12). *Departmentalized* means that you are certified to teach only one subject, like mathematics. This type of credential is different from a Multiple Subject Teaching Credential, which gives you the authority to teach all subjects in a self-contained classroom (Kindergarten to Grade 12). This type of credential is mostly used in elementary schools (Kindergarten to Grade 6). Finally, an Educational Specialist Instruction Credential gives you the authority to teach any subject to students from Kindergarten to Grade 12 who have a specific disability or impairment.

According to the CDE guidelines, to earn any of the three teaching credentials (Single Subject, Multiple Subject, and Education Specialist), candidates need to verify their subject matter competency in one of the following stipulated ways:

- Complete a California Commission on Teacher Credentialing (CCTC)-approved subject matter preparation program.
- Take and pass the appropriate subject matter examination or examinations.
- If trained in a state other than California, provide verification of appropriate experience or education.

The Goals and Scope of the CSET

The CCTC has developed a new series of subject matter examinations, including mathematics, for prospective teachers who choose to meet the subject matter competence requirement for certification by taking examinations (2006). New examinations have been developed to match the recently revised K–12 California Student Academic Content Standards. The new and revised CSET replaces the examinations used before (Single Subject Assessment for Teaching and Praxis II tests) as the CCTC-approved subject matter examinations.

According to the CDE, the CCTC, National Evaluation System Inc. (NES), and California educators worked very closely to design the CSET program using the following goals as guidelines:

- "To develop tests specifically for credential candidates based on the unique needs and requirements of classroom teaching in California
- "To develop subject matter requirements to guide both the credential program and the examinations
- "To align tests with California student standards and curriculum frameworks
- "To provide for the repeated and significant participation of California teachers and teacher educators throughout the test development process
- "To prevent bias and ensure diversity in testing materials for the program
- "To provide support materials to examinees to help them prepare for the tests and interpret their results
- "To provide support materials to teacher education programs to help them relate test results to their instructional programs
- "To develop tests that are equitable to all examinees
- "To offer all examinees uniform and positive testing experiences
- "To provide California state policymakers with information to guide program and policy modifications"

(2006–2007 CSET Registration Bulletin retrieved May 27, 2007 from www.cset.nesinc.com/CS12_overview.asp).

Criterion-Referenced Tests

Another important CSET distinction is that the tests are criterion-referenced. Criterion-referenced tests determine what candidates know in relation to an established standard, not how they compare to other candidates. In other words, this type of test reports how well candidates are doing relative to a pre-established performance level. A cut-off score of passing or not passing the CSET has been pre-established, and no norms have been established. By passing the CSET, a candidate demonstrates that he or she has met the established standard in terms of subject matter knowledge and skills.

CSET Domains

The CSET are designed to measure pre-selected and pre-identified domains of knowledge. The content of each examination is defined by this set of subject matter requirements or content specifications. These domains are statements of important knowledge and skills and are selected and developed by groups of California educators: classroom teachers, teacher educators, school administrators, and other content and assessment specialists. A complete list of the domains for CSET: Mathematics is included in Part I of *CliffsTestPrep CSET: Mathematics*. This list was used as a framework to develop the test questions included in *CliffsTestPrep CSET: Mathematics'* practice tests. The domain for each item is indicated in the Answers and Explanations section provided after each practice test. Use these descriptions to discover your strengths and weaknesses as they relate to the different domains in the area of mathematics.

Exam Questions

According to the CDE, the CSET's exam questions are developed in consultation with groups of classroom teachers, teacher educators, administrators, and other content and assessment specialists using various resources, including text-books, California curriculum syllabi, teacher education curricula, and teacher credential standards. The questions included in *CliffsTestPrep CSET: Mathematics* for Practice CSET: Math Test I and Practice CSET: Math Test II were developed by these same means.

Administration of the CSET

Subsections in this section cover time allotment, retaking the CSET, and requirements for test admission.

CSET Subtest Time Allotment

The CSET: Mathematics contains three subtests that are described in more detail later in this chapter. Candidates taking the CSET: Mathematics receive five uninterrupted hours of testing time. The subtests are not individually timed; all subtests should be completed within the allotted five hours time span. The CSET: Mathematics Examination, Subtest II, which allows the use of a graphing calculator, is always administered first in the test session. Because of this, you might want to start with Subtest II of the *CliffsTestPrep CSET: Mathematics* practice examinations and spend as much of the five hours as you need on each subtest.

Requirements for Test Admission

You need to pre-register to take the CSET, after which you receive an admission ticket containing important identification information, as well as the date, time, and location of your test session. You are required to present that admission ticket when you arrive at the test site. You are scheduled for the morning and/or afternoon session, depending on the subtest or subtests that you are registered to take. CSET: Mathematics is typically administered during the afternoon test sessions on the test administration day. Upon completion of the test, you need to hand in all test materials that were used during the session. This procedure is in place to protect the integrity and security of the testing process.

The CSET Web site (www.cset.nesinc.com) indicates that you must bring to the test administration a current, government-issued identification, in the name in which you registered, bearing your photograph and signature. Copies are not accepted. Acceptable forms of government-issued identification include photo-bearing driver's licenses and passports. The Department of Motor Vehicles provides acceptable photo-bearing identification cards for individuals who do not have a driver's license. Unacceptable forms of government-issued identification include student and employee identification cards, social security cards, draft classification cards, and credit cards. If you have any questions regarding acceptable photographic identification, call CSET (916-445-7254 or, if outside the 916 area code, you may call toll free at 888-921-2682) before the test date. If the name on your identification differs from the name in which you are registered, you must bring official verification of the change (for example, marriage certificate, court order).

If you do not have proper identification as described, you must bring a current, accurate photograph of yourself; report directly to the Information table at your test site; complete a personal identification information form; and certify, under penalty of perjury, that you are the person you purport to be. You may also be asked to provide your fingerprints on the day of the test. Your photograph is kept, and your official score report is not released unless you present the proper identification as described previously *no later than 16 calendar days after the test date*. In addition, you are not able to access your unofficial scores online. Instructions for providing proper identification after the test date are provided at the test site. If you do not provide documentation of your identification within 16 calendar days after the test date, your scores are permanently voided and are not reported to you or to the CCTC. Enhanced security measures, including additional security screenings, may be required by test site facilities. If an additional screening is conducted, only screened persons are admitted to the test site. If you do not proceed through the security screening, you are not allowed to test, and you do not receive a refund or credit of any kind.

Retaking the CSET

If you pass a CSET: Mathematics subtest, you do not have to take that subtest again as long as you use the score toward certification within five years of the test date. If you do not pass the subtest, you may register and retake that subtest on a subsequent test date. You can register and retake a subtest as many times as necessary. For the Practice CSET: Mathematics tests, we recommend that you take them as a whole (all three subtests) even if you pass one, two, or all of the three subtests. This approach provides you with more consistency and real-time practice.

Content Specifications in CSET: Mathematics

As indicated before, the CSET: Mathematics consists of three subtests that are scored separately and can be taken separately. Each subtest is composed of both multiple-choice and constructed-response items. Notice that there are 30 multiple-choice items, and 4 constructed-response items per subtest for a total of 102 items altogether. Algebra, Geometry, and Calculus make up about 70 percent of the total CSET: Mathematics content. The two Practice CSET: Mathematics tests included in *CliffsTestPrep CSET: Mathematics* follow the same content specifications.

Subtest	Domains	Number of Multiple-Choice Items	Number of Constructed-Response Items (short [focused] responses)
I	Algebra	24	3
	Number Theory	6	1
	Subtest Total	**30**	**4**
II	Geometry	22	3
	Probability and Statistics	8	1
	Subtest Total	**30**	**4**
III	Calculus	26	3
	History of Mathematics	4	1
	Subtest Total	**30**	**4**
	Total Number of Items	**90**	**12**

Candidates verifying subject matter competence by examination for a credential in Foundation-Level Mathematics are required to take and pass CSET Subtests I and II only.

Types of Questions

The CSET: Mathematics includes three types of questions: multiple-choice, enhanced multiple-choice, and written responses. The items are intended to be straightforward. They are not attempts to trick you or make you get the wrong answer. You should not try to overthink your answers to the questions.

Multiple-Choice Questions

This type of item presents a question or an incomplete statement that may be answered or completed correctly by only one of four possible alternatives: A, B, C, or D. You need to identify the *best* possible answer to the question from these four alternatives. The key word here is "best." If you cannot find the best answer, try eliminating as many options as possible. This approach increases your chances of being right, but always attempt to find the best choice first. Multiple-choice items might be accompanied by supplementary or additional information such as a passage, drawing, table, graph, or diagram to provide necessary background or information for an item. The inclusion of such items might require you to think critically about the question or material presented and could require comparisons, applications, judgments, and/or analyses. Mark your responses carefully on your answer sheet to help in avoiding errors in the electronic scoring process. Incomplete erasures and extraneous marks might cause the electronic scorer to indicate a false error. If you have to change an answer, erase the old answer completely and brush off erasure dust. You should keep your answer sheet free of extraneous marks and have only your answer choices marked (one per item).

Enhanced Multiple-Choice Questions

Some of the multiple-choice questions in this book have been identified as **ENHANCED**. This term is used to indicate that these items are complex multiple-choice questions, which require 2–3 minutes each to complete. Enhanced multiple-choice questions are not identified on the actual CSET: Mathematics test. The solution manual for each practice test included in this book identifies the enhanced multiple-choice items for your convenience.

Constructed-Response Questions

Four constructed-response questions (also known as written-response questions) are asked in each of the three subtests. Each of these written-response items is designed so that you can complete the answer within a short amount of time (approximately 10 to 15 minutes each). For the written-response questions or constructed-response questions, you generally are presented with introductory information, which could include or take the form of a map, sketch, graph, paragraph, table, quotation, excerpt, and/or drawing. This information is followed by a specific assignment. For example, you might be asked to prove, discuss, analyze, explain, compare, transform, or evaluate the information. You should read very carefully and address all parts of the constructed-response questions. They usually require more than one task. During the actual test, you write your answers in a written response sheet. In the practice tests, you will use extra lined paper to write your answers.

Scoring Information

The CDE uses electronic scoring for the multiple-choice items and hand scoring for constructed-response items. Candidates' multiple-choice answers are scored using computer programs that read candidates' bubbled answers and score them based on an answer key. No penalty is assessed for guessing the answers to questions. A blank answer has the same weight as a wrong answer. However, you should try to solve a problem or narrow down to the possible best answer before you try to guess. In other words, you might want to make a more educated guess instead of just a wild guess.

The constructed questions are scored differently than the multiple-choice questions. Qualified and trained California educators read and evaluate candidates' answers to the written-response questions. They use answer keys and **rubrics** (criteria) that have been established and validated by the California educators. The rubrics are **focused holistic scoring rubrics**. A focused holistic rubric is used to assign a single score or rating for an entire written response based on an overall impression of a student's work. In essence, this type of evaluation rubric combines all the important ingredients of a written response to arrive at an overall single judgment of quality. Using these rubrics, the evaluators judge the overall correctness and quality of each response while focusing on a set of performance characteristics that have been identified as important. Each response is assigned a score based on an approved scoring scale presented later in this section.

The following table includes the performance characteristics that guide the scoring of your responses on each of the 12 constructed-response items in each subtest (4 items per each of 3 subtests):

Performance Characteristics for CSET: Mathematics Subtests I, II, and II	
Purpose	The extent to which the response addresses the constructed-response assignment's charge in relation to relevant CSET subject matter requirements.
Subject Matter Knowledge	The application of accurate subject matter knowledge as described in the relevant CSET subject matter requirements.
Support	The appropriateness and quality of the supporting evidence in relation to relevant CSET subject matter requirements.
Depth and Breadth of Understanding	The degree to which the response demonstrates understanding of the relevant CSET subject matter requirements.

The following table includes the scoring scale that is used to score your answers to the constructed-response questions on each of the CSET: Mathematics subtests:

Scoring Scale for CSET: Mathematics Subtests I, II, and III	
Score Point	**Score Point Description**
4	The "4" response reflects a thorough command of the relevant knowledge and skills as defined in the subject matter requirements for CSET: Mathematics. ■ The purpose of the assignment is fully achieved. ■ There is a substantial and accurate application of relevant subject matter knowledge. ■ The supporting evidence is sound; there are high-quality, relevant examples. ■ The response reflects a comprehensive understanding of the assignment.
3	The "3" response reflects a general command of the relevant knowledge and skills as defined in the subject matter requirements for CSET: Mathematics. ■ The purpose of the assignment is largely achieved. ■ There is a largely accurate application of relevant subject matter knowledge. ■ The supporting evidence is adequate; there are some acceptable, relevant examples. ■ The response reflects an adequate understanding of the assignment.
2	The "2" response reflects a limited command of the relevant knowledge and skills as defined in the subject matter requirements for CSET: Mathematics. ■ The purpose of the assignment is partially achieved. ■ There is limited accurate application of relevant subject matter knowledge. ■ The supporting evidence is limited; there are few relevant examples. ■ The response reflects a limited understanding of the assignment.
1	The "1" response reflects little or no command of the relevant knowledge and skills as defined in the subject matter requirements for CSET: Mathematics. ■ The purpose of the assignment is not achieved. ■ There is little or no accurate application of relevant subject matter knowledge. ■ The supporting evidence is weak; there are no or few relevant examples. ■ The response reflects little or no understanding of the assignment.
U	The "U" (Unscorable) is assigned to a response that is unrelated to the assignment, illegible, primarily in a language other than English, or does not contain a sufficient amount of original work to score.
B	The "B" (Blank) is assigned to a response that is blank.

You should get acquainted with the performance characteristics and scoring scale that are used to score the constructed-response questions. The total score that a candidate may receive is a combination of the total points received for the constructed-response questions and the multiple-choice questions for each of the CSET: Mathematics subtests.

After taking the test, your score report provides information about your scoring for each subtest taken, your passing status, and—if you did not pass—your total subtest score. It also includes summary information about CSET: Mathematics subtests passed to date. The reverse side contains diagnostic information for each subtest taken to provide you with information about your areas of strength and weakness in each subtest section. Use this information if you need to retake any of the subtests.

Each of the CSET: Mathematics subtests is scored separately. To pass an examination, you must achieve a passing score on each of the examination's required subtests: Algebra/Number Theory, Geometry/Probability and Statistics, and Calculus/History of Mathematics. The minimum passing score for each subtest was established by the CCTC based on recommendations from California teachers and teacher educators and on the basis of total subtest performance. Test results are reported as scaled scores, which are based on the number of raw score points earned on each section (multiple-choice section and/or constructed-response section) and the weighting of each section. Raw scores for each subtest are converted to a scale of 100 to 300. The scaled score of 220 represents the minimum passing score for each section.

A passing subtest score must be achieved at a single CSET administration for each subtest. Your performance on each of the three subtests of the CSET: Mathematics cannot be combined across administrations. After you pass a subtest, you do not have to take that subtest again as long as you use the score toward certification within five years of the test date. You may register to retake all sections or some sections of the CSET: Mathematics. All necessary registration information and forms are provided in the current CSET Registration Bulletin or via the Internet at www.cset.nesinc.com.

Use of Approved Graphing Calculator

You need and are allowed to use a calculator for CSET: Mathematics Subtest II: Geometry and Probability and Statistics. You must bring your own graphing calculator to the test administration, and it must be one of the approved models listed in the current version of the CSET registration bulletin (www.cset.nesinc.com). Since the approved list of calculators might change, you should check for possible changes. The following table contains the approved graphing calculators at the time of this book's publication. Remember that the test administration staff clears the memory of your calculator both before and after testing. You should make sure that you back up the memory of your calculator, including applications, to an external device before arriving at the test site. **Note:** You are not allowed to bring the calculator's manual to the testing place. You must follow the same graphing calculator rules for your Practice CSET: Mathematics Subtest II in this book. Make sure you are familiar and know how to use the calculator you are planning to bring to the test site. This practice helps you simulate the testing conditions that you will have on your testing date, and your confidence in passing this section of the test should improve.

Manufacturer	Approved Models
Casio	FX 1.0 PLUS, fx-7400G, fx-7400G PLUS, fx-9750G PLUS, CFX-9850G, CFX-9850G PLUS, CFX-9850Ga, CFX-9850Ga PLUS, CFX-9850GB PLUS, CFX-9850GB PLUS(WE), CFX-9850GC PLUS, CFX-9970G, Algebra FX 2.0 (ALGFX2.0)
Sharp	EL-9300, EL-9600, EL-9600c, EL-9900
Texas Instruments	TI-73, TI-80, TI-81, TI-82, TI-83, TI-83 Plus, TI-83 Plus Silver, TI-84, TI-84 Plus, TI-84 Plus Silver, TI-85, TI-86, TI-89, TI-89 Titanium
Hewlett-Packard	HP 9g, HP 40g, HP 49g, HP 49 g PLUS

Test-Taking Strategies

The following are some tips for you to consider during the preparation period before taking the CSET: Mathematics. These ideas should help you analyze and focus your preparation time as you get ready to take the test.

Develop a Focusing Process

The practice tests provided in this book will help you prepare to take the actual CSET: Mathematics. It is a good idea that you read all the background information provided in this book and identify all the areas that the actual test covers: Algebra, Number Theory, Geometry, Probability and Statistics, Calculus, and History of Mathematics. Check the "Content Specifications in CSET: Mathematics" section (earlier in this chapter) for more details regarding the number of items per topic. This overall picture helps you in concentrating on the areas that are important for this test.

Take a close look at "CSET Mathematics Content Areas and Domains" in Part I of this book. This section helps you to focus your studies before you take the practice tests and to prepare for taking the actual test. After reviewing these domains, you should make a list of mathematics topics, skills, and concepts for which you feel you need more background or practice and for which you feel less familiar and confident. We have also included a section with sample practice items that deal with mathematical topics which are often more difficult. The two full-length practice exams also should help you get acquainted with the format of the CSET: Mathematics' multiple-choice and constructed-response questions. Also, take a look at the glossary of important mathematics terms and descriptions of important mathematical formulas sections in the back of this book. Then, using all of this information, set priorities based on this list of mathematics ideas and check the resources you need to start studying in more detail. Study each of the topics covered in the test, starting with the ones you need more time to study according to your priority list. At the end, you should have studied all areas, both those in which you are familiar and less familiar. Do not leave any topic out and spend sufficient time on each topic.

Setting aside time for your studies before you take the practice tests is very important. You want to have terms, formulas, concepts, and skills fresh in your mind for the practice and actual tests. Select the resources that work best for you to be used during this study time. You might also need a tutor, teacher, mentor, advisor, or a study group for support and extra help. However, you should take into account your preferences and study habits as you set a sound study plan.

After carefully studying for the test, find a quiet place (no phone, cell phone, television, radio, stereo, or other forms of electronic entertainment), take the first practice test, and spend five uninterrupted hours answering the questions. You should probably use a desk for this and avoid any disruption. This gives you an idea on how to time yourself. You might want to start with Subtest II using your graphing calculator. You may address multiple-choice questions and written-response questions within each subtest in the order that you prefer, but you must finish one subtest completely before moving on to another subtest. Remember, Subtest II is the ONLY subtest in which you can use a calculator.

Remember that every person is different in terms of timing. You need to know yourself and the speed that is comfortable for you. During the actual test, do not pay attention to what others do. Remember to use your graphing calculator for only Subtest II, prepare several number-2 sharpened pencils, and write your answers in the given test answer book for later review. You should write your solution process as you work on the questions as detailed and clearly as possible. These notes are very helpful when you start evaluating your solutions. Check the answers for the first practice test and see whether you had any problems by subtest and domain. You should check for correctness as well as quality of your responses to the questions. Are there any major areas of concern or priority? This gives you another opportunity to narrow down and focus your preparation priorities. We recommend that you go back and study everything a bit more, with an emphasis on the areas of need. Once again, after carefully studying for the test, find a quiet place and take the second practice test. Check the answers for the second practice test and, if you need to, study other subtest and domain areas before taking the actual test.

After these focusing exercises, you should have a better idea of how and when you are ready to take the actual CSET: Mathematics. You may decide to register for and attempt during a test session only some of the CSET: Mathematics subtests, leaving one or two subtests for another time. This allows you to spend more preparation time or coursework on the areas you judge you need to later.

Check the Resources You Need

After you set and focus your preparation priorities, you are ready to find the resources you need. Think about your coursework background and find any college mathematics textbooks; secondary mathematics textbooks; Web links; class notes; videos; publications from local, state, and national professional organizations; or other material that might help you study for the test. We have included a list of resources in this book that you can use to help with this selection process. You should organize the resources you have in terms of your preparation priorities and used them in that order. Remember to review all the topics—even those you feel you know well.

Refer to the Solution Manual

An answer/explanation section is provided at the end of each practice CSET: Mathematics test. Use this section to help you understand possible solutions and improve your test-taking ability. You might have used a different path for a solution to a specific problem. This is okay; if you get to the same answer, and the procedures you used are mathematically accurate, you don't need to have the same solution process. It is good to also learn other ways to solve the problem, however.

You should not take more than one practice exam per day. You need some time in between taking the exams to review your answers and possibly to readdress your study priorities.

Get R-E-A-D-Y before the test! The following are some ideas to keep in mind before you take the test, which are partly based on information provided by CSET registration bulletin (www.cset.nesinc.com):

- **R**est and sleep well several days before the test. You will not do as well if you are not rested and feel tired or tense.
- **E**at well. A nutritious and balanced breakfast and lunch (if the test is taken in the afternoon) can go a long way. If you will be taking examinations during both the morning and afternoon testing sessions, you might want to bring along something to eat during the break. Food is not allowed in the testing room.
- **A**ccessories you need for the test:

  Several number-2 sharpened pencils

  You need your own graphing calculator ready to be used for part II of the test only. Remember that the test administration staff will clear the memory of your calculator both before and after testing. You should make sure that you back up the memory of your calculator, including applications, to an external device before arriving at the test site. Remember that no scrap paper is allowed for any section of the test. All computation needs to be done directly on the test book that is provided at the site.

  You also need the admission ticket you receive after registering for a test date. You must bring to the test administration a current, government-issued identification, in the name in which you registered, bearing your photograph and signature. Copies are not accepted. See the previous section for more details regarding the identification requirements from the CSET registration bulletin.
- **D**ress comfortably and in layers so you can adapt to the testing room conditions. It is better to wear soft-soled shoes so that you do not disturb others if you need to leave your seat.
- **Y**ou need to relax and get **R-E-A-D-Y**. Leave plenty of time to get to the test session without pressure or anxiety. That way, you will arrive on time and be as relaxed as possible and ready to begin the test.

Get double R-E-A-D-Y during the test! The following are some additional ideas to keep in mind during the test:

- **R**ead and review the directions carefully (at least twice). Make sure that you understand and follow the instructions for the test and for each item of the test. This first step is crucial. When answering multiple-choice questions, make sure that you read all of the answer choices before choosing an answer. Remember that you are selecting the best possible answer out of four choices.
- **E**stimate and use common sense before calculating problems; this should give you a rough idea of what the answer should be before you start to work on the problem. You can also use your estimate to check your final answer and calculation errors. Sometimes, with multiple-choice items, you can eliminate one or two of the choices that contain errors or don't make sense and then choose the best answer out of the remaining choices. You should mark an answer to the multiple-choice items, even if you are not sure of the correct answer. Your score is not reduced because of wrong answers. However, you should attempt to figure out the best answer before guessing. Remember that the CSET: Mathematics has three subtests, but Subtest II is always administered first in the test session. If you are completing two or three sections, work on one subtest at a time. You receive one test booklet for each subtest that you are taking. You can allocate your time within the subtests on your own, spending more time on one subtest than on another.

- **A**lways refer to the original directions and context of the problem, especially when an answer doesn't make sense. You might have missed something about the problem setting. The test booklet contains general directions for the examination as a whole and specific directions for the individual questions and, in some cases, groups of questions. If you do not understand a specific direction, raise your hand and ask the test administrator.

- **D**ouble-check your answer choice and work. Don't skip steps. Work carefully and avoid accidental computational or reasoning errors. Check the accuracy of your answers for the multiple-choice items, and make sure that they were marked appropriately. Also, check the quality, legibility, and completeness of your answers to the constructed-response questions. However, don't overdo your checking. Remember to time and pace yourself. Timing yourself is very important in this test since you are responsible for setting your own pace. You should have developed a plan regarding how much time you will devote on each subtest that you are taking (assuming you are taking more than one). Try to stick to your plan and finish each subtest within your planned time. At the end of the five hours, you are required to stop working and return all test materials to the test administrator. You should make plans to stay for the full five hours that you are given to complete the test, even if it could take you less time to complete the exam. Do not rush to finish.

- **Y**ou can do it! You are **R-E-A-D-Y**!

Important Considerations for This TestPrep Book

Unlike other test prep books for the CSET: Mathematics already on the market, *CliffsTestPrep CSET: Mathematics* offers targeted information on the format and structure of the exam (rather than sacrificing a great amount of space on review), and provides two full-length practice tests. After each practice test, a detailed description of answers is provided to help you thoroughly understand each item. The intention of the authors is to make this book a tool you can use to practice and learn more about the CSET: Mathematics. This book is not intended as a substitute for quality learning from courses and other experiences, but provides in-depth practice of test-taking skills needed for the successful completion of the CSET for this certification area.

After a list of respective content areas and domains for the CSET: Mathematics, practice items relating to topics that tend to be more difficult are included in Part I of the book. At the end of *CliffsTestPrep CSET: Mathematics* are three more sections related to the CSET: Mathematics—a glossary of important mathematical terms, a description of important formulas, and a list of resources. You should study all of these sections before you complete the two Practice CSET: Mathematics Tests. This approach can help you learn more quickly and increase the effectiveness of the materials provided in this book.

This book concentrates on presenting information and practice tests related to the new revisions made to the CSET for Single Subject Teaching Credential in the area of mathematics (referred to in this document as CSET: Mathematics). More information is available from the CSET registration bulletin and the CSET Web site (www.cset.nesinc.com). Also, changes to the CSET program that modify or supplement information presented in this book are disseminated through the CSET Web site.

The two practice tests in *CliffsTestPrep CSET: Mathematics* are, like the test itself, divided in three subtests. We recommend that you set aside five uninterrupted hours to complete each Practice CSET: Mathematics Test. We have included an answer key and explanation for each item's possible responses; however, we recommend and encourage you to initially take the practice tests without looking at these sections of this book. You should record your responses on a separate sheet of paper and review your answers with the provided responses afterward.

CONTENT AREAS, DOMAINS, AND PRACTICE ITEMS

This section contains the Mathematics subject matter requirements arranged according to the domains covered by each subtest of CSET: Mathematics. In parentheses after each named domain is the CCTC-assigned domain code from the Mathematics subject matter requirements (2002, by CCTC and NES). This same content is presented in the correct order at www.cset.nesinc.com/PDFs/CS_mathematics_SMR.pdf.

Mathematics Subtest I: Algebra and Number Theory

Part I: Content Domains for Subject Matter Understanding and Skill in Mathematics (Algebra and Number Theory)

Algebra (SMR Domain 1)

Candidates demonstrate an understanding of the foundations of the algebra contained in the Mathematics Content Standards for California Public Schools (1997) as outlined in the Mathematics Framework for California Public Schools: Kindergarten through Grade Twelve (1999) from an advanced standpoint. To ensure a rigorous view of algebra and its underlying structures, candidates have a deep conceptual knowledge. They are skilled at symbolic reasoning and use algebraic skills and concepts to model a variety of problem-solving situations. They understand the power of mathematical abstraction and symbolism.

0001 Algebraic Structures (SMR 1.1)

a. Know why the real and complex numbers are each a field and that particular rings are not fields (for example, integers, polynomial rings, matrix rings).

b. Apply basic properties of real and complex numbers in constructing mathematical arguments (for example, if $a < b$ and $c < 0$, then $ac > bc$).

c. Know that the rational numbers and real numbers can be ordered and that the complex numbers cannot be ordered, but that any polynomial equation with real coefficients can be solved in the complex field.

(Mathematics Content Standards for California Public Schools, Grade 6, Number Sense: 1.0, 2.0; Grade 7, Algebra and Functions: 1.0; Algebra I: 1.0, 3.0–7.0, 9.0–15.0, 24.0, 25.0; Geometry: 1.0, 17.0; Algebra II: 1.0–8.0, 11.0, 24.0, 25.0; Trigonometry: 17.0; Mathematical Analysis: 2.0; Linear Algebra: 9.0, 11.0)

0002 Polynomial Equations and Inequalities (SMR 1.2)

a. Know why graphs of linear inequalities are half planes and be able to apply this fact (for example, linear programming).

b. Prove and use the following:

- The Rational Root Theorem for polynomials with integer coefficients
- The Factor Theorem
- The Conjugate Roots Theorem for polynomial equations with real coefficients
- The Quadratic Formula for real and complex quadratic polynomials
- The Binomial Theorem

c. Analyze and solve polynomial equations with real coefficients using the Fundamental Theorem of Algebra.

(Mathematics Content Standards for California Public Schools, Grade 7, Algebra and Functions: 2.0–4.0; Algebra I: 1.0, 2.0, 4.0–10.0, 12.0–15.0, 17.0–23.0; Algebra II: 2.0–11.0, 16.0, 17.0; Trigonometry: 17.0, 18.0; Mathematical Analysis: 4.0, 6.0)

0003 Functions (SMR 1.3)

a. Analyze and prove general properties of functions (that is, domain and range, one-to-one, onto, inverses, composition, and differences between relations and functions).

b. Analyze properties of polynomial, rational, radical, and absolute value functions in a variety of ways (for example, graphing, solving problems).

c. Analyze properties of exponential and logarithmic functions in a variety of ways (for example, graphing, solving problems).

(Mathematics Content Standards for California Public Schools, Grade 6, Algebra and Functions: 1.0; Grade 7, Number Sense: 1.0, 2.0; Algebra and Functions: 3.0; Algebra I: 3.0–6.0, 10.0, 13.0, 15.0–18.0, 21.0–23.0; Algebra II: 1.0–4.0, 6.0–17.0, 24.0, 25.0; Trigonometry: 2.0, 4.0–8.0, 19.0; Mathematical Analysis: 6.0, 7.0; Calculus: 9.0)

0004 Linear Algebra (SMR 1.4)

a. Understand and apply the geometric interpretation and basic operations of vectors in two and three dimensions, including their scalar multiples and scalar (dot) and cross products.

b. Prove the basic properties of vectors (for example, perpendicular vectors have zero dot product).

c. Understand and apply the basic properties and operations of matrices and determinants (for example, to determine the solvability of linear systems of equations).

(Mathematics Content Standards for California Public Schools, Algebra I: 9.0; Algebra II: 2.0; Mathematical Analysis: 1.0; Linear Algebra: 1.0–12.0)

Number Theory (SMR Domain 3)

Candidates demonstrate an understanding of the number theory and a command of the number sense contained in the Mathematics Content Standards for California Public Schools (1997) as outlined in the Mathematics Framework for California Public Schools: Kindergarten through Grade Twelve (1999) from an advanced standpoint. To ensure a rigorous view of number theory and its underlying structures, candidates have a deep conceptual knowledge. They prove and use properties of natural numbers. They formulate conjectures about the natural numbers using inductive reasoning and verify conjectures with proofs.

0005 Natural Numbers (SMR 3.1)

a. Prove and use basic properties of natural numbers (for example, properties of divisibility).

b. Use the Principle of Mathematical Induction to prove results in number theory.

c. Know and apply the Euclidean Algorithm.

d. Apply the Fundamental Theorem of Arithmetic (for example, find the greatest common factor and the least common multiple, show that every fraction is equivalent to a unique fraction in which the numerator and denominator are relatively prime, prove that the square root of any number, not a perfect square number, is irrational).

(Mathematics Content Standards for California Public Schools, Grade 6, Number Sense: 2.0; Grade 7, Number Sense: 1.0; Algebra I: 1.0, 2.0, 12.0, 24.0, 25.0; Geometry: 1.0; Algebra II: 21.0, 23.0, 25.0; Mathematical Analysis: 3.0)

Part II: Subject Matter Skills and Abilities Applicable to the Content Domains in Mathematics (Algebra and Number Theory)

Candidates for Single Subject Teaching Credentials in mathematics use inductive and deductive reasoning to develop, analyze, and draw conclusions and validate conjectures and arguments. As they reason, they use counterexamples, construct proofs using contradictions, and create multiple representations of the same concept. They know the interconnections among mathematical ideas and use techniques and concepts from different domains and subdomains to model the same problem. They explain mathematical interconnections with other disciplines. They are able to communicate their mathematical thinking clearly and coherently to others, orally, graphically, and in writing, through the use of precise language and symbols.

Candidates solve routine and complex problems by drawing from a variety of strategies while demonstrating an attitude of persistence and reflection in their approaches. They analyze problems through pattern recognition and the use of analogies. They formulate and prove conjectures and test conclusions for reasonableness and accuracy. They use counterexamples to disprove conjectures.

Candidates select and use different representational systems (for example, coordinates, graphs). They understand the usefulness of transformations and symmetry to help analyze and simplify problems. They make mathematical models to analyze mathematical structures in real contexts. They use spatial reasoning to model and solve problems that cross disciplines.

(Mathematics Content Standards for California Public Schools, Grade 6, Mathematical Reasoning: 1.0–3.0; Grade 7, Mathematical Reasoning: 1.0–3.0)

Mathematics Subtest II: Geometry and Probability and Statistics

Part I: Content Domains for Subject Matter Understanding and Skill in Mathematics (Geometry and Probability and Statistics)

Geometry (SMR Domain 2)

Candidates demonstrate an understanding of the foundations of the geometry contained in the Mathematics Content Standards for California Public Schools (1997) as outlined in the Mathematics Framework for California Public Schools: Kindergarten through Grade Twelve (1999) from an advanced standpoint. To ensure a rigorous view of geometry and its underlying structures, candidates have a deep conceptual knowledge. They demonstrate an understanding of axiomatic systems and different forms of logical arguments. Candidates understand, apply, and prove theorems relating to a variety of topics in two- and three-dimensional geometry, including coordinate, synthetic, non-Euclidean, and transformational geometry.

0001 Parallelism (SMR 2.1)

a. Know the Parallel Postulate and its implications and justify its equivalents (for example, the Alternate Interior Angle Theorem, the angle sum of every triangle is 180 degrees).

b. Know that variants of the Parallel Postulate produce non-Euclidean geometries (for example, spherical, hyperbolic).

(Mathematics Content Standards for California Public Schools, Algebra I: 8.0, 24.0; Geometry: 1.0–3.0, 7.0, 13.0)

0002 Plane Euclidean Geometry (SMR 2.2)

a. Prove theorems and solve problems involving similarity and congruence.

b. Understand, apply, and justify properties of triangles (for example, the Exterior Angle Theorem, concurrence theorems, trigonometric ratios, Triangle Inequality, Law of Sines, Law of Cosines, the Pythagorean Theorem, and its converse).

c. Understand, apply, and justify properties of polygons and circles from an advanced standpoint (for example, derive the area formulas for regular polygons and circles from the area of a triangle).

d. Justify and perform the classical constructions (for example, angle bisector, perpendicular bisector, replicating shapes, regular n-gons for n equal to 3, 4, 5, 6, and 8).

e. Use techniques in coordinate geometry to prove geometric theorems.

(Mathematics Content Standards for California Public Schools, Grade 6, Algebra and Functions: 2.0, 3.0; Measurement and Geometry: 2.0; Grade 7, Measurement and Geometry: 1.0–3.0; Algebra I: 8.0, 24.0; Geometry: 1.0–6.0, 8.0–16.0, 18.0-21.0; Algebra II: 16.0, 17.0; Trigonometry: 12.0–14.0, 18.0, 19.0; Mathematical Analysis: 5.0)

0003 Three-Dimensional Geometry (SMR 2.3)

a. Demonstrate an understanding of parallelism and perpendicularity of lines and planes in three dimensions.

b. Understand, apply, and justify properties of three-dimensional objects from an advanced standpoint (for example, derive the volume and surface area formulas for prisms, pyramids, cones, cylinders, and spheres).

(Mathematics Content Standards for California Public Schools, Grade 6, Measurement and Geometry: 1.0; Grade 7, Measurement and Geometry: 2.0; Algebra I: 24.0; Geometry: 2.0, 3.0, 12.0, 17.0; Mathematical Analysis: 5.0)

0004 Transformational Geometry (SMR 2.4)

a. Demonstrate an understanding of the basic properties of isometries in two- and three-dimensional space (for example, rotation, translation, reflection).

b. Understand and prove the basic properties of dilations (for example, similarity transformations or change of scale).

(Mathematics Content Standards for California Public Schools, Geometry: 11.0, 22.0)

Probability and Statistics (SMR Domain 4)

Candidates demonstrate an understanding of the statistics and probability distributions for advanced placement statistics contained in the Mathematics Content Standards for California Public Schools (1997) as outlined in the Mathematics Framework for California Public Schools: Kindergarten through Grade Twelve (1999) from an advanced standpoint. To ensure a rigorous view of probability and statistics and their underlying structures, candidates have a deep conceptual knowledge. They solve problems and make inferences using statistics and probability distributions.

0005 Probability (SMR 4.1)

a. Prove and apply basic principles of permutations and combinations.

b. Illustrate finite probability using a variety of examples and models (for example, the fundamental counting principles).

c. Use and explain the concept of conditional probability.

d. Interpret the probability of an outcome.

e. Use normal, binomial, and exponential distributions to solve and interpret probability problems.

(Mathematics Content Standards for California Public Schools, Grade 6, Statistics, Data Analysis, and Probability: 3.0; Algebra II: 18.0–20.0; Probability and Statistics: 1.0–4.0; Advanced Probability and Statistics: 1.0–4.0, 7.0, 9.0, 17.0, 18.0)

0006 Statistics (SMR 4.2)

a. Compute and interpret the mean, median, and mode of both discrete and continuous distributions.

b. Compute and interpret quartiles, range, variance, and standard deviation of both discrete and continuous distributions.

c. Select and evaluate sampling methods appropriate to a task (for example, random, systematic, cluster, convenience sampling) and display the results.

d. Know the method of least squares and apply it to linear regression and correlation.

e. Know and apply the chi-square test.

(Mathematics Content Standards for California Public Schools, Grade 6, Statistics, Data Analysis, and Probability: 1.0, 2.0; Grade 7, Statistics, Data Analysis, and Probability: 1.0; Probability and Statistics: 5.0–7.0; Advanced Probability and Statistics: 4.0–6.0, 8.0, 10.0–13.0, 15.0–17.0, 19.0)

Part II: Subject Matter Skills and Abilities Applicable to the Content Domains in Mathematics (Geometry and Probability and Statistics)

Candidates for Single Subject Teaching Credentials in mathematics use inductive and deductive reasoning to develop, analyze, draw conclusions, and validate conjectures and arguments. As they reason, they use counterexamples, construct proofs using contradictions, and create multiple representations of the same concept. They know the interconnections among mathematical ideas and use techniques and concepts from different domains and sub-domains to model the same problem. They explain mathematical interconnections with other disciplines. They are able to communicate their mathematical thinking clearly and coherently to others, orally, graphically, and in writing, through the use of precise language and symbols.

Candidates solve routine and complex problems by drawing from a variety of strategies while demonstrating an attitude of persistence and reflection in their approaches. They analyze problems through pattern recognition and the use of analogies. They formulate and prove conjectures and test conclusions for reasonableness and accuracy. They use counterexamples to disprove conjectures.

Candidates select and use different representational systems (for example, coordinates, graphs). They understand the usefulness of transformations and symmetry to help analyze and simplify problems. They make mathematical models to analyze mathematical structures in real contexts. They use spatial reasoning to model and solve problems that cross disciplines.

(Mathematics Content Standards for California Public Schools, Grade 6, Mathematical Reasoning: 1.0–3.0; Grade 7, Mathematical Reasoning: 1.0–3.0)

Mathematics Subtest III: Calculus and History of Mathematics

Part I: Content Domains for Subject Matter Understanding and Skill in Mathematics (Calculus and History of Mathematics)

Calculus (SMR Domain 5)

Candidates demonstrate an understanding of the trigonometry and calculus contained in the Mathematics Content Standards for California Public Schools (1997) as outlined in the Mathematics Framework for California Public Schools: Kindergarten through Grade Twelve (1999) from an advanced standpoint. To ensure a rigorous view of trigonometry and calculus and their underlying structures, candidates have a deep conceptual knowledge. They apply the concepts of trigonometry and calculus to solving problems in real-world situations.

0001 Trigonometry (SMR 5.1)

a. Prove that the Pythagorean Theorem is equivalent to the trigonometric identity $\sin^2 x + \cos^2 x = 1$ and that this identity leads to $1 + \tan^2 x = \sec^2 x$ and $1 + \cot^2 x = \csc^2 x$.

b. Prove the sine, cosine, and tangent sum formulas for all real values and derive special applications of the sum formulas (for example, double angle, half angle).

c. Analyze properties of trigonometric functions in a variety of ways (for example, graphing and solving problems).

d. Know and apply the definitions and properties of inverse trigonometric functions (that is, arcsin, arccos, and arctan).

e. Understand and apply polar representations of complex numbers (for example, DeMoivre's Theorem).

(Mathematics Content Standards for California Public Schools, Algebra I: 24.0; Geometry: 3.0, 14.0, 18.0, 19.0; Algebra II: 24.0, 25.0; Trigonometry: 1.0–6.0, 8.0–11.0, 19.0; Mathematical Analysis: 1.0, 2.0; Calculus: 18.0, 20.0)

0002 Limits and Continuity (SMR 5.2)

a. Derive basic properties of limits and continuity, including the Sum, Difference, Product, Constant Multiple, and Quotient Rules, using the formal definition of a limit.

b. Show that a polynomial function is continuous at a point.

c. Know and apply the Intermediate Value Theorem, using the geometric implications of continuity.

(Mathematics Content Standards for California Public Schools, Algebra I: 24.0; Geometry: 3.0; Algebra II: 1.0, 15.0; Mathematical Analysis: 8.0; Calculus: 1.0–4.0)

0003 Derivatives and Applications (SMR 5.3)

a. Derive the rules of differentiation for polynomial, trigonometric, and logarithmic functions using the formal definition of derivative.

b. Interpret the concept of derivative geometrically, numerically, and analytically (that is, slope of the tangent, limit of difference quotients, extrema, Newton's method, and instantaneous rate of change).

c. Interpret both continuous and differentiable functions geometrically and analytically and apply Rolle's Theorem, the Mean Value Theorem, and L'Hôpital's rule.

d. Use the derivative to solve rectilinear motion, related rate, and optimization problems.

e. Use the derivative to analyze functions and planar curves (for example, maxima, minima, inflection points, concavity).

f. Solve separable first-order differential equations and apply them to growth and decay problems.

(Mathematics Content Standards for California Public Schools, Algebra I: 5.0–8.0, 10.0, 11.0, 13.0, 21.0, 23.0; Geometry: 3.0; Algebra II: 1.0, 9.0, 10.0, 12.0, 15.0; Trigonometry: 7.0, 15.0–19.0; Mathematical Analysis: 5.0, 7.0; Calculus: 1.0, 4.0–12.0, 27.0)

0004 Integrals and Applications (SMR 5.4)

a. Derive definite integrals of standard algebraic functions using the formal definition of integral.

b. Interpret the concept of a definite integral geometrically, numerically, and analytically (for example, limit of Riemann sums).

c. Prove the Fundamental Theorem of Calculus and use it to interpret definite integrals as antiderivatives.

d. Apply the concept of integrals to compute the length of curves and the areas and volumes of geometric figures.

(Mathematics Content Standards for California Public Schools, Algebra I: 24.0; Geometry: 9.0; Calculus: 13.0–23.0)

0005 Sequences and Series (SMR 5.5)

a. Derive and apply the formulas for the sums of finite arithmetic series and finite and infinite geometric series (for example, express repeating decimals as a rational number).

b. Determine convergence of a given sequence or series using standard techniques (for example, Ratio, Comparison, Integral Tests).

c. Calculate Taylor series and Taylor polynomials of basic functions.

(Mathematics Content Standards for California Public Schools, Algebra I: 24.0, 25.0; Algebra II: 21.0–23.0; Mathematical Analysis: 8.0; Calculus: 23.0–26.0)

History of Mathematics (SMR Domain 6)

Candidates understand the chronological and topical development of mathematics and the contributions of historical figures of various times and cultures. Candidates know important mathematical discoveries and their impact on human society and thought. These discoveries form a historical context for the content contained in the Mathematics Content Standards for California Public Schools (1997) as outlined in the Mathematics Framework for California Public Schools: Kindergarten through Grade Twelve (1999; for example, numeration systems, algebra, geometry, calculus).

0006 Chronological and Topical Development of Mathematics (SMR 6.1)

a. Demonstrate understanding of the development of mathematics, its cultural connections, and its contributions to society.

b. Demonstrate understanding of the historical development of mathematics, including the contributions of diverse populations as determined by race, ethnicity, culture, geography, and gender.

Part II: Subject Matter Skills and Abilities Applicable to the Content Domains in Mathematics (Calculus and History of Mathematics)

Candidates for Single Subject Teaching Credentials in mathematics use inductive and deductive reasoning to develop, analyze, draw conclusions, and validate conjectures and arguments. As they reason, they use counterexamples, construct proofs using contradictions, and create multiple representations of the same concept. They know the interconnections among mathematical ideas and use techniques and concepts from different domains and sub-domains to model the same problem. They explain mathematical interconnections with other disciplines. They are able to communicate their mathematical thinking clearly and coherently to others, orally, graphically, and in writing, through the use of precise language and symbols.

Candidates solve routine and complex problems by drawing from a variety of strategies while demonstrating an attitude of persistence and reflection in their approaches. They analyze problems through pattern recognition and the use of analogies. They formulate and prove conjectures and test conclusions for reasonableness and accuracy. They use counterexamples to disprove conjectures.

Candidates select and use different representational systems (for example, coordinates, graphs). They understand the usefulness of transformations and symmetry to help analyze and simplify problems. They make mathematical models to analyze mathematical structures in real contexts. They use spatial reasoning to model and solve problems that cross disciplines.

(Mathematics Content Standards for California Public Schools, Grade 6, Mathematical Reasoning: 1.0–3.0; Grade 7, Mathematical Reasoning: 1.0–3.0)

Practice Items

Fourteen content domains are part of the CSET: Mathematics exam. From the content in those domains, several mathematical concepts stand out as generally more difficult to understand. For those areas, we have chosen to provide additional explanation and practice. You should use them as you feel they are necessary for review as you prepare for the test. Within the content domains chosen, the subdomains that are more problematic have been addressed here. The domains included in this section are the following: 1.4 Linear Algebra, 5.1 Trigonometry, and 5.3 Derivatives and Applications. For areas not addressed here, consult the resource section included in this book for further assistance.

Content Domain 1.4: Linear Algebra

Subsection a: Understand and apply the geometric interpretation and basic operations of vectors in two and three dimensions, including their scalar multiples and scalar (dot) and cross products.

A **vector** is a quantity that has both direction and magnitude. It is a directed line segment and is generally represented by an arrow. The length of the arrow corresponds to the magnitude of the vector. The direction in which the arrow points corresponds to the direction of the vector, generally given as an angle from a horizontal line. You can represent given vectors in various ways depending upon the point at which the vector begins (See Figure 3–1).

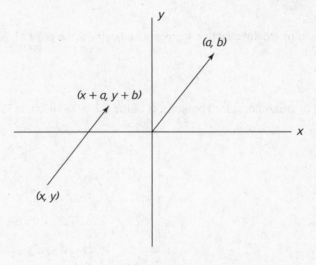

Figure 3–1

A **two-dimensional vector** is an ordered pair $\langle a, b \rangle$ of real numbers. A **three-dimensional vector** is an ordered triple $\langle a, b, c \rangle$ of real numbers. The values a, b, and c are **components** of the vector. When representing a three-dimensional vector, three-dimensional coordinates are used. If the vector begins at the origin, it is the **position vector,** and the endpoint of the vector is at the point (a, b). If the vector begins at a place other than the origin, the vector can be found by examining the coordinates of the points where the vector begins and ends.

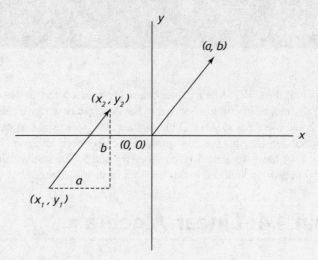

Figure 3–2

The position vector given in Figure 3–2 can be named as $\vec{a} = \langle a, b \rangle$. When repositioned to begin at the point $\langle x_1, y_1 \rangle$, the value of a and b can be found. $a = x_2 - x_1$, and $b = y_2 - y_1$. Therefore, the vector $\vec{a} = \langle a, b \rangle$ can be also named as $\vec{a} = \langle x_2 - x_1, y_2 - y_1 \rangle$. Given the initial and terminal points, the vector can be found by subtracting the corresponding coordinates of the initial point from the terminal point. The order in which the subtraction is completed is important, as reversing the subtraction would give a vector in the opposite direction.

Example:

Find the vector represented by the directed line segment that begins at the point (3, 5) and ends at the point (–2, –5).

Solution:

The vector can be found by determining the components of the vector as shown in Figure 3–3.

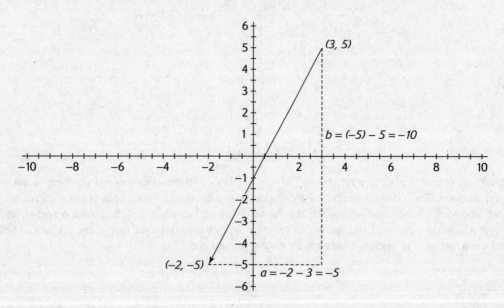

Figure 3–3

The vector can be represented by finding the difference of the *x*-coordinates and *y*-coordinates. The direction of the vector is down and to the left, so the components should both be negative to indicate the direction as well as the magnitude of the vector. In this case, the vector $\vec{a} = \langle -5, -10 \rangle$.

Magnitude and Direction

The definition of a vector involves both magnitude and direction. These can be found using the Pythagorean Theorem and trigonometry (see Figure 3–4).

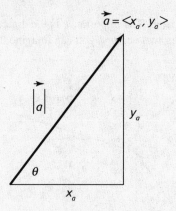

Figure 3–4

$$magnitude = \left|\vec{a}\right| = \sqrt{x_a^2 + y_a^2}$$

$$direction = \theta = \tan^{-1}\left(\frac{y_a}{x_a}\right)$$

Example:

Find the magnitude and direction of the vector $\vec{a} = \langle 4, 4\sqrt{3} \rangle$.

Solution:

The magnitude is the length of the vector and is found by

$$\left|\vec{a}\right| = \sqrt{x_a^2 + y_a^2} = \sqrt{(4)^2 + \left(4\sqrt{3}\right)^2} = \sqrt{16 + 48} = \sqrt{64} = 8.$$

The direction can be found with $\theta = \tan^{-1}\left(\frac{y_a}{x_a}\right) = \tan^{-1}\left(\frac{4\sqrt{3}}{4}\right) = \tan^{-1}\left(\sqrt{3}\right) = 60° = \frac{\pi}{3}$.

The direction and magnitude can also be found by examining the right triangle. Here, the vector would look like the following (see Figure 3–5):

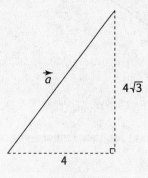

Figure 3–5

This fits the pattern for 30-60-90 right triangles, so you can use that relationship to find the magnitude, or the length of the hypotenuse, and the direction, or the angle with the horizontal. In this case, the magnitude is 8, and the direction is $60°$ or $\frac{\pi}{3}$.

After you know how to name a vector and find its magnitude and direction, you can perform operations on the vector, namely addition of vectors and multiplication of a vector by a scalar. These operations are expanded upon here.

Addition of Vectors

Vectors can be positioned anywhere in the plane. The importance is the direction and magnitude, but the starting point is not determined by the vector. When adding two vectors, you can imagine the second vector starts where the first left off (see Figure 3–6).

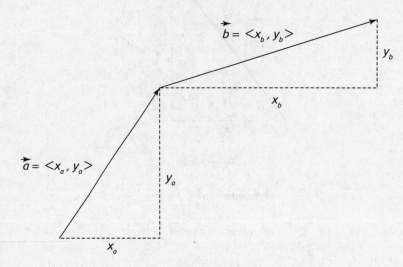

Figure 3–6

The sum would start where vector $\vec{a}$ begins and end where vector $\vec{b}$ ends (see Figure 3–7).

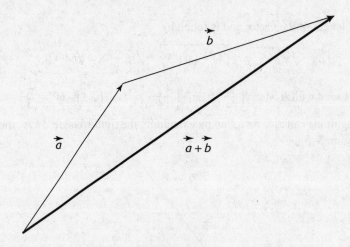

Figure 3–7

The vector $\vec{a} + \vec{b}$ can then be written as $\langle x_{a+b}, y_{a+b} \rangle$. (See Figure 3–8.)

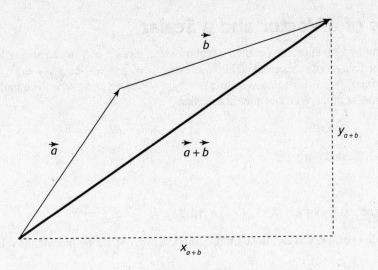

Figure 3–8

Using the prior two figures, you can write $x_{a+b} = x_a + x_b$ and $y_{a+b} = y_a + y_b$.

Therefore, when you add two vectors together, you can say that if you define $\vec{a} = \langle x_a, y_a \rangle$ and $\vec{b} = \langle x_b, y_b \rangle$, you can say $\vec{a} + \vec{b} = \langle x_a + x_b, \ y_a + y_b \rangle$.

Example:

Find the sum of the vectors $\vec{c} = \langle 4, 6 \rangle$ and $\vec{d} = \langle 2, 8 \rangle$.

Solution:

First, if you were to graph these vectors, you would have the following (see Figure 3–9):

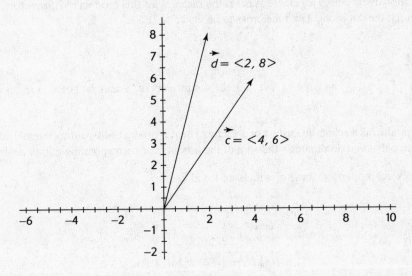

Figure 3–9

You know that you can reposition vector $\vec{d}$ so that it begins at the point (4, 6). This would make the vector $\vec{d}$ end at the point (4 + 2, 6 + 8), or (6, 14). The sum of the two vectors would start at the origin and end at the point (6, 14), so you can say $\vec{c} + \vec{d} = \langle 6, 14 \rangle$. Using the addition of vectors rule, you arrive at the same conclusion by saying $\vec{c} + \vec{d} = \langle x_c + x_d, \ y_c + y_d \rangle = \langle 4 + 2, 6 + 8 \rangle = \langle 6, 14 \rangle$.

Multiplication of a Vector and a Scalar

You can multiply a vector by a real number c, called a **scalar,** which gives $c\vec{a}$. You can also write this as $c<x_a, y_a>$. Multiplication can also be thought of as repeated addition, so $c<x_a,y_a> = <x_a,y_a> + <x_a,y_a> + <x_a,y_a> + <x_a,y_a> + <x_a,y_a> \ldots$ until you have added c times. This is the same as saying $c<x_a, y_a> = <cx_a, cy_a>$, so when you multiply by a scalar, you can multiply each component of the vector by the same scalar.

Example:

If the vector $\vec{a} = \langle 3,8 \rangle$, find $4\vec{a}$.

Solution:

Since $\vec{a} = \langle 3,8 \rangle$, you can find $4\vec{a} = \langle 4 \cdot 3, 4 \cdot 8 \rangle = \langle 12,32 \rangle$.

After you know these relationships, you can solve more complicated problems by piecing the relationships together.

Example:

If $\vec{a} = \langle 1,5 \rangle$ and $\vec{b} = \langle 2,-3 \rangle$, find $3\vec{a} - 2\vec{b}$.

Solution:

Using the properties of multiplying a vector by a scalar and adding vectors together, you can find $3\vec{a} = \langle 3 \cdot 1, 3 \cdot 5 \rangle = \langle 3,15 \rangle$ and $2\vec{b} = \langle 2 \cdot 2, 2 \cdot -3 \rangle = \langle 4,-6 \rangle$.

Now, you want $3\vec{a} - 2\vec{b}$. Subtracting is equivalent to adding the negative, so you can say $3\vec{a} + \left(-2\vec{b} \right)$, so $-2\vec{b} = \langle -2 \cdot 2, -2 \cdot -3 \rangle = \langle -4,6 \rangle$. Then you have $3\vec{a} - 2\vec{b} = 3\vec{a} + \left(-2\vec{b} \right) = \langle 3,15 \rangle + \langle -4,6 \rangle = \langle 3-4, 15+6 \rangle = \langle -1,21 \rangle$.

Thus far, we have discussed adding and subtracting vectors and multiplying a vector by a scalar. This sequence begs the question, can one multiply two vectors together? What is the meaning of this product? With vectors, you have two such ways to multiply vectors: the dot product and the cross product.

Dot Product

Given two vectors, $\vec{a} = \langle x_a, y_a, z_a \rangle$ and $\vec{b} = \langle x_b, y_b, z_b \rangle$, the dot product of $\vec{a}$ and $\vec{b}$, noted $\vec{a} \cdot \vec{b}$, is defined as $\vec{a} \cdot \vec{b} = x_a x_b + y_a y_b + z_a z_b$.

The result of the dot product is a scalar quantity, not a vector. The dot product of two-dimensional vectors is defined in the same way, but with only two coordinates—the sum of the products of corresponding components.

The dot product has several properties, some of which are listed here.

$$\vec{a} \cdot \vec{a} = \left| \vec{a} \right|^2$$

$$\vec{a} \cdot \vec{b} = \vec{b} \cdot \vec{a}$$

$$\vec{a} \cdot \left(\vec{b} + \vec{c} \right) = \vec{a} \cdot \vec{b} + \vec{a} \cdot \vec{c}$$

These can be proven with the definition of the dot product. If $\vec{a} = \langle x_a, y_a, z_a \rangle$, $\vec{b} = \langle x_b, y_b, z_b \rangle$, and $\vec{c} = \langle x_c, y_c, z_c \rangle$; then . . .

$$\vec{a} \cdot \vec{a} = x_a x_a + y_a y_a + z_a z_a = x_a^2 + y_a^2 + z_a^2 = \left(\sqrt{x_a^2 + y_a^2 + z_a^2} \right)^2 = \left| \vec{a} \right|^2$$

$$\vec{a} \cdot \vec{b} = x_a x_b + y_a y_b + z_a z_b = x_b x_a + y_b y_a + z_b z_a = \vec{b} \cdot \vec{a}$$

$$\vec{a} \cdot \left(\vec{b} + \vec{c} \right) = x_a \left(x_b + x_c \right) + y_a \left(y_b + y_c \right) + z_a \left(z_b + z_c \right) = x_a x_b + x_a x_c + y_a y_b + y_a y_c + z_a z_b + z_a z_c$$

$$= \left(x_a x_b + y_a y_b + z_a z_b \right) + \left(x_a x_c + y_a y_c + z_a z_c \right) = \vec{a} \cdot \vec{b} + \vec{a} \cdot \vec{c}.$$

Geometrically, the dot product of two vectors can be related to the angle between the vectors when both are positioned at the origin, as noted in Figure 3–10.

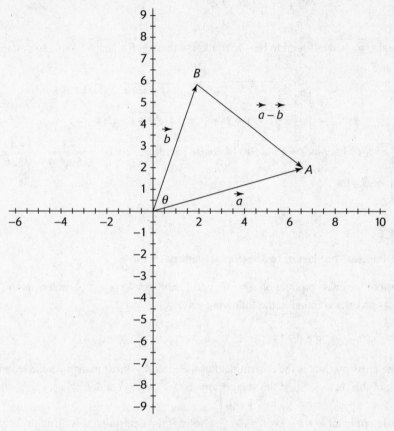

Figure 3–10

By applying the law of cosines to this triangle, you get the following:

$$\left|\vec{a}-\vec{b}\right|^2 = \left|\vec{a}\right|^2 + \left|\vec{b}\right|^2 - 2\left|\vec{a}\right|\left|\vec{b}\right|\cos\theta$$

Using the given properties, you can say the following:

$$\left|\vec{a}-\vec{b}\right|^2 = \left(\vec{a}-\vec{b}\right)\cdot\left(\vec{a}-\vec{b}\right) = \vec{a}\cdot\vec{a} - \vec{a}\cdot\vec{b} - \vec{b}\cdot\vec{a} + \vec{b}\cdot\vec{b} = \left|\vec{a}\right|^2 - 2\,\vec{a}\cdot\vec{b} + \left|\vec{b}\right|^2$$

Therefore, the law of cosines becomes

$$\left|\vec{a}\right|^2 - 2\,\vec{a}\cdot\vec{b} + \left|\vec{b}\right|^2 = \left|\vec{a}\right|^2 + \left|\vec{b}\right|^2 - 2\left|\vec{a}\right|\left|\vec{b}\right|\cos\theta$$

$$-2\,\vec{a}\cdot\vec{b} = -2\left|\vec{a}\right|\left|\vec{b}\right|\cos\theta$$

$$\vec{a}\cdot\vec{b} = \left|\vec{a}\right|\left|\vec{b}\right|\cos\theta.$$

Example 1:

Find the dot product of the vectors $\vec{a} = \langle 1, -3, 7\rangle$ and $\vec{b} = \langle -2, 3, 1\rangle$.

Solution:

$$\vec{a}\cdot\vec{b} = (1)(-2) + (-3)(3) + (7)(1) = -2 - 9 + 7 = -11 + 7 = -4$$

Example 2:

Find the angle between the vectors $\vec{a} = \langle 1, -3, 7 \rangle$ and $\vec{b} = \langle -2, 3, 1 \rangle$ when both are positioned at the origin.

Solution:

In the prior example, $\vec{a} \cdot \vec{b}$ was found to be –4. You know that $\vec{a} \cdot \vec{b} = |\vec{a}||\vec{b}|\cos\theta$, so you need to find the magnitude of $\vec{a}$ and $\vec{b}$.

$$|\vec{a}| = \sqrt{1^2 + (-3)^2 + 7^2} = \sqrt{1 + 9 + 49} = \sqrt{59}$$

$$|\vec{b}| = \sqrt{(-2)^2 + 3^2 + 1^2} = \sqrt{4 + 9 + 1} = \sqrt{14}$$

Then $\vec{a} \cdot \vec{b} = |\vec{a}||\vec{b}|\cos\theta$ becomes $-4 = \sqrt{59}\sqrt{14}\cos\theta$. Therefore, $\cos\theta = \dfrac{-4}{\sqrt{59}\sqrt{14}} = \dfrac{-4}{\sqrt{826}}$, so $\theta = \cos^{-1}\left(\dfrac{-4}{\sqrt{826}}\right)$, or $\theta = 98°$.

Cross Product

Unlike the dot product, the cross product of two vectors is another vector.

The geometric definition of the cross product of $\vec{a} = \langle x_a, y_a, z_a \rangle$ and $\vec{b} = \langle x_b, y_b, z_b \rangle$, noted $\vec{a} \times \vec{b}$, is perpendicular to both $\vec{a}$ and $\vec{b}$. The cross product is found in the following way:

$$\vec{a} \times \vec{b} = \langle y_a z_b - z_a y_b,\ z_a x_b - x_a z_b,\ x_a y_b - y_a x_b \rangle$$

One interpretation of the cross product is the determinant of the three-by-three matrix whose second and third rows are the components of each of the vectors. So, if the vectors are $\vec{a} = \langle x_a, y_a, z_a \rangle$ and $\vec{b} = \langle x_b, y_b, z_b \rangle$, the cross product can be found by taking the determinant $\vec{a} \times \vec{b} = \begin{vmatrix} \mathbf{i} & \mathbf{j} & \mathbf{k} \\ x_a & y_a & z_a \\ x_b & y_b & z_b \end{vmatrix}$. (Note: If the determinant is difficult for you, look at the extra practice section for **SMR** 1.4 Matrices and Determinants). So,

$$\vec{a} \times \vec{b} = \begin{vmatrix} \mathbf{i} & \mathbf{j} & \mathbf{k} \\ x_a & y_a & z_a \\ x_b & y_b & z_b \end{vmatrix} = \mathbf{i}\begin{vmatrix} y_a & z_a \\ y_b & z_b \end{vmatrix} - \mathbf{j}\begin{vmatrix} x_a & z_a \\ x_b & z_b \end{vmatrix} + \mathbf{k}\begin{vmatrix} x_a & y_a \\ x_b & y_b \end{vmatrix} = \mathbf{i}(y_a z_b - z_a y_b) - \mathbf{j}(x_a z_b - z_a x_b) + \mathbf{k}(x_a y_b - y_a x_b)$$

$$= \langle y_a z_b - z_a y_b,\ z_a x_b - x_a z_b,\ x_a y_b - y_a x_b \rangle.$$

Example:

Find the cross product of $\vec{a} = \langle 2, 3, -1 \rangle$ and $\vec{b} = \langle -3, 2, 4 \rangle$.

Solution:

Just using the fact that $\vec{a} \times \vec{b} = \langle y_a z_b - z_a y_b,\ z_a x_b - x_a z_b,\ x_a y_b - y_a x_b \rangle$, you can find the cross product as follows:

$$\vec{a} \times \vec{b} = \langle (3)(4) - (-1)(2),\ (-1)(-3) - (2)(4),\ (2)(2) - (3)(3)(-3) \rangle = \langle (12 - (-2)),\ (3 - 8),\ (4 - (-9)) \rangle$$

$$= \langle 14, -5, 13 \rangle$$

Alternatively, you can find the cross product using determinants.

$$\vec{a} \times \vec{b} = \begin{vmatrix} \mathbf{i} & \mathbf{j} & \mathbf{k} \\ 2 & 3 & -1 \\ -3 & 2 & 4 \end{vmatrix} = \mathbf{i}\begin{vmatrix} 3 & -1 \\ 2 & 4 \end{vmatrix} - \mathbf{j}\begin{vmatrix} 2 & -1 \\ -3 & 4 \end{vmatrix} + \mathbf{k}\begin{vmatrix} 2 & 3 \\ -3 & 2 \end{vmatrix} = \mathbf{i}(12 - (-2)) - \mathbf{j}(8 - 3) + \mathbf{k}(4 - (-9))$$

$$= 14\mathbf{i} - 5\mathbf{j} + 13\mathbf{k} = \langle 14, -5, 13 \rangle$$

Length of the Cross Product

The length of the cross product can be found by using algebraic properties.

$$\left|\vec{a}\times\vec{b}\right|^2 = \left(y_a z_b - z_a y_b\right)^2 + \left(z_a x_b - x_a z_b\right)^2 + \left(x_a y_b - y_a x_b\right)^2$$

$$= \left(y_a^2 z_b^2 - 2y_a z_a y_b z_b + z_a^2 y_b^2\right) + \left(z_a^2 x_b^2 - 2x_a z_a x_b z_b + x_a^2 z_b^2\right) + \left(x_a^2 y_b^2 - 2x_a y_a x_b y_b + y_a^2 x_b^2\right)$$

$$= \left(x_a^2 + y_a^2 + z_a^2\right)\left(x_b^2 + y_b^2 + z_b^2\right) - \left(x_a x_b + y_a y_b + z_a z_b\right)^2$$

$$= \left|\vec{a}\right|^2\left|\vec{b}\right|^2 - \left(\vec{a}\cdot\vec{b}\right)^2 = \left|\vec{a}\right|^2\left|\vec{b}\right|^2 - \left|\vec{a}\right|^2\left|\vec{b}\right|^2\cos^2\theta = \left|\vec{a}\right|^2\left|\vec{b}\right|^2\left(1 - \cos^2\theta\right) = \left|\vec{a}\right|^2\left|\vec{b}\right|^2\sin^2\theta$$

So, $\left|\vec{a}\times\vec{b}\right| = \left|\vec{a}\right|\left|\vec{b}\right|\sin\theta$ if $0 \le \theta \le \pi$.

So, the cross product of $\vec{a}$ and $\vec{b}$ can be thought of as the vector that is perpendicular to both $\vec{a}$ and $\vec{b}$ and has a length of $\left|\vec{a}\right|\left|\vec{b}\right|\sin\theta$.

Geometrically, if you consider a parallelogram whose sides are vectors $\vec{a}$ and $\vec{b}$, you can find the area of this parallelogram by finding the height of the parallelogram as shown in Figure 3–11.

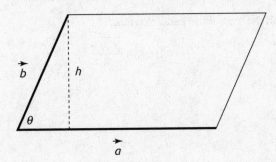

Figure 3–11

The height of the figure can be found with $\sin\theta = \dfrac{h}{\left|\vec{b}\right|}$, so $h = \left|\vec{b}\right|\sin\theta$. Then the area of the parallelogram can be found with $A = bh = \left|\vec{a}\right|\left|\vec{b}\right|\sin\theta = \left|\vec{a}\times\vec{b}\right|$. Thus, the magnitude of the cross product can be interpreted as the area of a parallelogram whose sides are the vectors.

Example 1:

Find the area of the parallelogram whose sides are made by the vectors $\vec{a} = \langle 3, -2, -1\rangle$ and $\vec{b} = \langle -4, 5, 1\rangle$.

Solution:

The area of the parallelogram is found by finding the magnitude of the cross product. Therefore, you need to first find the cross product. You will use determinants in this case.

$$\vec{a}\times\vec{b} = \begin{vmatrix} \mathbf{i} & \mathbf{j} & \mathbf{k} \\ 3 & -2 & -1 \\ -4 & 5 & 1 \end{vmatrix} = \mathbf{i}\begin{vmatrix} -2 & -1 \\ 5 & 1 \end{vmatrix} - \mathbf{j}\begin{vmatrix} 3 & -1 \\ -4 & 1 \end{vmatrix} + \mathbf{k}\begin{vmatrix} 3 & -2 \\ -4 & 5 \end{vmatrix} = \mathbf{i}\left(-2 - (-5)\right) - \mathbf{j}(3 - 4) + \mathbf{k}(15 - 8)$$

$$= 3\mathbf{i} + \mathbf{j} + 7\mathbf{k} = \langle 3, 1, 7\rangle$$

The area of the parallelogram is the magnitude of this vector. Therefore,

$$Area = \sqrt{3^2 + 1^2 + 7^2} = \sqrt{9 + 1 + 49} = \sqrt{59}.$$

Example 2:

Find the area of the triangle, which is determined by the vectors $\vec{a} = \langle 1, 2, -4 \rangle$ and $\vec{b} = \langle 2, -3, -1 \rangle$.

Solution:

The area of a triangle is half the area of the parallelogram formed by the same vectors. First, find the area of the parallelogram and then find the area of the triangle. To find the area of the parallelogram, first find the cross product.

$$\vec{a} \times \vec{b} = \begin{vmatrix} \mathbf{i} & \mathbf{j} & \mathbf{k} \\ 1 & 2 & -4 \\ 2 & -3 & -1 \end{vmatrix} = \mathbf{i} \begin{vmatrix} 2 & -4 \\ -3 & -1 \end{vmatrix} - \mathbf{j} \begin{vmatrix} 1 & -4 \\ 2 & -1 \end{vmatrix} + \mathbf{k} \begin{vmatrix} 1 & 2 \\ 2 & -3 \end{vmatrix} = \mathbf{i}(-2 - 12) - \mathbf{j}(-1 - (-8)) + \mathbf{k}(-3 - 4)$$

$$= 14\mathbf{i} + -7\mathbf{j} - 7\mathbf{k} = \langle -14, -7, -7 \rangle$$

The area of the parallelogram is the magnitude of the cross product.

$$Area_{par} = \sqrt{(-14)^2 + (-7)^2 + (-7)^2} = \sqrt{196 + 49 + 49} = \sqrt{294}$$

The area of the triangle is half the area of the parallelogram, so

$$Area_{tri} = \frac{\sqrt{294}}{2}.$$

Practice Problems

1. Find the vector represented by the directed line segment from point (2, –6) to point (–3, 4).

2. Find the magnitude and direction of the vector from problem 1.

For problems 3–12, use the fact that $\vec{a} = \langle -3, 6 \rangle$ and $\vec{b} = \langle 4, -2 \rangle$.

3. Find $\vec{a} + \vec{b}$.

4. Find $\left| \vec{a} + \vec{b} \right|$.

5. Find $\vec{a} - \vec{b}$.

6. Find $\left| \vec{a} - \vec{b} \right|$.

7. Find $2\vec{a} + 3\vec{b}$.

8. Find $-3\vec{a} - 6\vec{b}$.

9. Find $\vec{a} \cdot \vec{b}$.

10. Find the angle between $\vec{a}$ and $\vec{b}$.

11. Find $\vec{a} \times \vec{b}$.

12. Find the area of the triangle formed by vectors $\vec{a}$ and $\vec{b}$.

Solutions

1. The vector begins at the point (2, –6) and ends at the point (–3, 4). If you graphed this vector, it would look like Figure 3–12:

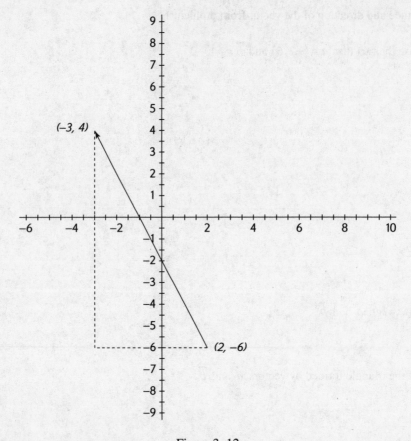

Figure 3–12

The horizontal component is five units to the left, and the vertical component is 10 units up. Therefore, the vector can be defined as $\langle -5, 10 \rangle$. An alternative method is to use the definition of the vector to say $\langle -3 - 2, 4 - (-6) \rangle = \langle -5, 10 \rangle$.

2. The magnitude and direction are found using the Pythagorean Theorem and trigonometry. Using the preceding figure, the magnitude can be found by using the Pythagorean Theorem. So

$$magnitude = \sqrt{(-5)^2 + (10)^2} = \sqrt{25 + 100} = \sqrt{125}.$$

The direction can be found by using inverse tangent. So

$$direction = \theta = \tan^{-1}\left(\frac{10}{-5}\right) = \tan^{-1}(-2) = -63°.$$

Since the vector is pointing up and to the right, the angle is between 90 and 180. Therefore, the direction would be about 117°.

For problems 3–8, use the fact that $\vec{a} = \langle -3, 6 \rangle$ and $\vec{b} = \langle 4, -2 \rangle$.

3. To find $\vec{a} + \vec{b}$, add the corresponding components of each of the vectors, so

$$\vec{a} + \vec{b} = \langle -3, 6 \rangle + \langle 4, -2 \rangle = \langle -3 + 4, 6 + (-2) \rangle = \langle 1, 4 \rangle.$$

4. To find $\left|\vec{a} + \vec{b}\right|$, use the prior result. This means you want to find

$$\left|\langle 1, 4 \rangle\right| = \sqrt{1^2 + 4^2} = \sqrt{1 + 16} = \sqrt{17}.$$

5. To find $\vec{a} - \vec{b}$, subtract the corresponding components of each of the vectors, so

$$\vec{a} - \vec{b} = \langle -3, 6 \rangle - \langle 4, -2 \rangle = \langle -3 - 4, 6 - (-2) \rangle = \langle -7, 8 \rangle.$$

6. To find $\left| \vec{a} - \vec{b} \right|$, again use the prior result. This means you want to find

$$\left| \langle -7, 8 \rangle \right| = \sqrt{(-7)^2 + 8^2} = \sqrt{49 + 64} = \sqrt{113}.$$

7. Find $2\vec{a} + 3\vec{b}$. Since $\vec{a} = \langle -3, 6 \rangle$, $2\vec{a} = \langle (2)(-3), (2)(6) \rangle = \langle -6, 12 \rangle$. Since $\vec{b} = \langle 4, -2 \rangle$,

$3\vec{b} = \langle (3)(4), (3)(-2) \rangle = \langle 12, -6 \rangle$. You want to add these together, so

$2\vec{a} + 3\vec{b} = \langle -6, 12 \rangle + \langle 12, -6 \rangle = \langle -6 + 12 \ 12 + (-6) \rangle = \langle 6, 6 \rangle.$

8. Find $-3\vec{a} - 6\vec{b}$. Since $\vec{a} = \langle -3, 6 \rangle$, $-3\vec{a} = \langle (-3)(-3), (-3)(6) \rangle = \langle 9, -18 \rangle$. Since $\vec{b} = \langle 4, -2 \rangle$,

$-6\vec{b} = \langle (-6)(4), (-6)(-2) \rangle = \langle -24, 12 \rangle$. You want to add these together, so

$-3\vec{a} - 6\vec{b} = \langle 9, -18 \rangle + \langle -24, 12 \rangle = \langle 9 + (-24), -18 + 12 \rangle = \langle -15, -6 \rangle.$

9. Find $\vec{a} \cdot \vec{b}$. Since $\vec{a} = \langle -3, 6 \rangle$ and $\vec{b} = \langle 4, -2 \rangle$, $\vec{a} \cdot \vec{b} = (-3)(4) + (6)(-2) = -12 - 12 = -24.$

10. To find the angle between $\vec{a}$ and $\vec{b}$, use the dot product. So $\vec{a} \cdot \vec{b} = \left| \vec{a} \right| \left| \vec{b} \right| \cos\theta$.

You need to find the magnitude of each of the vectors. Therefore, $\left| \vec{a} \right| = \sqrt{(-3)^2 + (6)^2} = \sqrt{9 + 36} = \sqrt{45} = 3\sqrt{5}$

and $\left| \vec{b} \right| = \sqrt{(4)^2 + (-2)^2} = \sqrt{16 + 4} = \sqrt{20} = 2\sqrt{5}$. Then $\vec{a} \cdot \vec{b} = \left| \vec{a} \right| \left| \vec{b} \right| \cos\theta$ becomes $-24 = (3\sqrt{5})(2\sqrt{5})\cos\theta$.

Then $\cos\theta = \dfrac{-24}{30} = \dfrac{-4}{5}$. Therefore, $\theta = \cos^{-1}\left(\dfrac{-4}{5}\right)$ and $\theta =$ approximately $143°$.

11. To find $\vec{a} \times \vec{b}$, set up a determinant to evaluate.

$$\vec{a} \times \vec{b} = \begin{vmatrix} \mathbf{i} & \mathbf{j} & \mathbf{k} \\ -3 & 6 & 0 \\ 4 & -2 & 0 \end{vmatrix} = \mathbf{i}\begin{vmatrix} 6 & 0 \\ -2 & 0 \end{vmatrix} - \mathbf{j}\begin{vmatrix} -3 & 0 \\ 4 & 0 \end{vmatrix} + \mathbf{k}\begin{vmatrix} -3 & 6 \\ 4 & -2 \end{vmatrix} = \mathbf{i}(0-0) - \mathbf{j}(0-0) + \mathbf{k}(6-24)$$

$= 0\mathbf{i} + 0\mathbf{j} - 18\mathbf{k} = \langle 0, 0, -18 \rangle$

12. The area of the triangle is half the area of the corresponding parallelogram. The area of the parallelogram is the magnitude of the cross product found in problem 11. The magnitude of the cross product is 18, so the area of the triangle is 9.

Vectors have several basic properties. They are listed here, and one is given a proof. The others are left to you to prove the property in the practice exercises.

Properties of Vectors

If $\vec{a}$, $\vec{b}$, and $\vec{c}$ are vectors and c and d are scalars, then

1. $\vec{a} + \vec{b} = \vec{b} + \vec{a}$
2. $\vec{a} + \left(\vec{b} + \vec{c} \right) = \left(\vec{a} + \vec{b} \right) + \vec{c}$
3. $\vec{a} + \vec{0} = \vec{a}$
4. $\vec{a} + \left(-\vec{a} \right) = \vec{0}$
5. $c \left(\vec{a} + \vec{b} \right) = c\,\vec{a} + c\,\vec{b}$
6. $(c + d)\vec{a} = c\,\vec{a} + d\,\vec{a}$
7. $(cd)\vec{a} = c \left(d\,\vec{a} \right)$
8. $1\,\vec{a} = \vec{a}$

Example:

Prove property number 5: $c \left(\vec{a} + \vec{b} \right) = c\,\vec{a} + c\,\vec{b}$.

Solution:

Suppose $\vec{a} = \langle x_a, y_a, z_a \rangle$ and $\vec{b} = \langle x_b, y_b, z_b \rangle$. You can find $\vec{a} + \vec{b} = \langle x_a + x_b,\ y_a + y_b,\ z_a + z_b \rangle$. Then

$$c \left(\vec{a} + \vec{b} \right) = \langle c\left(x_a + x_b \right),\ c\left(y_a + y_b \right),\ c\left(z_a + z_b \right) \rangle = \langle cx_a + cx_b,\ cy_a + cy_b,\ cz_a + cz_b \rangle$$

$$= \langle cx_a, cy_a, cz_a \rangle + \langle cx_b, cy_b, cz_b \rangle = c\,\vec{a} + c\,\vec{b}.$$

Therefore, $c \left(\vec{a} + \vec{b} \right) = c\,\vec{a} + c\,\vec{b}$.

Properties of the Dot Product

If $\vec{a}$, $\vec{b}$, and $\vec{c}$ are vectors and c and d are scalars, then the following properties of the dot product hold true.

1. $\vec{a} \cdot \vec{a} = \left| \vec{a} \right|^2$
2. $\vec{a} \cdot \vec{b} = \vec{b} \cdot \vec{a}$
3. $\vec{a} \cdot \left(\vec{b} + \vec{c} \right) = \vec{a} \cdot \vec{b} + \vec{a} \cdot \vec{c}$
4. $\left(c\,\vec{a} \right) \cdot \vec{b} = c \left(\vec{a} \cdot \vec{b} \right) = \vec{a} \cdot \left(c\,\vec{b} \right)$
5. $\vec{0} \cdot \vec{a} = 0$

Example:

Prove property number 3: $\vec{a} \cdot \left(\vec{b} + \vec{c} \right) = \vec{a} \cdot \vec{b} + \vec{a} \cdot \vec{c}$.

Solution:

Suppose $\vec{a} = \langle x_a, y_a, z_a \rangle, \vec{b} = \langle x_b, y_b, z_b \rangle$, and $\vec{c} = \langle x_c, y_c, z_c \rangle$.

Then $\vec{b} + \vec{c} = \langle x_b + x_c,\ y_b + y_c,\ z_b + z_c \rangle$ and $\vec{a} \cdot \left(\vec{b} + \vec{c} \right) = x_a \left(x_b + x_c \right) + y_a \left(y_b + y_c \right) + z_a \left(z_b + z_c \right)$.

Distributing and recombining terms gives:

$$\vec{a} \cdot \left(\vec{b} + \vec{c} \right) = x_a x_b + x_a x_c + y_a y_b + y_a y_c + z_a z_b + z_a z_c = \left(x_a x_b + y_a y_b + z_a z_b \right) + \left(x_a x_c + y_a y_c + z_a z_c \right) =$$
$$\vec{a} \cdot \vec{b} + \vec{a} \cdot \vec{c}$$

Therefore, $\vec{a} \cdot \left(\vec{b} + \vec{c} \right) = \vec{a} \cdot \vec{b} + \vec{a} \cdot \vec{c}$.

Properties of Cross Product

If $\vec{a}$, $\vec{b}$, and $\vec{c}$ are vectors and c and d are scalars, then the following properties of the cross product hold true.

1. $\vec{a} \times \vec{b} = -\vec{b} \times \vec{a}$
2. $\left(c\,\vec{a} \right) \times \vec{b} = c \left(\vec{a} \times \vec{b} \right) = \vec{a} \times \left(c\,\vec{b} \right)$
3. $\vec{a} \times \left(\vec{b} + \vec{c} \right) = \left(\vec{a} \times \vec{b} \right) + \left(\vec{a} \times \vec{c} \right)$
4. $\left(\vec{a} + \vec{b} \right) \times \vec{c} = \left(\vec{a} \times \vec{c} \right) + \left(\vec{b} \times c \right)$
5. $\vec{a} \cdot \left(\vec{b} \times \vec{c} \right) = \left(\vec{a} \times \vec{b} \right) \cdot \vec{c}$
6. $\vec{a} \times \left(\vec{b} \times \vec{c} \right) = \left(\vec{a} \cdot \vec{c} \right) \vec{b} - \left(\vec{a} \cdot \vec{b} \right) \vec{c}$

Example:

Prove property number 2: $\left(c\,\vec{a} \right) \times \vec{b} = c \left(\vec{a} \times \vec{b} \right) = \vec{a} \times \left(c\,\vec{b} \right)$.

Solution:

Suppose $\vec{a} = \langle x_a, y_a, z_a \rangle, \vec{b} = \langle x_b, y_b, z_b \rangle$, and $\vec{c} = \langle x_c, y_c, z_c \rangle$.

Then $c\,\vec{a} = \langle cx_a, cy_a, cz_a \rangle$, so $\left(c\,\vec{a} \right) \times \vec{b} = \begin{vmatrix} \mathbf{i} & \mathbf{j} & \mathbf{k} \\ cx_a & cy_a & cz_a \\ x_b & y_b & z_b \end{vmatrix}$. Evaluating this determinant gives

$$\mathbf{i} \begin{vmatrix} cy_a & cz_a \\ y_b & z_b \end{vmatrix} - \mathbf{j} \begin{vmatrix} cx_a & cz_a \\ x_b & z_b \end{vmatrix} + \mathbf{k} \begin{vmatrix} cx_a & cy_a \\ x_b & y_b \end{vmatrix} = \mathbf{i} \left(cy_a z_b - cz_a y_b \right) - \mathbf{j} \left(cx_a z_b - cz_a x_b \right) + \mathbf{k} \left(cx_a y_b - cy_a x_b \right) =$$
$$\langle cy_z z_b - cz_a y_b,\ cx_a z_b - cz_a y_b,\ cx_a y_b - cy_a x_b \rangle.$$

There is a common factor of c throughout, so $\left(c\,\vec{a} \right) \times \vec{b}$ becomes

$$\langle c \left(y_a z_b - z_a y_b \right),\ c \left(x_a z_b - z_a x_b \right),\ c \left(x_a y_b - y_a x_b \right) \rangle = c \left(\vec{a} \times \vec{b} \right).$$

Therefore, $\left(c\,\vec{a} \right) \times \vec{b} = c \left(\vec{a} \times \vec{b} \right)$. You can also return to $\left(c\,\vec{a} \right) \times \vec{b}$ and reorganize the vector. Then

$$\langle cy_a z_b - cz_a y_b,\ cx_a z_b - cz_a x_b,\ cx_a y_b - cy_a x_b \rangle = \langle y_a \left(cz_b \right) - z_a \left(cy_b \right),\ x_a \left(cz_b \right) - z_a \left(cx_b \right),\ x_a \left(cy_b \right) - y_a \left(cx_b \right) \rangle =$$
$$\vec{a} \times \left(c\,\vec{b} \right). \text{ Therefore, } \left(c\,\vec{a} \right) \times \vec{b} = c \left(\vec{a} \times \vec{b} \right) = \vec{a} \times \left(c\,\vec{b} \right).$$

Practice Problems

If $\vec{a}$, $\vec{b}$, and $\vec{c}$ are vectors and c and d are scalars, then prove the following:

1. $\vec{a} + \vec{b} = \vec{b} + \vec{a}$

2. $\vec{a} + \left(\vec{b} + \vec{c} \right) = \left(\vec{a} + \vec{b} \right) + \vec{c}$

3. $\vec{a} + \vec{0} = \vec{a}$

4. $\vec{a} + \left(-\vec{a} \right) = \vec{0}$

5. $(c + d)\vec{a} = c\,\vec{a} + d\,\vec{a}$

6. $(cd)\vec{a} = c\left(d\,\vec{a} \right)$

7. $1\vec{a} = \vec{a}$

8. $\vec{a} \cdot \vec{a} = \left| \vec{a} \right|^2$

9. $\vec{a} \cdot \vec{b} = \vec{b} \cdot \vec{a}$

10. $\left(c\,\vec{a} \right) \cdot \vec{b} = c\left(\vec{a} \cdot \vec{b} \right) = \vec{a} \cdot \left(c\,\vec{b} \right)$

11. $\vec{0} \cdot \vec{a} = 0$

12. $\vec{a} \times \vec{b} = -\vec{b} \times \vec{a}$

13. $\vec{a} \times \left(\vec{b} + \vec{c} \right) = \left(\vec{a} \times \vec{b} \right) + \left(\vec{a} \times \vec{c} \right)$

14. $\left(\vec{a} + \vec{b} \right) \times \vec{c} = \left(\vec{a} \times \vec{b} \right) + \left(\vec{b} \times \vec{c} \right)$

15. $\vec{a} \cdot \left(\vec{b} \times \vec{c} \right) = \left(\vec{a} \times \vec{b} \right) \cdot \vec{c}$

16. $\vec{a} \times \left(\vec{b} \times \vec{c} \right) = \left(\vec{a} \cdot \vec{c} \right)\vec{b} - \left(\vec{a} \cdot \vec{b} \right)\vec{c}$

Solutions

1. Prove: $\vec{a} + \vec{b} = \vec{b} + \vec{a}$.

Suppose $\vec{a} = \langle x_a, y_a, z_a \rangle$ and $\vec{b} = \langle x_b, y_b, z_b \rangle$. Then $\vec{a} + \vec{b} = \langle x_a + x_b,\ y_a + y_b,\ z_a + z_b \rangle = \langle x_b + x_a,\ y_b + y_a,\ z_b + z_a \rangle = \vec{b} + \vec{a}$. Therefore, $\vec{a} + \vec{b} = \vec{b} + \vec{a}$.

2. Prove: $\vec{a} + \left(\vec{b} + \vec{c} \right) = \left(\vec{a} + \vec{b} \right) + \vec{c}$.

Suppose $\vec{a} = \langle x_a, y_a, z_a \rangle, \vec{b} = \langle x_b, y_b, z_b \rangle$, and $\vec{c} = \langle x_c, y_c, z_c \rangle$. Then $\left(\vec{b} + \vec{c} \right) = \langle x_b + x_c,\ y_b + y_c,\ z_b + z_c \rangle$. Then $\vec{a} + \left(\vec{b} + \vec{c} \right) = \langle x_a + (x_b + x_c),\ y_a + (y_b + y_c),\ z_a + (z_b + z_c) \rangle$. This can be written as $\langle (x_a + x_b) + x_c,\ (y_a + y_b) + y_c,\ (z_a + z_b) + z_c \rangle = \left(\vec{a} + \vec{b} \right) + \vec{c}$. Therefore, $\vec{a} + \left(\vec{b} + \vec{c} \right) = \left(\vec{a} + \vec{b} \right) + \vec{c}$.

3. Prove: $\vec{a} + \vec{0} = \vec{a}$.

Suppose $\vec{a} = \langle x_a, y_a, z_a \rangle$. The vector $\vec{0} = \langle 0, 0, 0 \rangle$. Then $\vec{a} + \vec{0} = \langle x_a + 0,\ y_a + 0,\ z_a + 0 \rangle = \langle x_a, y_a, z_a \rangle = \vec{a}$. Therefore, $\vec{a} + \vec{0} = \vec{a}$.

4. Prove: $\vec{a} + \left(-\vec{a} \right) = \vec{0}$.

Suppose $\vec{a} = \langle x_a, y_a, z_a \rangle$. Then $-\vec{a} = (-1)\vec{a} = \langle -x_a, -y_a, -z_a \rangle$. Then $\vec{a} + \left(-\vec{a} \right) = \langle x_a + (-x_a),\ y_a + (-y_a),\ z_a + (-z_a) \rangle = \langle 0, 0, 0 \rangle = \vec{0}$. Therefore, $\vec{a} + \left(-\vec{a} \right) = \vec{0}$.

5. Prove: $(c + d)\vec{a} = c\,\vec{a} + d\,\vec{a}$.

Suppose $\vec{a} = \langle x_a, y_a, z_a \rangle$. Then $(c + d)\vec{a} = \langle (c + d)x_a,\ (c + d)y_a,\ (c + d)z_a \rangle = \langle cx_a + dx_a,\ cy_a + dy_a,\ dz_a + dz_a \rangle$. This can be written as $\langle cx_a, cy_a, cz_a \rangle + \langle dx_a, dy_a, dz_a \rangle = c\,\vec{a} + d\,\vec{a}$. Therefore, $(c + d)\vec{a} = c\,\vec{a} + d\,\vec{a}$.

6. Prove: $(cd)\vec{a} = c\left(d\,\vec{a} \right)$.

Suppose $\vec{a} = \langle x_a, y_a, z_a \rangle$. Then $(cd)\vec{a} = \langle (cd)x_a,\ (cd)y_a,\ (cd)z_a \rangle = \langle c(dx_a),\ c(dy_a),\ c(dz_a) \rangle = c\left(d\,\vec{a} \right)$. Therefore, $(cd)\vec{a} = c\left(d\,\vec{a} \right)$.

7. Prove: $1\,\vec{a} = \vec{a}$.

Suppose $\vec{a} = \langle x_a, y_a, z_a \rangle$. Then $1\,\vec{a} = \langle 1(x_a),\ 1(y_a),\ 1(z_a) \rangle = \langle x_a, y_a, z_a \rangle = \vec{a}$. Therefore, $1\,\vec{a} = \vec{a}$.

8. Prove: $\vec{a} \cdot \vec{a} = \left| \vec{a} \right|^2$.

Suppose $\vec{a} = \langle x_a, y_a, z_a \rangle$. Then $\vec{a} \cdot \vec{a} = x_a x_a + y_a y_a + z_a z_a = x_a^2 + y_a^2 + z_a^2 = \left(\sqrt{x_a^2 + y_a^2 + z_a^2} \right)^2 = \left| \vec{a} \right|^2$. Therefore, $\vec{a} \cdot \vec{a} = \left| \vec{a} \right|^2$.

9. Prove: $\vec{a} \cdot \vec{b} = \vec{b} \cdot \vec{a}$.

Suppose $\vec{a} = \langle x_a, y_a, z_a \rangle$ and $\vec{b} = \langle x_b, y_b, z_b \rangle$. Then $\vec{a} \cdot \vec{b} = x_a x_b + y_a y_b + z_a z_b = x_b x_a + y_b y_a + z_b z_a = \vec{b} \cdot \vec{a}$. Therefore, $\vec{a} \cdot \vec{b} = \vec{b} \cdot \vec{a}$.

10. Prove: $\left(c\,\vec{a} \right) \cdot \vec{b} = c\left(\vec{a} \cdot \vec{b} \right) = \vec{a} \cdot \left(c\,\vec{b} \right)$.

Suppose $\vec{a} = \langle x_a, y_a, z_a \rangle$ and $\vec{b} = \langle x_b, y_b, z_b \rangle$. Then $c\,\vec{a} = \langle cx_a, cy_a, cz_a \rangle$. Thus, $\left(c\,\vec{a} \right) \cdot \vec{b} = (cx_a)x_b + (cy_a)y_b + (cz_a)z_b$. This can be written as $c(x_a x_b) + c(y_a y_b) + c(z_a z_b) = c\left(\vec{a} \cdot \vec{b} \right)$. Therefore, $\left(c\,\vec{a} \right) \cdot \vec{b} = c\left(\vec{a} \cdot \vec{b} \right)$. Similarly, $\left(c\,\vec{a} \right) \cdot \vec{b} = (cx_a)x_b + (cy_a)y_b + (cz_a)z_b = x_a(cx_b) + y_a(cy_b) + z_a(cz_b) = \vec{a} \cdot \left(c\,\vec{b} \right)$. Therefore, $\left(c\,\vec{a} \right) \cdot \vec{b} = c\left(\vec{a} \cdot \vec{b} \right) = \vec{a} \cdot \left(c\,\vec{b} \right)$.

11. Prove: $\vec{0} \cdot \vec{a} = 0$.

Suppose $\vec{a} = \langle x_a, y_a, z_a \rangle$. The vector $\vec{0} = \langle 0, 0, 0 \rangle$. Therefore, $\vec{0} \cdot \vec{a} = 0(x_a) + 0(x_b) + 0(x_c) = 0 + 0 + 0 = 0$. Therefore, $\vec{0} \cdot \vec{a} = 0$.

12. Prove: $\vec{a} \times \vec{b} = -\vec{b} \times \vec{a}$.

Suppose $\vec{a} = \langle x_a, y_a, z_a \rangle$ and $\vec{b} = \langle x_b, y_b, z_b \rangle$. So $-\vec{b} = \langle -x_b, -y_b, -z_b \rangle$. Then we can write

$\vec{a} \times \vec{b} = \begin{vmatrix} y_a & z_a \\ y_b & z_b \end{vmatrix} \mathbf{i} - \begin{vmatrix} x_a & z_a \\ x_b & z_b \end{vmatrix} \mathbf{j} + \begin{vmatrix} x_a & y_a \\ x_b & y_b \end{vmatrix} \mathbf{k} = (y_a z_b - z_a y_b) \mathbf{i} - (x_a z_b - z_a x_b) \mathbf{j} + (x_a y_b - y_a x_b) \mathbf{k}$. Similarly,

$-\vec{b} \times \vec{a} = \begin{vmatrix} -y_b & -z_b \\ y_a & z_a \end{vmatrix} \mathbf{i} - \begin{vmatrix} -x_b & -z_b \\ x_a & z_a \end{vmatrix} \mathbf{j} + \begin{vmatrix} -x_b & -y_b \\ x_a & y_a \end{vmatrix} \mathbf{k} =$

$\left(-z_a y_b - (-y_a z_b) \right) \mathbf{i} - \left(-z_a x_b - (-x_a z_b) \right) \mathbf{j} + \left(-y_a x_b - (-x_a y_b) \right) \mathbf{k}$,

which can be written as

$\left(-z_a y_b + y_a z_b \right) \mathbf{i} - \left(-z_a x_b + x_a z_b \right) \mathbf{j} + \left(-y_a x_b + x_a y_b \right) \mathbf{k}$

$= \left(y_a z_b - z_a y_b \right) \mathbf{i} - \left(x_a z_b - z_a x_b \right) \mathbf{j} + \left(x_a y_b - y_a x_b \right) \mathbf{k} = \vec{a} \times \vec{b}$.

Therefore, $\vec{a} \times \vec{b} = -\vec{b} \times \vec{a}$.

13. Prove: $\vec{a} \times \left(\vec{b} + \vec{c} \right) = \left(\vec{a} \times \vec{b} \right) + \left(\vec{a} \times \vec{c} \right)$.

Suppose $\vec{a} = \langle x_a, y_a, z_a \rangle, \vec{b} = \langle x_b, y_b, z_b \rangle$, and $\vec{c} = \langle x_c, y_c, z_c \rangle$. Then $\vec{b} + \vec{c} = \langle x_b + x_c, \, y_b + y_c, \, z_b + z_c \rangle$. Therefore,

$\vec{a} \times \left(\vec{b} + \vec{c} \right) = \begin{vmatrix} \mathbf{i} & \mathbf{j} & \mathbf{k} \\ x_a & y_a & z_a \\ x_b + x_c & y_b + y_c & z_b + z_c \end{vmatrix} = \begin{vmatrix} y_a & z_a \\ y_b + y_c & z_b + z_c \end{vmatrix} \mathbf{i} - \begin{vmatrix} x_a & z_a \\ x_b + x_c & z_b + z_c \end{vmatrix} \mathbf{j} + \begin{vmatrix} x_a & y_a \\ x_b + x_c & y_b + y_c \end{vmatrix} \mathbf{k}$

$= \left(y_a (z_b + z_c) - z_a (y_b + y_c) \right) \mathbf{i} - \left(x_a (z_b + z_c) - z_a (x_b + x_c) \right) \mathbf{j} + \left(x_a (y_b + y_c) - y_a (x_b + x_c) \right) \mathbf{k}$

$= \left((y_a z_b + y_a z_c) - z_a y_b - z_a y_c \right) \mathbf{i} - \left((x_a z_b + x_a z_c) - z_a x_b - z_a x_c \right) \mathbf{j} + \left((x_a y_b + x_a y_c) - y_a x_b - y_a x_c \right) \mathbf{k}$

$= \left((y_a z_b - z_a y_b) + (y_a z_c - z_a y_c) \right) \mathbf{i} - \left((x_a z_b - z_a x_b) + (x_a z_c - z_a x_c) \right) \mathbf{j} + \left((x_a y_b - y_a x_b) + (x_a y_c - y_a x_c) \right) \mathbf{k}$

$= \left((y_a z_b - z_a y_b) \mathbf{i} - (x_a z_b - z_a x_b) \mathbf{j} + (x_a y_b - y_a x_b) \mathbf{k} \right) + \left((y_a z_c - z_a y_c) \mathbf{i} - (x_a z_c - z_a x_c) \mathbf{j} + (x_a y_c - y_a x_c) \mathbf{k} \right)$

$= \left(\vec{a} \times \vec{b} \right) + \left(\vec{a} \times \vec{c} \right)$.

Therefore, $\vec{a} \times \left(\vec{b} + \vec{c} \right) = \left(\vec{a} \times \vec{b} \right) + \left(\vec{a} \times \vec{c} \right)$.

14. Prove: $\left(\vec{a} + \vec{b} \right) \times \vec{c} = \left(\vec{a} \times \vec{c} \right) + \left(\vec{b} \times \vec{c} \right)$.

Suppose $\vec{a} = \langle x_a, y_a, z_a \rangle, \vec{b} = \langle x_b, y_b, z_b \rangle$, and $\vec{c} = \langle x_c, y_c, z_c \rangle$. Then $\vec{a} + \vec{b} = \langle x_a + x_b, \, y_a + y_b, \, z_a + z_b \rangle$. Therefore,

$\left(\vec{a} + \vec{b} \right) \times \vec{c} = \begin{vmatrix} \mathbf{i} & \mathbf{j} & \mathbf{k} \\ x_a + x_b & y_a + y_b & z_a + z_b \\ x_c & y_c & z_c \end{vmatrix} = \begin{vmatrix} y_a + y_b & z_a + z_b \\ y_c & z_c \end{vmatrix} \mathbf{i} - \begin{vmatrix} x_a + x_b & z_a + z_b \\ x_c & z_c \end{vmatrix} \mathbf{j} + \begin{vmatrix} x_a + x_b & y_a + y_b \\ x_c & y_c \end{vmatrix} \mathbf{k}$

$= \left((y_a + y_b) z_c - (z_a + z_b) y_c \right) \mathbf{i} - \left((x_a + x_b) z_c - (z_a + z_b) x_c \right) \mathbf{j} + \left((x_a + x_b) y_c - (y_a + y_b) x_c \right) \mathbf{k}$

$= \left((y_a z_c + y_b z_c) - z_a y_c - z_b y_c \right) \mathbf{i} - \left((x_a z_c + x_b z_c) - z_a x_c - z_b x_c \right) \mathbf{j} + \left((x_a y_c + x_b y_c) - y_a x_c - y_b x_c \right) \mathbf{k}$

$= \left((y_a z_c - z_a y_c) + (y_b z_c - z_b y_c) \right) \mathbf{i} - \left((x_a z_c - z_a x_c) + (x_b z_c - z_b x_c) \right) \mathbf{j} + \left((x_a y_c - y_a x_c) + x_b y_c - y_b x_c \right) \mathbf{k}$

$= \left((y_a z_c - z_a y_c) \mathbf{i} - (x_a z_c - z_a x_c) \mathbf{j} + (x_a y_c - y_a x_c) \mathbf{k} \right) + \left((y_b z_c - z_b y_c) \mathbf{i} - (x_b z_c - z_b x_c) \mathbf{j} + (x_b y_c - y_b x_c) \mathbf{k} \right)$

$= \left(\vec{a} \times \vec{c} \right) + \left(\vec{b} \times \vec{c} \right)$.

Therefore, $\left(\vec{a} + \vec{b} \right) \times \vec{c} = \left(\vec{a} \times \vec{c} \right) + \left(\vec{b} \times \vec{c} \right)$.

15. Prove: $\vec{a} \cdot \left(\vec{b} \times \vec{c} \right) = \left(\vec{a} \times \vec{b} \right) \cdot \vec{c}$.

Suppose $\vec{a} = \langle x_a, y_a, z_a \rangle, \vec{b} = \langle x_b, y_b, z_b \rangle$, and $\vec{c} = \langle x_c, y_c, z_c \rangle$. Then

$$\vec{b} \times \vec{c} = \begin{vmatrix} \mathbf{i} & \mathbf{j} & \mathbf{k} \\ x_b & y_b & z_b \\ x_c & y_c & z_c \end{vmatrix} = \begin{vmatrix} y_b & z_b \\ y_c & z_c \end{vmatrix} \mathbf{i} - \begin{vmatrix} x_b & z_b \\ x_c & z_c \end{vmatrix} \mathbf{j} + \begin{vmatrix} x_b & y_b \\ x_c & y_c \end{vmatrix} \mathbf{k} = \left(y_b z_c - z_b y_c \right) \mathbf{i} - \left(x_b z_c - z_b x_c \right) \mathbf{j} + \left(x_b y_c - y_b x_c \right) \mathbf{k}.$$

Then $\vec{a} \cdot \left(\vec{b} \times \vec{c} \right) = x_a \left(y_b z_c - z_b y_c \right) - y_a \left(x_b z_c - z_b x_c \right) + z_a \left(x_b y_c - y_b x_c \right)$. This can be rewritten and grouped so that the components of $\vec{c}$ are common factors. This gives

$$\vec{a} \cdot \left(\vec{b} \times \vec{c} \right) = \left(y_a z_b x_c - z_a y_b x_c \right) + \left(z_a x_b y_c - x_a z_b y_c \right) + \left(x_a y_b z_c - y_a x_b z_c \right)$$

$$= \left(y_a z_b - z_a y_b \right) x_c - \left(x_a z_b - z_a x_b \right) y_c + \left(x_a y_b - y_a x_b \right) z_c$$

$$= \left(\vec{a} \times \vec{b} \right) \cdot \vec{c}.$$

Therefore, $\vec{a} \cdot \left(\vec{b} \times \vec{c} \right) = \left(\vec{a} \times \vec{b} \right) \cdot \vec{c}$.

16. Prove: $\vec{a} \times \left(\vec{b} \times \vec{c} \right) = \left(\vec{a} \cdot \vec{c} \right) \vec{b} - \left(\vec{a} \cdot \vec{b} \right) \vec{c}$.

Suppose $\vec{a} = \langle x_a, y_a, z_a \rangle, \vec{b} = \langle x_b, y_b, z_b \rangle$, and $\vec{c} = \langle x_c, y_c, z_c \rangle$. Then

$$\vec{b} \times \vec{c} = \begin{vmatrix} \mathbf{i} & \mathbf{j} & \mathbf{k} \\ x_b & y_b & z_b \\ x_c & y_c & z_c \end{vmatrix} = \left(y_b z_c - z_b y_c \right) \mathbf{i} - \left(x_b z_c - z_b x_c \right) \mathbf{j} + \left(x_b y_c - y_b x_c \right) \mathbf{k}. \text{ Then}$$

$$\vec{a} \times \left(\vec{b} \times \vec{c} \right) = \begin{vmatrix} \mathbf{i} & \mathbf{j} & \mathbf{k} \\ x_a & y_a & z_a \\ y_b z_c - z_b y_c & z_b x_c - x_b z_c & x_b y_c - y_b x_c \end{vmatrix}$$

$$= \left(y_a \left(x_b y_c - y_b x_c \right) - z_a \left(z_b x_c - x_b z_c \right) \right) \mathbf{i} - \left(x_a \left(x_b y_c - y_b x_c \right) - z_a \left(y_b z_c - z_b y_c \right) \right) \mathbf{j} +$$

$$\left(x_a \left(z_b x_c - x_b z_c \right) - y_a \left(y_b z_c - z_b y_c \right) \right) \mathbf{k}$$

$$= \left(y_a x_b y_c - y_a y_b x_c - z_a z_b x_c + z_a x_b z_c \right) \mathbf{i} + \left(x_a y_b x_c - x_a x_b y_c + z_a y_b z_c - z_a z_b y_c \right) \mathbf{j} +$$

$$\left(x_a z_b x_c - x_a x_b z_c - y_a y_b z_c + y_a z_b y_c \right) \mathbf{k}.$$

If you look ahead at the direction you want to go, you can add and subtract identical quantities to each component of this vector so that you have all the pieces of the dot product. Since you add and subtract the same amount, you have not changed the vector.

This gives $\left(y_a x_b y_c + z_a x_b z_c + z_a z_b z_c - x_a x_b x_c - y_a y_b x_c - z_a z_b x_c \right) \mathbf{i} +$
$\left(x_a y_b x_c + y_a y_b y_c + z_a y_b z_c - x_a x_b y_c - y_a y_b y_c - z_a z_b y_c \right) \mathbf{j} + \left(x_a z_b x_c + y_a z_b y_c + z_a z_b z_c - x_a x_b z_c - z_a z_b z_c \right) \mathbf{k}.$

The right side of the property has vectors $\vec{b}$ and $\vec{c}$, so you can split this vector into two vectors based on the components of vectors $\vec{b}$ and $\vec{c}$. This gives

$$\langle \left(y_a y_c + z_a z_c + x_a x_c \right) x_b, \left(x_a x_c + y_a y_z + z_a z_c \right) y_b, \left(x_a x_c + y_a y_c + z_a z_c \right) z_b \rangle -$$

$$\langle \left(x_a x_b + y_a y_b + z_a z_b \right) x_c, \left(x_a x_b + y_a y_b - z_a z_b \right) y_c, \left(x_a x_b + y_a y_b + z_a z_b \right) z_c \rangle.$$

This can be written as

$$\left(x_a x_c + y_a y_c + z_a z_c \right) \langle x_b, y_b, z_b \rangle - \left(x_a x_b + y_a y_b + z_a z_b \right) \langle x_c, y_c, z_c \rangle = \left(\vec{a} \cdot \vec{c} \right) \vec{b} - \left(\vec{a} \cdot \vec{b} \right) \vec{c}. \text{ Therefore,}$$

$$\vec{a} \times \left(\vec{b} \times \vec{c} \right) = \left(\vec{a} \cdot \vec{c} \right) \vec{b} - \left(\vec{a} \cdot \vec{b} \right) \vec{c}.$$

Subsection c: Understand and apply the basic properties and operations of matrices and determinants (for example, to determine the solvability of linear systems of equations).

A **matrix (plural is matrices)** is a rectangular array of numbers that can be added and multiplied. The individual numbers within a matrix are called **entries.** A matrix has dimensions given in rows and columns. The dimensions of a matrix are given as the number of rows by number of columns. For example, a matrix with 3 rows and 4 columns is a 3×4 matrix. The number of rows is always given first followed by the number of columns.

Example 1:

Find the dimensions of the following matrices:

a) $A = \begin{bmatrix} 2 & 3 & 1 \\ 5 & 3 & 8 \\ 7 & 19 & -3 \\ -1 & 2.5 & -3.8 \end{bmatrix}$
b) $B = \begin{bmatrix} 2 & -3 & \frac{3}{4} & 1.6 \end{bmatrix}$
c) $C = \begin{bmatrix} 2 & 10 \\ 9 & 6 \\ -3 & -5 \\ 1.5 & -5 \\ 0 & -2 \\ 1.7 & -3.2 \\ -8 & 19 \end{bmatrix}$

Solution:

Part a: There are 4 rows and 3 columns, so A is a 4×3 matrix.

Part b: There are 1 row and 4 columns, so B is a 1×4 matrix.

Part c: There are 7 rows and 2 columns, so C is a 7×2 matrix.

The entries in a matrix can be referred to individually and are usually given a subscript that corresponds to the row number and column number within which the entry is contained. For example, entry $A_{2,1}$ is found in row 2 and column 1 of the matrix A.

Example 2: For the matrices given in example 1, find the number associated with each entry.

a) $A_{2,3}$ c) $B_{1,2}$ e) $C_{5,1}$

b) $A_{3,1}$ d) $B_{1,4}$ f) $C_{6,2}$

Solution:

a) $A_{2,3}$ corresponds to the entry in row 2, column 3 of matrix A. This is 8.

b) $A_{3,1}$ corresponds to the entry in row 3, column 1 of matrix A. This is 7.

c) $B_{1,2}$ corresponds to the entry in row 1, column 2 of matrix B. This is -3.

d) $B_{1,4}$ corresponds to the entry in row 1, column 4 of matrix B. This is 1.6.

e) $C_{5,1}$ corresponds to the entry in row 5, column 1 of matrix C. This is 0.

f) $C_{6,2}$ corresponds to the entry in row 6, column 2 of matrix C. This is -3.2.

Adding and Subtracting Matrices

Matrices can be added and subtracted by adding or subtracting corresponding entries. Since you are adding or subtracting corresponding entries, you can only add or subtract matrices with the same dimensions. The solution has the same dimensions as the original matrices.

Example 1:

$$\text{Given } A = \begin{bmatrix} -2 & 1 \\ 4 & -5 \\ 3 & 7 \\ -1 & 8 \end{bmatrix} \text{ and } B = \begin{bmatrix} 3 & 1 \\ -2 & 5 \\ 1 & -6 \\ 3 & 0 \end{bmatrix},$$

Find $A + B$ and $A - B$.

Solution:

To add the matrices A and B, add corresponding entries. So

$$A + B = \begin{bmatrix} -2+3 & 1+1 \\ 4+(-2) & -5+5 \\ 3+1 & 7+(-6) \\ -1+3 & 8+0 \end{bmatrix} = \begin{bmatrix} 1 & 2 \\ 2 & 0 \\ 4 & 1 \\ 2 & 8 \end{bmatrix}.$$

To subtract matrices A and B, subtract corresponding entries. So

$$A - B = \begin{bmatrix} -2-3 & 1-1 \\ 4-(-2) & -5-5 \\ 3-1 & 7-(-6) \\ -1-3 & 8-0 \end{bmatrix} = \begin{bmatrix} -5 & 0 \\ 6 & -10 \\ 2 & 13 \\ -4 & 8 \end{bmatrix}.$$

The fact you can add and subtract matrices raises two questions. Is matrix addition commutative? Is matrix subtraction commutative? The answers to these questions follow.

Given matrix A and matrix B with the same dimensions, say 2×3. You could define matrix A and matrix B as follows:

$$A = \begin{bmatrix} a_{1,1} & a_{1,2} \\ a_{2,1} & a_{2,2} \\ a_{3,1} & a_{3,2} \end{bmatrix} \text{ and } B = \begin{bmatrix} b_{1,1} & b_{1,2} \\ b_{2,1} & b_{2,2} \\ b_{3,1} & b_{3,2} \end{bmatrix}$$

Then, $A + B = \begin{bmatrix} a_{1,1}+b_{1,1} & a_{1,2}+b_{1,2} \\ a_{2,1}+b_{2,1} & a_{2,2}+b_{2,2} \\ a_{3,1}+b_{3,1} & a_{3,2}+b_{3,2} \end{bmatrix} = \begin{bmatrix} b_{1,1}+a_{1,1} & b_{1,2}+a_{1,2} \\ b_{2,1}+a_{2,1} & b_{2,2}+a_{2,2} \\ b_{3,1}+a_{3,1} & b_{3,2}+a_{3,2} \end{bmatrix} = B + A.$ You can extend this process to any size matrix,

so you can demonstrate that the matrix addition is commutative.

Similarly, you can subtract the matrices, and you would get

$$A - B = \begin{bmatrix} a_{1,1}-b_{1,1} & a_{1,2}-b_{1,2} \\ a_{2,1}-b_{2,1} & a_{2,2}-b_{2,2} \\ a_{3,1}-b_{3,1} & a_{3,2}-b_{3,2} \end{bmatrix} = \begin{bmatrix} -\left(b_{1,1}-a_{1,1}\right) & -\left(b_{1,2}-a_{1,2}\right) \\ -\left(b_{2,1}-a_{2,1}\right) & -\left(b_{2,2}-a_{2,2}\right) \\ -\left(b_{3,1}-a_{3,1}\right) & -\left(b_{3,2}-a_{3,2}\right) \end{bmatrix} \neq B - A.$$

This demonstrates that matrix subtraction is not commutative.

Multiplication of Matrices

You can combine multiplication and matrices in two ways. The first is multiplying a matrix by a scalar. In this case, each entry in the matrix is multiplied by the scalar. This is similar to multiplying a vector by a scalar, discussed in a prior section.

Example 1:

Given $A = \begin{bmatrix} 2 & 1 & 8 \\ -3 & 4 & -2 \\ 9 & 0 & -6 \end{bmatrix}$. Find $4A$.

Solution:

Since $A = \begin{bmatrix} 2 & 1 & 8 \\ -3 & 4 & -2 \\ 9 & 0 & -6 \end{bmatrix}$, you can find $4A$ by multiplying each entry in A by 4. So

$$4A = \begin{bmatrix} 4(2) & 4(1) & 4(8) \\ 4(-3) & 4(4) & 4(-2) \\ 4(9) & 4(0) & 4(-6) \end{bmatrix} = \begin{bmatrix} 8 & 4 & 32 \\ -12 & 16 & -8 \\ 36 & 0 & -24 \end{bmatrix}.$$

The second way to incorporate multiplication with matrices is by multiplying matrices. When multiplying two matrices, say A and B, the entries in one row of matrix A are multiplied by the corresponding entries in one column of matrix B. These products are then added together to find the corresponding entry in the product. Because of this relationship, the number of columns in the first matrix must equal the number of rows of the second matrix. So, if A has dimensions $m \times n$, then matrix B must have dimensions $n \times p$ with p not necessarily equal to m. The product will have dimensions $m \times p$. When finding entries in the product, you begin with the position in the product. If you are looking for the entry in row 3, column 2 of the product, you will take the first entry of row 3 of A and multiply it by the first entry of column 2 of B. Then take the second entry of row 3 of A and multiply it by the second entry of column 2 of B. This continues until all the entries have been used. These products are then added together to find the entry in row 3, column 2 of the product AB.

Example 2:

If $A = \begin{bmatrix} -2 & -1 \\ 3 & 2 \\ 0 & 1 \end{bmatrix}$ and $B = \begin{bmatrix} 1 & 2 & -4 & 3 \\ 0 & 4 & -1 & -2 \end{bmatrix}$, find AB.

Solution:

Matrix A has dimensions 3×2. Matrix B has dimensions 2×4. Therefore, AB will have dimensions 3×4.

$$AB = \begin{bmatrix} (-2)(1)+(-1)(0) & (-2)(2)+(-1)(4) & (-2)(-4)+(-1)(-1) & (-2)(3)+(-1)(-2) \\ (3)(1)+(2)(0) & (3)(2)+(2)(4) & (3)(-4)+(2)(-1) & (3)(3)+(2)(-2) \\ (0)(1)+(1)(0) & (0)(2)+(1)(4) & (0)(-4)+(1)(-1) & (0)(3)+(1)(-2) \end{bmatrix}$$

$$= \begin{bmatrix} -2+0 & -4+(-4) & 8+1 & -6+2 \\ 3+0 & 6+8 & -12+(-2) & 9+(-4) \\ 0+0 & 0+4 & 0+(-1) & 0+(-2) \end{bmatrix} = \begin{bmatrix} -2 & -8 & 9 & -4 \\ 3 & 14 & -14 & 5 \\ 0 & 4 & -1 & -2 \end{bmatrix}$$

Because of the relationship that needs to exist in order to be able to multiply matrices and the method used to multiply them, multiplication of matrices is generally not commutative. If A has dimensions 3×4 and B has dimensions 4×2, you can calculate AB, but BA does not exist. If A has dimensions 3×4 and B has dimension 4×3, you can calculate AB and get a 3×3 matrix. When you calculate BA, you get a 4×4 matrix. These will never be equal, so multiplication of matrices is not commutative.

Determinants

Every square matrix (where the number of rows equals the number of columns) has a corresponding determinant. The determinant of a matrix is a scalar number. The dimensions of the determinant determine the difficulty in calculating the determinant.

2 × 2 Determinant

For a given 2×2 matrix A, given as $A = \begin{bmatrix} a & b \\ c & d \end{bmatrix}$, the determinant of A, noted $\det(A)$ or $|A|$, can be written as $\begin{vmatrix} a & b \\ c & d \end{vmatrix}$.

The value of the determinant can be found by calculating $ad - bc$.

Example:

Find the value of the determinant of A, if $A = \begin{bmatrix} 2 & 1 \\ -5 & 8 \end{bmatrix}$.

Solution:

$$\det(A) = |A| = \begin{vmatrix} 2 & 1 \\ -5 & 8 \end{vmatrix} = (2)(8) - (1)(-5) = 16 - (-5) = 21.$$

3 × 3 Determinant

For a given 3×3 matrix A, given as $A = \begin{bmatrix} a & b & c \\ d & e & f \\ g & h & i \end{bmatrix}$, the determinant of A, noted $\det(A)$ or $|A|$, can be written as $\begin{vmatrix} a & b & c \\ d & e & f \\ g & h & i \end{vmatrix}$. The value of the determinant can be found by expanding the determinant along any row or column. The signs used in finding the determinant follow the pattern of $\begin{vmatrix} + & - & + \\ - & + & - \\ + & - & + \end{vmatrix}$. So, if you use row one to expand the determinant, the first element will be added; then you will subtract the second element and add the third element. Similarly, if you chose to use column two to expand the determinant, the first element will be subtracted, the second added, and the third subtracted. The elements are determined by 2×2 determinants that correspond to the entries in the 3×3 matrix. The entry is multiplied by the determinant determined by ignoring the row and column in which the entry is located. This is continued across the row or down the column selected to expand the determinant. Generally, the first row is used to expand the determinant; however, if entries have a value 0, other rows or columns may be helpful to use to minimize the calculations necessary. The 3×3 determinant is found in the following way if the first row is used to expand the determinant:

$$\det(A) = \begin{vmatrix} a & b & c \\ d & e & f \\ g & h & i \end{vmatrix} = a\begin{vmatrix} e & f \\ h & i \end{vmatrix} - b\begin{vmatrix} d & f \\ g & i \end{vmatrix} + c\begin{vmatrix} d & e \\ g & h \end{vmatrix} = a(ei - fh) - b(di - gf) + c(dh - eg)$$

If, for example, the second column was used to expand the determinant, the calculation would be as follows:

$$\det(A) = \begin{vmatrix} a & b & c \\ d & e & f \\ g & h & i \end{vmatrix} = -b\begin{vmatrix} d & f \\ g & i \end{vmatrix} + e\begin{vmatrix} a & c \\ g & i \end{vmatrix} - h\begin{vmatrix} a & c \\ d & f \end{vmatrix} = -b(di - gf) + e(ai - gc) - h(af - cd)$$

Example:

Find the determinant of $A = \begin{bmatrix} -1 & 2 & 5 \\ 3 & -2 & 8 \\ 1 & -4 & -2 \end{bmatrix}$.

Solution:

For the matrix $A = \begin{bmatrix} -1 & 2 & 5 \\ 3 & -2 & 8 \\ 1 & -4 & -2 \end{bmatrix}$, the corresponding determinant will be

$$\det(A) = |A| = \begin{vmatrix} -1 & 2 & 5 \\ 3 & -2 & 8 \\ 1 & -4 & -2 \end{vmatrix} = -1 \begin{vmatrix} -2 & 8 \\ -4 & -2 \end{vmatrix} - 2 \begin{vmatrix} 3 & 8 \\ 1 & -2 \end{vmatrix} + 5 \begin{vmatrix} 3 & -2 \\ 1 & -4 \end{vmatrix}$$

$$= (-1)\big(4 - (-32)\big) - 2(-6 - 8) + 5\big(-12 - (-2)\big)$$

$$= (-1)(36) - 2(-14) + 5(-10) = -36 + 28 - 50 = -58.$$

Solving Systems of Equations

The entries in a matrix can be correlated with coefficients of linear equations, so matrices are often used to solve systems of equations. The determinant is important in order to determine whether a system of equations has a solution. If you take the coefficients of the variables in each equation of the system and create a coefficient matrix, the determinant of this matrix will tell you whether the system has a solution. If a system is given as $\begin{cases} ax + by + cz = d \\ ex + fy + gz = h \\ mx + ny + pz = r \end{cases}$, this can be modeled with matrices in the following way:

$$\begin{bmatrix} a & b & c \\ e & f & g \\ m & n & p \end{bmatrix} \begin{bmatrix} x \\ y \\ z \end{bmatrix} = \begin{bmatrix} d \\ h \\ r \end{bmatrix}$$

In order for this system to have a solution, you need to be able to divide by the coefficient matrix. Dividing by matrices is done by multiplying by the inverse. In order to have an inverse matrix, the determinant of the matrix cannot be zero. If the determinant of the matrix is zero, the matrix is not invertible, and no solution exists to the system of equations. So, to determine whether a system has a solution, first find the determinant of the coefficient matrix.

Example:

Determine whether the system $\begin{cases} 2x + 3y - z = 4 \\ 3x + 2y - 2z = 3 \\ x + y + z = 2 \end{cases}$ has a solution.

Solution:

Find the determinant of the coefficient matrix $\begin{bmatrix} 2 & 3 & -1 \\ 3 & 2 & -2 \\ 1 & 1 & 1 \end{bmatrix}$. So, find $\begin{vmatrix} 2 & 3 & -1 \\ 3 & 2 & -2 \\ 1 & 1 & 1 \end{vmatrix}$.

$$\begin{vmatrix} 2 & 3 & -1 \\ 3 & 2 & -2 \\ 1 & 1 & 1 \end{vmatrix} = 2 \begin{vmatrix} 2 & -2 \\ 1 & 1 \end{vmatrix} - 3 \begin{vmatrix} 3 & -2 \\ 1 & 1 \end{vmatrix} - 1 \begin{vmatrix} 3 & 2 \\ 1 & 1 \end{vmatrix} = 2\big(2 - (-2)\big) - 3\big(3 - (-2)\big) - 1(3 - 2)$$

$$= 2(4) - 3(5) - 1(1) = 8 - 15 - 1 = -8$$

Since the determinant is not zero, the system of equations has a solution.

Practice Problems

Given the following matrices:

$$A = \begin{bmatrix} 3 & 1 & 4 \\ 2 & 1 & -3 \\ 1 & -2 & -1 \\ -1 & 3 & -4 \end{bmatrix}, \quad B = \begin{bmatrix} 2 & -1 & 3 \\ -4 & 0 & 1 \\ -2 & -3 & 5 \\ 1 & -2 & 4 \end{bmatrix}, \quad C = \begin{bmatrix} -1 & -2 & -5 & 1 \\ 3 & 2 & 4 & -2 \\ 4 & -1 & 2 & 3 \end{bmatrix}, \text{ and } D = \begin{bmatrix} -1 & 3 \\ 0 & 4 \\ -2 & 1 \end{bmatrix}$$

1. Find the dimensions of A, B, C, and D.

2. Find $A + B$.

3. Find $B + A$.

4. Find $A + C$.

5. Find $A - B$.

6. Find $B - A$.

7. Find $C - D$.

8. Find $2B$.

9. Find $-4C$.

10. Find $-1A$.

11. Find BC.

12. Find AD.

13. Find CB.

14. If $A = \begin{bmatrix} 2 & 3 \\ 1 & 5 \end{bmatrix}$, find $\det(A)$.

15. If $A = \begin{bmatrix} -1 & 4 & -2 \\ 3 & 2 & 5 \\ 1 & 3 & -2 \end{bmatrix}$, find $\det(A)$.

16. Determine whether the system of equations given by $\begin{cases} x - y + z = 3 \\ 2x - 2y + 2z = 5 \\ x + 2y - 3z = 1 \end{cases}$ has a solution.

Solutions

$$A = \begin{bmatrix} 3 & 1 & 4 \\ 2 & 1 & -3 \\ 1 & -2 & -1 \\ -1 & 3 & -4 \end{bmatrix}, \quad B = \begin{bmatrix} 2 & -1 & 3 \\ -4 & 0 & 1 \\ -2 & -3 & 5 \\ 1 & -2 & 4 \end{bmatrix}, \quad C = \begin{bmatrix} -1 & -2 & -5 & 1 \\ 3 & 2 & 4 & -2 \\ 4 & -1 & 2 & 3 \end{bmatrix}, \text{ and } D = \begin{bmatrix} -1 & 3 \\ 0 & 4 \\ -2 & 1 \end{bmatrix}.$$

1. The dimensions of A are 4×3; the dimensions of B are 4×3; the dimensions of C are 3×4; the dimensions of D are 3×2.

2. $A + B = \begin{bmatrix} 3+2 & 1+(-1) & 4+3 \\ 2+(-4) & 1+0 & -3+1 \\ 1+(-2) & -2+(-3) & -1+5 \\ -1+1 & 3+(-2) & -4+4 \end{bmatrix} = \begin{bmatrix} 5 & 0 & 7 \\ -2 & 1 & -2 \\ -1 & -5 & 4 \\ 0 & 1 & 0 \end{bmatrix}.$

3. $B + A = \begin{bmatrix} 2+3 & -1+1 & 3+4 \\ -4+2 & 0+1 & 1+(-3) \\ -2+1 & -3+(-2) & 5+(-1) \\ 1+(-1) & -2+3 & 4+(-4) \end{bmatrix} = \begin{bmatrix} 5 & 0 & 7 \\ -2 & 1 & -2 \\ -1 & -5 & 4 \\ 0 & 1 & 0 \end{bmatrix}.$

4. Matrix A is 4×3. Matrix C is 3×4. These are different dimensions, so the sum of A and C is undefined.

5. $A - B = \begin{bmatrix} 3-2 & 1-(-1) & 4-3 \\ 2-(-4) & 1-0 & -3-1 \\ 1-(-2) & -2-(-3) & -1-5 \\ -1-1 & 3-(-2) & -4-4 \end{bmatrix} = \begin{bmatrix} 1 & 2 & 1 \\ 6 & 1 & -4 \\ 3 & 1 & -6 \\ -2 & 5 & -8 \end{bmatrix}.$

6. $B - A = \begin{bmatrix} 2-3 & -1-1 & 3-4 \\ -4-2 & 0-1 & 1-(-3) \\ -2-1 & -3-(-2) & 5-(-1) \\ 1-(-1) & -2-3 & 4-(-4) \end{bmatrix} = \begin{bmatrix} -1 & -2 & -1 \\ -6 & -1 & 4 \\ -3 & -1 & 6 \\ 2 & -5 & 8 \end{bmatrix}.$

7. Matrix C is 3×4. Matrix D is 3×2. These are different dimensions, so the difference of C and D is undefined.

8. Since $B = \begin{bmatrix} 2 & -1 & 3 \\ -4 & 0 & 1 \\ -2 & -3 & 5 \\ 1 & -2 & 4 \end{bmatrix}$, you can find $2B$ by multiplying each entry in B by 2. So,

$$2B = \begin{bmatrix} 2(2) & 2(-1) & 2(3) \\ 2(-4) & 2(0) & 2(1) \\ 2(-2) & 2(-3) & 2(5) \\ 2(1) & 2(-2) & 2(4) \end{bmatrix} = \begin{bmatrix} 4 & -2 & 6 \\ -8 & 0 & 2 \\ -4 & -6 & 10 \\ 2 & -4 & 8 \end{bmatrix}.$$

9. Since $C = \begin{bmatrix} -1 & -2 & -5 & 1 \\ 3 & 2 & 4 & -2 \\ 4 & -1 & 2 & 3 \end{bmatrix}$, you can find $-4C$ by multiplying each entry in C by -4. So,

$$-4C = \begin{bmatrix} (-4)(-1) & (-4)(-2) & (-4)(-5) & (-4)(1) \\ (-4)(3) & (-4)(2) & (-4)(4) & (-4)(-2) \\ (-4)(4) & (-4)(-1) & (-4)(2) & (-4)(3) \end{bmatrix} = \begin{bmatrix} 4 & 8 & 20 & -4 \\ -12 & -8 & -16 & 8 \\ -16 & 4 & -8 & -12 \end{bmatrix}.$$

10. Since $A = \begin{bmatrix} 3 & 1 & 4 \\ 2 & 1 & -3 \\ 1 & -2 & -1 \\ -1 & 3 & -4 \end{bmatrix}$, you can find $-1A$ by multiplying each entry in A by -1. So,

$$-1A = \begin{bmatrix} (-1)(3) & (-1)(1) & (-1)(4) \\ (-1)(2) & (-1)(1) & (-1)(-3) \\ (-1)(1) & (-1)(-2) & (-1)(-1) \\ (-1)(-1) & (-1)(3) & (-1)(-4) \end{bmatrix} = \begin{bmatrix} -3 & -1 & -4 \\ -2 & -1 & 3 \\ -1 & 2 & 1 \\ 1 & -3 & 4 \end{bmatrix}.$$

11. B has dimensions 4×3. C has dimensions 3×4. The product BC will have dimensions 4×4.

$$BC = \begin{bmatrix} (2)(-1)+(-1)(3)+(3)(4) & (2)(-2)+(-1)(2)+(3)(-1) & 2(-5)+(-1)(4)+(3)(2) & (2)(1)+(-1)(-2)+(3)(3) \\ (-4)(-1)+(0)(3)+(1)(4) & (-4)(-2)+(0)(2)+(1)(-1) & (-4)(-5)+(0)(4)+(1)(2) & (-4)(1)+(0)(-2)+(1)(3) \\ (-2)(-1)+(-3)(3)+(5)(4) & (-2)(-2)+(-3)(2)+(5)(-1) & (-2)(-5)+(-3)(4)+(5)(2) & (-2)(1)+(-3)(-2)+(5)(3) \\ (1)(-1)+(-2)(3)+(4)(4) & (1)(-2)+(-2)(2)+(4)(-1) & (1)(-5)+(-2)(4)+(4)(2) & (1)(1)+(-2)(-2)+(4)(3) \end{bmatrix}$$

$$= \begin{bmatrix} -2-3+12 & -4-2-3 & -10-4+6 & 2+2+9 \\ 4+0+4 & 8+0-1 & 20+0+2 & -4+0+3 \\ 2-9+20 & 4-6-5 & 10-12+10 & -2+6+15 \\ -1-6+16 & -2-4-4 & -5-8+8 & 1+4+12 \end{bmatrix} = \begin{bmatrix} 7 & -9 & -8 & 13 \\ 8 & 7 & 22 & -1 \\ 13 & -7 & 8 & 19 \\ 9 & -10 & -5 & 17 \end{bmatrix}$$

12. Matrix A has dimensions 4×3. Matrix D has dimensions 3×2. The product AD will have dimensions 4×2.

$$AD = \begin{bmatrix} (3)(-1)+(1)(0)+(4)(-2) & (3)(3)+(1)(4)+(4)(1) \\ (2)(-1)+(1)(0)+(-3)(-2) & (2)(3)+(1)(4)+(-3)(1) \\ (1)(-1)+(-2)(0)+(-1)(-2) & (1)(3)+(-2)(4)+(-1)(1) \\ (-1)(-1)+(3)(0)+(-4)(-2) & (-1)(3)+(3)(4)+(-4)(1) \end{bmatrix} = \begin{bmatrix} -3+0-8 & 9+4+4 \\ -2+0+6 & 6+4-3 \\ -1+0+2 & 3-8-1 \\ 1+0+8 & -3+12-4 \end{bmatrix} = \begin{bmatrix} -11 & 17 \\ 4 & 7 \\ 1 & -6 \\ 9 & 5 \end{bmatrix}$$

13. Matrix C has dimensions 3×4. Matrix B has dimensions 4×3. The product CB will have dimensions 3×3.

$$CB = \begin{bmatrix} (-1)(2)+(-2)(-4)+(-5)(-2)+(1)(1) & (-1)(-1)+(-2)(0)+(-5)(-3)+(1)(-2) & (-1)(3)+(-2)(1)+(-5)(5)+(1)(4) \\ (3)(2)+(2)(-4)+(4)(-2)+(-2)(1) & (3)(-1)+(2)(0)+(4)(-3)+(-2)(-2) & (3)(3)+(2)(1)+(4)(5)+(-2)(4) \\ (4)(2)+(-1)(-4)+(2)(-2)+(3)(1) & (4)(-1)+(-1)(0)+(2)(-3)+(3)(-2) & (4)(3)+(-1)(1)+(2)(5)+(3)(4) \end{bmatrix}$$

$$= \begin{bmatrix} -2+8+10+1 & 1+0+15-2 & -3-2-25+4 \\ 6-8-8-2 & -3+0-12+4 & 9+2+20-8 \\ 8+4-4+3 & -4+0-6-6 & 12-1+10+12 \end{bmatrix} = \begin{bmatrix} 17 & 14 & -26 \\ -12 & -11 & 23 \\ 11 & -16 & 33 \end{bmatrix}$$

14. $\det(A) = \begin{vmatrix} 2 & 3 \\ 1 & 5 \end{vmatrix} = (2)(5) - (3)(1) = 10 - 3 = 7.$

15. $\det(A) = \begin{vmatrix} -1 & 4 & -2 \\ 3 & 2 & 5 \\ 1 & 3 & -2 \end{vmatrix} = (-1) \begin{vmatrix} 2 & 5 \\ 3 & -2 \end{vmatrix} - (4) \begin{vmatrix} 3 & 5 \\ 1 & -2 \end{vmatrix} + (-2) \begin{vmatrix} 3 & 2 \\ 1 & 3 \end{vmatrix}$

$= (-1)\big((2)(-2) - (5)(3)\big) - 4\big((3)(-2) - (5)(1)\big) - 2\big((3)(3) - (2)(1)\big)$

$= (-1)(-4 - 15) - 4(-6 - 5) - 2(9 - 2) = (-1)(-19) - 4(-11) - 2(7) = 19 + 44 - 14 = 63 - 14 = 49.$

16. You want to find the determinant of $\begin{vmatrix} 1 & -1 & 1 \\ 2 & -2 & 2 \\ 1 & 2 & -3 \end{vmatrix}$. So,

$\begin{vmatrix} 1 & -1 & 1 \\ 2 & -2 & 2 \\ 1 & 2 & -3 \end{vmatrix} = 1 \begin{vmatrix} -2 & 2 \\ 2 & -3 \end{vmatrix} - (-1) \begin{vmatrix} 2 & 2 \\ 1 & -3 \end{vmatrix} + 1 \begin{vmatrix} 2 & -2 \\ 1 & 2 \end{vmatrix} = 1(6 - 4) + 1(-6 - 2) + 1\big(4 - (-2)\big) = 2 - 8 + 6 = 0.$

Since the determinant is zero, there is no solution to the system of equations.

Content Domain 5.1: Trigonometry

The areas of this content domain that tend to be the most difficult are the areas involving proof. These are examined here. For further practice on the other subsections of this content domain, see the resources section included in this book.

Subsection a: Prove that the Pythagorean Theorem is equivalent to the trigonometric identity $\sin^2 x + \cos^2 x = 1$ and that this identity leads to $1 + \tan^2 x = \sec^2 x$ and $1 + \cot^2 x = \csc^2 x$.

The Pythagorean Theorem is based on the relationship between the sides of a right triangle. The Pythagorean Theorem states:

The sum of the squares of length of the legs of a right triangle is equal to the square of the length of the hypotenuse.

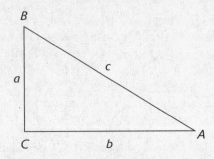

Figure 3–13

In the preceding figure, the Pythagorean Theorem can be written as $a^2 + b^2 = c^2$.

If you examine the triangle in the preceding figure, you can use trigonometric ratios, ($\sin A = \frac{a}{c}$ and $\cos A = \frac{b}{c}$), and rewrite the Pythagorean Theorem in terms of these ratios.

These can be rewritten as $a = c \sin A$ and $b = c \cos A$. Substituting this into the Pythagorean Theorem gives $(c \sin A)^2 + (c \cos A)^2 = c^2$. Simplifying gives $c^2 \sin^2 A + c^2 \cos^2 A = c^2$. Dividing both sides of this equation by c^2 gives $\sin^2 A + \cos^2 A = 1$, the first Pythagorean Identity. A similar substitution shows that this theorem is true for angle B as well.

After you have determined this form for the Pythagorean Theorem, you can manipulate this equation to determine the Pythagorean relationships with other trigonometric functions.

Beginning with $\sin^2 A + \cos^2 A = 1$, divide both sides of the equation by $\sin^2 A$. This gives $\frac{\sin^2 A}{\sin^2 A} + \frac{\cos^2 A}{\sin^2 A} = \frac{1}{\sin^2 A}$. Simplifying and using the reciprocal trigonometric functions gives $1 + \cot^2 A = \csc^2 A$, the second Pythagorean Identity.

In a similar way, the third Pythagorean Identity, $\tan^2 A + 1 = \sec^2 A$, can be derived from $\sin^2 A + \cos^2 A = 1$. This is included in the practice exercises at the end of this section.

These are the three Pythagorean Identities used in trigonometry. They, along with other trigonometric identities including double angle and half angle formulas, are useful in proving trigonometric identities. It is important to examine where these other identities come from as well.

Subsection b: Prove the sine, cosine, and tangent sum formulas for all real values and derive special applications of the sum formulas (for example, double angle, half angle).

To prove the formula for sin $(A + B)$, start with Figure 3–14:

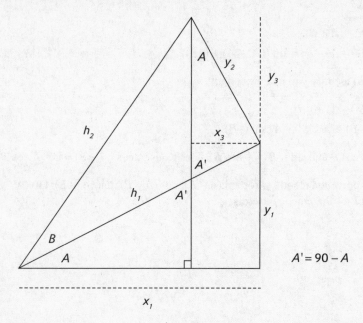

Figure 3–14

You are interested in describing sin $(A + B)$. Here's what you know:

$$\sin(A + B) = \frac{y_1 + y_3}{h_2}$$

$$\cos A = \frac{y_3}{y_2}$$

$$\sin A = \frac{y_1}{h_1}$$

$$\cos B = \frac{h_1}{h_2}$$

$$\sin B = \frac{y_2}{h_2}$$

These can be written as:

$y_3 = y_2 \cos A$

$y_1 = h_1 \sin A$

$h_1 = h_2 \cos B$

$y_2 = h_2 \sin B$

Substituting into sin $(A + B)$ gives

$$\sin(A + B) = \frac{y_1 + y_3}{h_2} = \frac{h_1 \sin A + y_2 \cos A}{h_2}$$

$$= \frac{(h_2 \cos B)\sin A + (h_2 \sin B)\cos A}{h_2} = \frac{h_2(\cos B \sin A + \sin B \cos A)}{h_2}$$

$$= \cos B \sin A + \sin B \cos A.$$

This can be rewritten to appear as you are used to seeing the sum formula as:

$$\sin (A + B) = \sin A \cos B + \cos A \sin B$$

To determine the $\cos (A + B)$ identity, you can use the $\sin (A + B)$ and the facts that $\cos A = \sin (90 - A)$ and $\sin A = \cos (90 - A)$. This leads to

$$\cos (A + B) = \sin (90 - (A + B))$$
$$\cos (A + B) = \sin ((90 - A) - B) = \sin ((90 - A) + (-B)).$$

Then, using the $\sin (A + B)$ identity you just proved gives

$$\cos (A + B) = \sin ((90 - A) + (-B))$$
$$= \sin (90 - A) \cos (-B) + \cos (90 - A) \sin (-B).$$

You know that $\cos (-B) = \cos B$ and $\sin (-B) = -\sin (B)$. This leads to $\cos (A + B) = \cos A \cos B - \sin A \sin B$.

There are similar ways to prove the identities for $\sin (A - B)$, $\cos (A - B)$, $\tan (A + B)$, $\tan (A - B)$, $\sin (2A)$, $\cos (2A)$, and $\tan (2A)$. These are left for the practice exercises.

Practice Problems

1. Use the Pythagorean Identity $\sin^2 A + \cos^2 A = 1$ to derive the trigonometric identity $\tan^2 A + 1 = \sec^2 A$.

2. Prove $\sin (A - B) = \sin A \cos B - \cos A \sin B$.

3. Prove $\cos (A - B) = \cos A \cos B + \sin A \sin B$.

4. Prove $\tan (A + B) = \dfrac{\tan A + \tan B}{1 - \tan A \tan B}$.

5. Prove $\sin (2A) = 2 \sin A \cos A$.

6. Prove $\cos (2A) = \cos^2 A - \sin^2 A$.

7. Prove $\tan (2A) = \dfrac{2 \tan A}{1 - \tan^2 A}$.

8. Prove $\sin \left(\dfrac{A}{2} \right) = \pm \sqrt{\dfrac{1 - \cos A}{2}}$.

9. Prove $\cos \left(\dfrac{A}{2} \right) = \pm \sqrt{\dfrac{1 + \cos A}{2}}$.

Solutions

1. Again, beginning with $\sin^2 A + \cos^2 A = 1$, divide both sides of the equation by $\cos^2 A$. This gives $\frac{\sin^2 A}{\cos^2 A} + \frac{\cos^2 A}{\cos^2 A} = \frac{1}{\cos^2 A}$. Simplifying and using the reciprocal trigonometric functions gives $\tan^2 A + 1 = \sec^2 A$.

2. In order to prove $\sin (A - B) = \sin A \cos B - \cos A \sin B$, start with $\sin (A + B) = \sin A \cos B + \cos A \sin B$. $\sin (A - B)$ can be written as $\sin (A + (-B))$. Using the sine sum identity, this becomes $\sin (A - B) = \sin (A + (-B)) = \sin A \cos (-B) + \cos A \sin (-B) = \sin A \cos B - \cos A \sin B$.

3. In order to prove $\cos (A - B) = \cos A \cos B + \sin A \sin B$, follow a procedure similar to practice exercise 2. $\cos(A - B) = \cos (A + (-B)) = \cos A \cos (-B) - \sin A \sin (-B) = \cos A \cos B \sin A \sin_B$.

4. Prove $\tan (A + B) = \frac{\tan A + \tan B}{1 - \tan A \tan B}$. Use $\sin (A + B)$ and $\cos (A + B)$.

$\tan (A + B) = \frac{\sin (A + B)}{\cos (A + B)} = \frac{\sin A \cos B + \cos A \sin B}{\cos A \cos B - \sin A \sin B}$. If you divide the numerator and denominator by $\cos A \cos B$, this gives

$$\tan (A + B) = \frac{\dfrac{\sin A \cos B}{\cos A \cos B} + \dfrac{\cos A \sin B}{\cos A \cos B}}{\dfrac{\cos A \cos B}{\cos A \cos B} - \dfrac{\sin A \sin B}{\cos A \cos B}} = \frac{\dfrac{\sin A}{\cos A} + \dfrac{\sin B}{\cos B}}{1 - \dfrac{\sin A}{\cos A} \dfrac{\sin B}{\cos B}} = \frac{\tan A + \tan B}{1 - \tan A \tan B}.$$

5. Prove $\sin (2A) = 2 \sin A \cos A$. Begin with $\sin (A + B)$. $\sin (A + B) = \sin A \cos B + \cos A \sin B$. Therefore, $\sin (2A) = \sin (A + A) = \sin A \cos A + \cos A \sin A = 2 \sin A \cos A$.

6. Prove $\cos (2A) = \cos^2 A - \sin^2 A$. Begin with $\cos (A + B)$. $\cos (A + B) = \cos A \cos B - \sin A \sin B$. Therefore, $\cos (2A) = \cos (A + A) = \cos A \cos A - \sin A \sin A = \cos^2 A - \sin^2 A$.

7. Prove $\tan (2A) = \frac{2 \tan A}{1 - \tan^2 A}$. Begin with $\tan (A + B)$. $\tan (A + B) = \frac{\tan A + \tan B}{1 - \tan A \tan B}$. Therefore,

$$\tan (2A) = \tan (A + A) = \frac{\tan A + \tan A}{1 - \tan A \tan A} = \frac{2 \tan A}{1 - \tan^2 A}.$$

8. Prove $\sin \left(\frac{A}{2} \right) = \pm \sqrt{\frac{1 - \cos A}{2}}$. Begin with $\cos (2A) = \cos^2 A - \sin^2 A$. This can be written as $\cos (2A) = (1 - \sin^2 A) - \sin^2 A = 1 - 2\sin^2 A$. If you want $\cos A$, you can say $\cos A = 1 - 2 \sin^2 \left(\frac{A}{2} \right)$. Solve this for $\sin \left(\frac{A}{2} \right)$, so $2 \sin^2 \left(\frac{A}{2} \right) = 1 - \cos A$. Continue, and you find

$$\sin^2 \left(\frac{A}{2} \right) = \frac{1 - \cos A}{2}$$

$$\sin \left(\frac{A}{2} \right) = \pm \sqrt{\frac{1 - \cos A}{2}}.$$

9. Prove $\cos \left(\frac{A}{2} \right) = \pm \sqrt{\frac{1 + \cos A}{2}}$. Using the same pattern as in problem 8, the identity $\cos (2A) = \cos^2 A - \sin^2 A$ can be written as $\cos (2A) = \cos^2 A - (1 - \cos^2 A) = 2\cos^2 A - 1$. As before, this can be written as $\cos A = 2 \cos^2 \left(\frac{A}{2} \right) - 1$. Solve this for $\cos \left(\frac{A}{2} \right)$, which gives

$$2 \cos^2 \left(\frac{A}{2} \right) = 1 + \cos A$$

$$\cos^2 \left(\frac{A}{2} \right) = \frac{1 + \cos A}{2}$$

$$\cos \left(\frac{A}{2} \right) = \pm \sqrt{\frac{1 + \cos A}{2}}.$$

Content Domain 5.3: Derivatives and Applications

Subsection a: Derive the rules of differentiation for polynomial, trigonometric, and logarithmic functions using the formal definition of a derivative.

Understanding the formal definition of a derivative is often overlooked. Although it is faster and, in some ways, easier to use the rules that derive from the formal definition, using the formal definition of a derivative can help you to formulate the shortcut rules you use most often.

Two methods exist for the formal definition of a derivative at a point. They vary based upon the labeling of a graph. The derivative can be defined as the slope of the tangent line to a curve at a given point. Because it is difficult to pinpoint what exactly is a tangent line, you use limits to help define the slope of a tangent line.

Examine Figure 3–15.

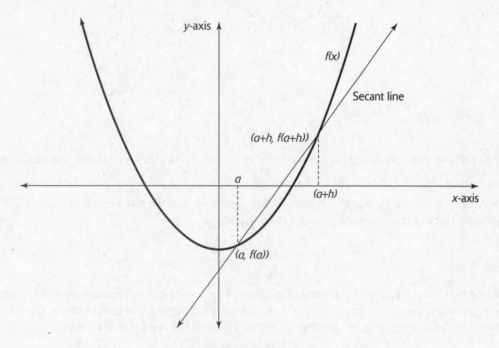

Figure 3–15

In this case, the point at which the tangent line is desired is labeled $(a, f(a))$. If you select another point on the graph that is h units away from a, you can label that point as $(a+h, f(a+h))$. The line that connects these two points is called a **secant line**. You can find the slope of this secant line using the formula for slope given two points (x_1, y_1) and (x_2, y_2), which is $m = \frac{y_2 - y_1}{x_2 - x_1}$. Using the points for the secant line, this becomes:

$$m = \frac{f(a+h) - f(a)}{(a+h) - a} = \frac{f(a+h) - f(a)}{h}$$

If you move the point $(a+h, f(a+h))$ closer to the point $(a, f(a))$, this line becomes closer to being considered a tangent line. When the two points coincide and h becomes zero, the line is then tangent. Therefore, you can define the derivative as the slope of a line tangent to a curve as:

$$f'(a) = \lim_{h \to 0} \frac{f(a+h) - f(a)}{h}$$

This is one way to define the derivative of a function at a point with the formal definition. The second is similar, but uses slightly different labels.

Examine Figure 3–16.

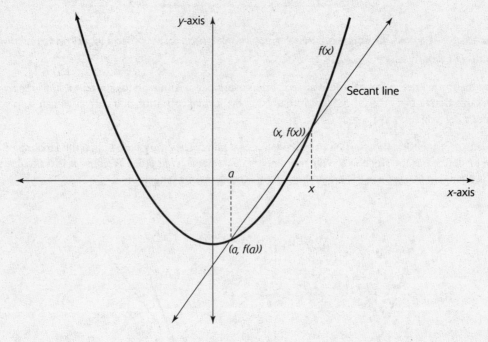

Figure 3–16

In this case, the point at which the tangent line is desired is now $(a, f(a))$, and the second point that makes the secant line is labeled $(x, f(x))$. Then the slope of the secant line can be written as $m = \dfrac{f(x) - f(a)}{x - a}$. To find the tangent line, you again move the point $(x, f(x))$ closer to the point $(a, f(a))$ until they coincide and x becomes equal to a. Then the slope of the tangent line to a curve at point $(a, f(a))$ can be defined as

$$f'(a) = \lim_{x \to a} \frac{f(x) - f(a)}{x - a}.$$

When examining the formal definition of the derivative, either of these methods will provide a correct solution. Sometimes one method is easier to work with than the other, so it is helpful to know both methods. Depending upon whether you are comfortable factoring or multiplying, one may be easier to work with than another.

Here are some examples worked out with both methods. Following that will be three problems for you to work out with step-by-step hints to help you. Then, there will be several example exercises for you to work on your own followed by solutions to those exercises.

Example 1:

Use the formal definition of a derivative to find the derivative of $f(x) = 3x - 5$ at the point $(a, f(a))$.

First method:

$$f(a) = 3a - 5$$
$$f(a + h) = 3(a + h) - 5$$

$$f'(a) = \lim_{h \to 0} \frac{f(a + h) - f(a)}{h} = \lim_{h \to 0} \frac{(3(a + h) - 5) - (3a - 5)}{h} = \lim_{h \to 0} \frac{3a + 3h - 5 - 3a + 5}{h} =$$

$$\lim_{h \to 0} \frac{3h}{h} = \lim_{h \to 0} 3 = 3$$

Second method:

$f(a) = 3a - 5$
$f(x) = 3x - 5$
$f'(a) = \lim\limits_{x \to a} \dfrac{f(x) - f(a)}{x - a} = \lim\limits_{x \to a} \dfrac{(3x - 5) - (3a - 5)}{x - a} = \lim\limits_{x \to a} \dfrac{3x - 5 - 3a + 5}{x - a} = \lim\limits_{x \to a} \dfrac{3x - 3a}{x - a} = \lim\limits_{x \to a} \dfrac{3(x - a)}{x - a} = \lim\limits_{x \to a} 3 = 3$

Both variations of the formal definition of the derivative give the same solution. In this case, the use of either variation of the definition is equally difficult. In some cases, one variation of the derivative may be easier to compute than the other, as in example 2.

Example 2:

Use the formal definition of the derivative to find the derivative of $f(x) = x^3 - 2x^2 + 5$ at the point $(a, f(a))$

First method:

$$f(a) = a^3 - 2a^2 + 5$$
$$f(a + h) = (a + h)^3 - 2(a + h)^2 + 5$$
$$\lim_{h \to 0} \frac{f(a + h) - f(a)}{h} = \lim_{h \to 0} \frac{\left((a + h)^3 - 2(a + h)^2 + 5\right) - (a^3 - 2a^2 + 5)}{h}$$
$$= \lim_{h \to 0} \frac{\left(a^3 + 3a^2h + 3ah^2 + h^3 - 2(a^2 + 2ah + h^2) + 5\right) - a^3 + 2a^2 - 5}{h}$$
$$= \lim_{h \to 0} \frac{a^3 + 3a^2h + 3ah^2 + h^3 - 2a^2 - 4ah - 2h^2 + 5 - a^3 + 2a^2 - 5}{h}$$
$$= \lim_{h \to 0} \frac{3a^2h + 3ah^2 + h^3 - 4ah - 2h^2}{h} = \lim_{h \to 0} \frac{h(3a^2 + 3ah + h^2 - 4a - 2h)}{h}$$
$$= \lim_{h \to 0} 3a^2 + 3ah + h^2 - 4a - 2h = 3a^2 - 4a$$

Second method:

$$f(x) = x^3 - 2x^2 + 5$$
$$f(a) = a^3 - 2a^2 + 5$$
$$\lim_{x \to a} \frac{f(x) - f(a)}{x - a} = \lim_{x \to a} \frac{(x^3 - 2x^2 + 5) - (a^3 - 2a^2 + 5)}{x - a}$$
$$= \lim_{x \to a} \frac{x^3 - 2x^2 + 5 - a^3 + 2a^2 - 5}{x - a}$$
$$= \lim_{x \to a} \frac{x^3 - a^3 - 2x^2 + 2a^2}{x - a} = \lim_{x \to a} \frac{\left((x - a)(x^2 + xa + a^2)\right) - 2(x^2 - a^2)}{x - a}$$
$$= \lim_{x \to a} \frac{\left((x - a)(x^2 + xa + a^2)\right) - 2\left((x + a)(x - a)\right)}{x - a}$$
$$= \lim_{x \to a} \frac{(x - a)\left(x^2 + xa + a^2 - 2(x + a)\right)}{x - a}$$
$$= \lim_{x \to a} x^2 + xa + a^2 - 2x - 2a$$
$$= a^2 + a^2 + a^2 - 2a - 2a$$
$$= 3a^2 - 4a$$

Again, in this example, the solutions are the same.

Here, the first method required expanding $(a + h)^3$ and $(a + h)^2$. If one knows binomial expansion rules, these are not difficult. The second method required factoring $(x^3 - a^3)$ and $(x^2 - a^2)$. Again, if one knows the pattern for factoring the difference of cubes and the difference of squares, this is not difficult. Here, the decision to choose one method over the other is preference. Most of the time, this is the case. Preference determines which variation of the definition should be used.

If the derivative at any point $(x, f(x))$ is what is desired, replace a by x and $f'(x)$ is then determined. Additionally, the first variation can be written as $f'(x) = \lim_{h \to 0} \dfrac{f(x+h) - f(x)}{h}$, which gives the derivative at any point $(x, f(x))$ outright.

Following is an example with step-by-step directions. Use these to help you as you solve the practice problems if you get stuck. Then there are several problems to practice using the formal definition of the derivative to find $f'(x)$. The solutions to those problems follow.

Example 3:

Find the derivative of $f(x) = 2x^2 - 4$ using the formal definition of the derivative.

Step 1: Do you prefer factoring or expanding binomials?

If you prefer factoring, use $f'(a) = \lim_{x \to a} \dfrac{f(x) - f(a)}{x - a}$.

If you prefer expanding, use $f'(a) = \lim_{h \to 0} \dfrac{f(a+h) - f(a)}{h}$ or $f'(x) = \lim_{h \to 0} \dfrac{f(x+h) - f(x)}{h}$.

Step 2: Define $f(x)$, $f(a)$, $f(a+h)$ depending upon which definition you are using.

$$f(x) = 2x^2 - 4$$
Here, $\quad f(a) = 2a^2 - 4$.
$$f(a+h) = 2(a+h)^2 - 4$$

Step 3: Substitute into the definition formula.

$f'(a) = \lim_{x \to a} \dfrac{f(x) - f(a)}{x - a}$ $= \lim_{x \to a} \dfrac{(2x^2 - 4) - (2a^2 - 4)}{x - a}$	$f'(a) = \lim_{h \to 0} \dfrac{f(a+h) - f(a)}{h}$ $= \lim_{h \to 0} \dfrac{(2(a+h)^2 - 4) - (2a^2 - 4)}{h}$

Step 4: Simplify and evaluate the limit.

$= \lim_{x \to a} \dfrac{2x^2 - 4 - 2a^2 + 4}{x - a}$ $= \lim_{x \to a} \dfrac{2x^2 - 2a^2}{x - a}$ $= \lim_{x \to a} \dfrac{2(x+a)(x-a)}{x - a}$ $= \lim_{x \to a} 2(x + a)$ $= 2(a + a) = 2(2a) = 4a$	$= \lim_{h \to 0} \dfrac{2(a^2 + 2ah + h^2) - 4 - 2a^2 + 4}{h}$ $= \lim_{h \to 0} \dfrac{2a^2 + 4ah + 2h^2 - 4 - 2a^2 + 4}{4}$ $= \lim_{h \to 0} \dfrac{4ah + 2h^2}{h}$ $= \lim_{h \to 0} \dfrac{2h(2a + h)}{h} = \lim_{h \to 0} 2(2a + h)$ $= 4a$

Step 5: If you want the derivative at x, substitute x for a in the derivative, so $f'(x) = 4x$.

Practice Problems

1. Find the derivative of $f(x) = 2x^3 - 4x + 7$ using the formal definition of the derivative.

2. Find the derivative of $f(x) = \sqrt{3x - 2}$ using the formal definition of the derivative.

3. Find the derivative of $f(x) = \frac{2x - 3}{x + 1}$ using the formal definition of the derivative.

4. Find the derivative of $f(x) = \sqrt{3x^2 - 2}$ using the formal definition of the derivative.

5. Find the derivative of $f(x) = \frac{2 - x^2}{x}$ using the formal definition of the derivative.

6. Find the derivative of $f(x) = \frac{1}{\sqrt{2x - 1}}$ using the formal definition of the derivative.

Solutions

1. $f(x) = 2x^3 - 4x + 7$, so $f(a) = 2a^3 - 4a + 7$ and $f(x + h) = 2(x + h)^3 - 4(x + h) + 7$.

First Method:

$$f'(x) = \lim_{h \to 0} \frac{f(x+h) - f(x)}{h}$$

$$= \lim_{h \to 0} \frac{2(x+h)^3 - 4(x+h) + 7 - (2x^3 - 4x + 7)}{h}$$

$$= \lim_{h \to 0} \frac{2(x^3 + 3x^2 h + 3xh^2 + h^3) - 4x - 4h + 7 - 2x^3 + 4x - 7}{h}$$

$$= \lim_{h \to 0} \frac{2x^3 + 6x^2 h + 6xh^2 + 2h^3 - 4x - 4h + 7 - 2x^3 + 4x - 7}{h}$$

$$= \lim_{h \to 0} \frac{6x^2 h + 6xh^2 + 2h^2 - 4h}{h} = \lim_{h \to 0} \frac{h(6x^2 + 6xh + 2h^2 - 4)}{h}$$

$$= \lim_{h \to 0} 6x^2 + 6xh + 2h^2 - 4$$

$$= 6x^2 - 4$$

Second Method:

$$f'(a) = \lim_{x \to a} \frac{f(x) - f(a)}{x - a}$$

$$= \lim_{x \to a} \frac{(2x^3 - 4x + 7) - (2a^3 - 4a + 7)}{x - a} = \lim_{x \to a} \frac{2x^3 - 4x + 7 - 2a^3 + 4a - 7}{x - a}$$

$$= \lim_{x \to a} \frac{(2x^3 - 2a^3) - 4x + 4a}{x - a} = \lim_{x \to a} \frac{2(x - a)(x^2 + xa + a^2) - 4(x - a)}{x - a}$$

$$= \lim_{x \to a} \frac{(x - a)(2(x^2 + xa + a^2) - 4)}{x - a} = \lim_{x \to a} 2x^2 + 2xa + 2a^2 - 4$$

$$= 2a^2 + 2aa + 2a^2 - 4 = 6a^2 - 4$$

So,

$$f'(x) = 6x^2 - 4.$$

2. $f(x) = \sqrt{3x - 2}$, so $f(a) = \sqrt{3a - 2}$ and $f(x + h) = \sqrt{3(x + h) - 2}$.

First Method:

$$f'(x) = \lim_{h \to 0} \frac{f(x+h) - f(x)}{h}$$

$$= \lim_{h \to 0} \frac{\sqrt{3(x+h) - 2} - \sqrt{3x - 2}}{h} = \lim_{h \to 0} \frac{\sqrt{3x + 3h - 2} - \sqrt{3x - 2}}{h}$$

$$= \lim_{h \to 0} \frac{(\sqrt{3x + 3h - 2} - \sqrt{3x - 2})(\sqrt{3x + 3h - 2} + \sqrt{3x - 2})}{h(\sqrt{3x + 3h - 2} + \sqrt{3x - 2})}$$

$$= \lim_{h \to 0} \frac{(3x + 3h - 2) - (3x - 2)}{h(\sqrt{3x + 3h - 2} + \sqrt{3x - 2})} = \lim_{h \to 0} \frac{3x + 3h - 2 - 3x + 2}{h(\sqrt{3x + 3h - 2} + \sqrt{3x - 2})}$$

$$= \lim_{h \to 0} \frac{3h}{h(\sqrt{3x + 3h - 2} + \sqrt{3x - 2})} = \lim_{h \to 0} \frac{3}{\sqrt{3x + 3h - 2} + \sqrt{3x - 2}}$$

$$= \frac{3}{\sqrt{3x - 2} + \sqrt{3x - 2}}$$

$$= \frac{3}{2\sqrt{3x - 2}}$$

Second Method:

$$f'(a) = \lim_{x \to a} \frac{f(x) - f(a)}{x - a} = \lim_{x \to a} \frac{\sqrt{3x-2} - \sqrt{3a-2}}{x - a}$$

$$= \lim_{x \to a} \frac{\left(\sqrt{3x-2} - \sqrt{3a-2}\right)\left(\sqrt{3x-2} + \sqrt{3a-2}\right)}{(x-a)\left(\sqrt{3x-2} + \sqrt{3a-2}\right)}$$

$$= \lim_{x \to a} \frac{(3x-2) - (3a-2)}{(x-a)\left(\sqrt{3x-2} + \sqrt{3a-2}\right)} = \lim_{x \to a} \frac{3x - 2 - 3a + 2}{(x-a)\left(\sqrt{3x-2} + \sqrt{3a-2}\right)}$$

$$= \lim_{x \to a} \frac{3x - 3a}{(x-a)\left(\sqrt{3x-2} + \sqrt{3a-2}\right)} = \lim_{x \to a} \frac{3(x-a)}{(x-a)\left(\sqrt{3x-2} + \sqrt{3a-2}\right)}$$

$$= \lim_{x \to a} \frac{3}{\left(\sqrt{3x-2} + \sqrt{3a-2}\right)} = \frac{3}{\sqrt{3a-2} + \sqrt{3a-2}} = \frac{3}{2\sqrt{3a-2}}$$

So,

$$f'(x) = \frac{3}{2\sqrt{3x-2}}.$$

3. $f(x) = \dfrac{2x-3}{x+1}$, so $f(a) = \dfrac{2a-3}{a+1}$ and $f(x+h) = \dfrac{2(x+h)-3}{(x+h)+1}$.

First Method:

$$f'(x) = \lim_{h \to 0} \frac{f(x+h) - f(x)}{h}$$

$$= \lim_{h \to 0} \frac{\dfrac{2(x+h)-3}{(x+h)+1} - \dfrac{2x-3}{x+1}}{h} = \lim_{h \to 0} \frac{\dfrac{2x+2h-3}{x+h+1} - \dfrac{2x-3}{x+1}}{h}$$

$$= \lim_{h \to 0} \frac{\dfrac{(2x+2h-3)(x+1)}{(x+h+1)(x+1)} - \dfrac{(2x-3)(x+h+1)}{(x+1)(x+h+1)}}{h}$$

$$= \lim_{h \to 0} \frac{\dfrac{(2x^2 + 2x + 2xh + 2h - 3x - 3) - (2x^2 + 2xh + 2x - 3x - 3h - 3)}{(x+h+1)(x+1)}}{h}$$

$$= \lim_{h \to 0} \frac{(2x^2 + 2x + 2xh + 2h - 3x - 3 - 2x^2 - 2xh - 2x + 3x + 3h + 3)}{(x+h+1)(x+1)h}$$

$$= \lim_{h \to 0} \frac{5h}{(x+h+1)(x+1)h} = \lim_{h \to 0} \frac{5}{(x+h+1)(x+1)} = \frac{5}{(x+1)(x+1)} = \frac{5}{(x+1)^2}$$

Second Method:

$$f'(a) = \lim_{x \to a} \frac{f(x) - f(a)}{x - a}$$

$$= \lim_{x \to a} \frac{\dfrac{2x-3}{x+1} - \dfrac{2a-3}{a+1}}{x-a} = \lim_{x \to a} \frac{\dfrac{(2x-3)(a+1)}{(x+1)(a+1)} - \dfrac{(2a-3)(x+1)}{(a+1)(x+1)}}{x-a}$$

$$= \lim_{x \to a} \frac{\dfrac{(2xa + 2x - 3a - 3) - (2xa + 2a - 3x - 3)}{(x+1)(a+1)}}{(x-a)}$$

$$= \lim_{x \to a} \frac{2xa + 2x - 3a - 3 - 2xa - 2a + 3x + 3}{(x+1)(a+1)(x-a)}$$

$$= \lim_{x \to a} \frac{5x - 5a}{(x+1)(a+1)(x-a)} = \lim_{x \to a} \frac{5(x-a)}{(x+1)(a+1)(x-a)}$$

$$= \lim_{x \to a} \frac{5}{(x+1)(a+1)} = \frac{5}{(a+1)(a+1)} = \frac{5}{(a+1)^2}$$

So, $f'(x) = \dfrac{5}{(x+1)^2}$.

4. $f(x) = \sqrt{3x^2 - 2}$, so $f(a) = \sqrt{3a^2 - 2}$ and $f(x+h) = \sqrt{3(x+h)^2 - 2}$.

First Method:

$$f'(x) = \lim_{h \to 0} \frac{f(x+h) - f(x)}{h}$$

$$= \lim_{h \to 0} \frac{\sqrt{3(x+h)^2 - 2} - \sqrt{3x^2 - 2}}{h} = \lim_{h \to 0} \frac{\sqrt{3(x^2 + 2xh + h^2) - 2} - \sqrt{3x^2 - 2}}{h}$$

$$= \lim_{h \to 0} \frac{\sqrt{3x^2 + 6xh + 3h^2 - 2} - \sqrt{3x^2 - 2}}{h}$$

$$= \lim_{h \to 0} \frac{\left(\sqrt{3x^2 + 6xh + 3h^2 - 2} - \sqrt{3x^2 - 2}\right)\left(\sqrt{3x^2 + 6xh + 3h^2 - 2} + \sqrt{3x^2 - 2}\right)}{h\left(\sqrt{3x^2 + 6xh + 3h^2 - 2} + \sqrt{3x^2 - 2}\right)}$$

$$= \lim_{h \to 0} \frac{(3x^2 + 6xh + 3h^2 - 2) - (3x^2 - 2)}{h\left(\sqrt{3x^2 + 6xh + 3h^2 - 2} + \sqrt{3x^2 - 2}\right)} = \lim_{h \to 0} \frac{3x^2 + 6xh + 3h^2 - 2 - 3x^2 + 2}{h\left(\sqrt{3x^2 + 6xh + 3h^2 - 2} + \sqrt{3x^2 - 2}\right)}$$

$$= \lim_{h \to 0} \frac{6xh + 3h^2}{h\left(\sqrt{3x^2 + 6xh + 3h^2 - 2} + \sqrt{3x^2 - 2}\right)} = \lim_{h \to 0} \frac{h(6x + 3h)}{h\left(\sqrt{3x^2 + 6xh + 3h^2 - 2} + \sqrt{3x^2 - 2}\right)}$$

$$= \lim_{h \to 0} \frac{6x + 3h}{\left(\sqrt{3x^2 + 6xh + 3h^2 - 2} + \sqrt{3x^2 - 2}\right)} = \frac{6x}{\sqrt{3x^2 - 2} + \sqrt{3x^2 - 2}} = \frac{6x}{2\sqrt{3x^2 - 2}} = \frac{3x}{\sqrt{3x^2 - 2}}$$

Second Method:

$$f'(a) = \lim_{x \to a} \frac{f(x) - f(a)}{x - a}$$

$$= \lim_{x \to a} \frac{\sqrt{3x^2 - 2} - \sqrt{3a^2 - 2}}{x - a} = \lim_{x \to a} \frac{\left(\sqrt{3x^2 - 2} - \sqrt{3a^2 - 2}\right)\left(\sqrt{3x^2 - 2} + \sqrt{3a^2 - 2}\right)}{(x-a)\left(\sqrt{3x^2 - 2} + \sqrt{3a^2 - 2}\right)}$$

$$= \lim_{x \to a} \frac{(3x^2 - 2) - (3a^2 - 2)}{(x-a)\left(\sqrt{3x^2 - 2} + \sqrt{3a^2 - 2}\right)} = \lim_{x \to a} \frac{3x^2 - 2 - 3a^2 + 2}{(x-a)\left(\sqrt{3x^2 - 2} + \sqrt{3a^2 - 2}\right)}$$

$$= \lim_{x \to a} \frac{3x^2 - 3a^2}{(x-a)\left(\sqrt{3x^2 - 2} + \sqrt{3a^2 - 2}\right)} = \lim_{x \to a} \frac{3(x+a)(x-a)}{(x-a)\left(\sqrt{3x^2 - 2} + \sqrt{3a^2 - 2}\right)}$$

$$= \lim_{x \to a} \frac{3(x+a)}{\left(\sqrt{3x^2 - 2} + \sqrt{3a^2 - 2}\right)} = \frac{3(a+a)}{\sqrt{3a^2 - 2} + \sqrt{3a^2 - 2}} = \frac{3(2a)}{2\sqrt{3a^2 - 2}} = \frac{3a}{\sqrt{3a^2 - 2}}$$

So,

$$f'(x) = \frac{3x}{\sqrt{3x^2 - 2}}.$$

5. $f(x) = \frac{2 - x^2}{x}$, so $f(a) = \frac{2 - a^2}{a}$ and $f(x+h) = \frac{2 - (x+h)^2}{(x+h)}$.

First Method:

$$f'(x) = \lim_{h \to 0} \frac{f(x+h) - f(x)}{h}$$

$$= \lim_{h \to 0} \frac{\frac{2 - (x+h)^2}{(x+h)} - \frac{2 - x^2}{x}}{h} = \lim_{h \to 0} \frac{\frac{2 - (x^2 + 2xh + h^2)}{(x+h)} - \frac{2 - x^2}{x}}{h}$$

$$= \lim_{h \to 0} \frac{\frac{(2 - x^2 - 2xh - h^2)(x)}{(x+h)(x)} - \frac{(2 - x^2)(x+h)}{x(x+h)}}{h}$$

$$= \lim_{h \to 0} \frac{\frac{2x - x^3 - 2x^2 h - xh^2 - (2x + 2h - x^3 - x^2 h)}{(x+h)(x)}}{h}$$

$$= \lim_{h \to 0} \frac{2x - x^3 - 2x^2 h - xh^2 - 2h + x^3 + x^2 h}{(x+h)(x)(h)}$$

$$= \lim_{h \to 0} \frac{-2x^2 h - xh^2 - 2h + x^2 h}{(x+h)(x)(h)} = \lim_{h \to 0} \frac{h(-2x^2 - xh - 2 + x^2)}{(x+h)(x)(h)}$$

$$= \lim_{h \to 0} \frac{-2x^2 - xh - 2 + x^2}{(x+h)(x)} = \frac{-2x^2 - 2 + x^2}{(x)(x)} = \frac{-x^2 - 2}{x}$$

Second Method:

$$f'(a) = \lim_{x \to a} \frac{f(x) - f(a)}{x - a}$$

$$= \lim_{x \to a} \frac{\frac{2 - x^2}{x} - \frac{2 - a^2}{a}}{x - a} = \lim_{x \to a} \frac{\frac{(2 - x^2)a}{xa} - \frac{(2 - a^2)x}{ax}}{x - a} = \lim_{x \to a} \frac{2a - x^2 a - (2x - xa^2)}{x - a}$$

$$= \lim_{x \to a} \frac{\frac{2a - x^2 a - 2x + xa^2}{ax}}{x - a} = \lim_{x \to a} \frac{2a - x^2 a - 2x + xa^2}{ax(x - a)} = \lim_{x \to a} \frac{-x^2 a + xa^2 - 2x + 2a}{ax(x - a)}$$

$$= \lim_{x \to a} \frac{(-ax(x - a)) - 2(x - a)}{ax(x - a)} = \lim_{x \to a} \frac{(x - a)(-ax - 2)}{ax(x - a)} = \lim_{x \to a} \frac{-ax - 2}{ax} = \frac{-a^2 - 2}{a^2}$$

So,

$$f'(x) = \frac{-x^2 - 2}{x^2}.$$

6. $f(x) = \dfrac{1}{\sqrt{2x-1}}$, so $f(a) = \dfrac{1}{\sqrt{2a-1}}$ and $f(x+h) = \dfrac{1}{\sqrt{2(x+h)-1}}$.

First Method:

$$f'(x) = \lim_{h \to 0} \frac{f(x+h) - f(x)}{h}$$

$$= \lim_{h \to 0} \frac{\dfrac{1}{\sqrt{2(x+h)-1}} - \dfrac{1}{\sqrt{2x-1}}}{h} = \lim_{h \to 0} \frac{\dfrac{\sqrt{2x-1}}{\sqrt{2(x+h)-1}\sqrt{2x-1}} - \dfrac{\sqrt{2(x+h)-1}}{\sqrt{2(x+h)-1}\sqrt{2x-1}}}{h}$$

$$= \lim_{h \to 0} \frac{\dfrac{\sqrt{2x-1} - \sqrt{2(x+h)-1}}{\sqrt{(2x-1)(2(x+h)-1)}}}{h} = \lim_{h \to 0} \frac{\sqrt{2x-1} - \sqrt{2x+2h-1}}{h\sqrt{(2x-1)(2x+2h-1)}}$$

$$= \lim_{h \to 0} \frac{\left(\sqrt{2x-1} - \sqrt{2x+2h-1}\right)\left(\sqrt{2x-1} + \sqrt{2x+2h-1}\right)}{h\sqrt{(2x-1)(2x+2h-1)}\left(\sqrt{2x-1} + \sqrt{2x+2h-1}\right)}$$

$$= \lim_{h \to 0} \frac{(2x-1) - (2x+2h-1)}{h\sqrt{(2x-1)(2x+2h-1)}\left(\sqrt{2x-1} + \sqrt{2x+2h-1}\right)} = \lim_{h \to 0} \frac{2x-1-2x-2h+1}{h\sqrt{(2x-1)(2x+2h-1)}\left(\sqrt{2x-1} + \sqrt{2x+2h-1}\right)}$$

$$= \lim_{h \to 0} \frac{-2h}{h\sqrt{(2x-1)(2x+2h-1)}\left(\sqrt{2x-1} + \sqrt{2x+2h-1}\right)} = \lim_{h \to 0} \frac{-2}{\sqrt{(2x-1)(2x+2h-1)}\left(\sqrt{2x-1} + \sqrt{2x+2h-1}\right)}$$

$$= \frac{-2}{\sqrt{(2x-1)(2x-1)}\left(\sqrt{2x-1} + \sqrt{2x-1}\right)} = \frac{-2}{(2x-1)\left(2\sqrt{2x-1}\right)}$$

$$= \frac{-1}{(2x-1)\sqrt{2x-1}}$$

Second Method:

$$\lim_{x \to a} \frac{f(x) - f(a)}{x - a}$$

$$= \lim_{x \to a} \frac{\dfrac{1}{\sqrt{2x-1}} - \dfrac{1}{\sqrt{2a-1}}}{x-a} = \lim_{x \to a} \frac{\dfrac{\sqrt{2a-1}}{\sqrt{2x-1}\sqrt{2a-1}} - \dfrac{\sqrt{2x-1}}{\sqrt{2a-1}\sqrt{2x-1}}}{x-a} = \lim_{x \to a} \frac{\dfrac{\sqrt{2a-1} - \sqrt{2x-1}}{\sqrt{(2x-1)(2a-1)}}}{x-a}$$

$$= \lim_{x \to a} \frac{\sqrt{2a-1} - \sqrt{2x-1}}{(x-a)\sqrt{(2x-1)(2a-1)}} = \lim_{x \to a} \frac{\left(\sqrt{2a-1} - \sqrt{2x-1}\right)\left(\sqrt{2a-1} + \sqrt{2x-1}\right)}{(x-a)\sqrt{(2x-1)(2a-1)}\left(\sqrt{2a-1} + \sqrt{2x-1}\right)}$$

$$= \lim_{x \to a} \frac{(2a-1) - (2x-1)}{(x-a)\sqrt{(2x-1)(2a-1)}\left(\sqrt{2a-1} + \sqrt{2x-1}\right)} = \lim_{x \to a} \frac{2a-1-2x+1}{(x-a)\sqrt{(2x-1)(2a-1)}\left(\sqrt{2a-1} + \sqrt{2x-1}\right)}$$

$$= \lim_{x \to a} \frac{2a-2x}{(x-a)\sqrt{(2x-1)(2a-1)}\left(\sqrt{2a-1} + \sqrt{2x-1}\right)} = \lim_{x \to a} \frac{-2(x-a)}{(x-a)\sqrt{(2x-1)(2a-1)}\left(\sqrt{2a-1} + \sqrt{2x-1}\right)}$$

$$= \lim_{x \to a} \frac{-2}{\sqrt{(2x-1)(2a-1)}\left(\sqrt{2a-1} + \sqrt{2x-1}\right)} = \frac{-2}{\left(\sqrt{(2a-1)(2a-1)}\right)\left(\sqrt{(2a-1)} + \sqrt{2a-1}\right)}$$

$$= \frac{-2}{(2a-1)(2)\sqrt{2a-1}} = \frac{-1}{(2a-1)\sqrt{2a-1}}$$

So,

$$f'(x) = \frac{-1}{(2x-1)\sqrt{2x-1}}.$$

CSET PRACTICE TESTS

Practice CSET: Mathematics Test I

Remember to read and follow the instructions carefully.

The set of multiple-choice questions and constructed-response questions presented in this Practice CSET: Mathematics Test I are similar to the questions you will see on the **Mathematics Subtest I: Algebra; Number Theory**. This subtest includes the same amount of items you will find on the actual CSET: Mathematics test. We have included an answer key and explanation for each item's possible responses; however, we recommend and encourage you to respond to the items without looking at these sections of this book. You should record your responses on a separate sheet of paper and review your answers with the provided responses afterward.

Note: The use of calculators is not allowed for the CSET: Mathematics Subtest I.

Practice CSET: Mathematics Subtest I

1. Assume that a, b, c, and d are consecutive positive integers. Find the value of $i^a + i^b + i^c + i^d$.

   A. -1
   B. 1
   C. 0
   D. i

2. Solve the following equation: $\sqrt{4n} + 9 = 5$.

   A. 4
   B. 1
   C. 16
   D. This equation has no solution.

3. You represent a complex number $z = 2 - 4i$ as a vector in the plane. What will happen if you multiply z by i?

   A. Rotate z counterclockwise by 90°.
   B. Translate z 2 units in the x-direction and 4 units in the y-direction.
   C. Reflect z over the y-axis.
   D. Reflect z over the x-axis.

GO ON TO THE NEXT PAGE

4. Use the graph below to answer the question that follows.

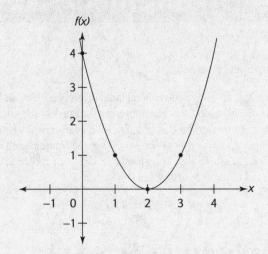

Which of the following is the equation of the graph shown above?

A. $y = 2x^2 + 4$
B. $y = x^2 - 4x + 4$
C. $y = x^2 + 4x + 4$
D. $y = x^2$

5. Indicate the value of $f(9)$ for $f(x) = -3\sqrt{x} - 3x^3$.

A. −19674
B. −19692
C. −2178
D. −2196

6. Identify whether one of the following vectors is equal to $\overline{MN}$ if $M = (2, 1)$ and $N = (3, -4)$:

$\overline{QR}$, where $Q = \langle -4, 5 \rangle$ and $R = \langle -3, 10 \rangle$

$\overline{LP}$, where $L = \langle 1, -1 \rangle$ and $P = \langle 2, 3 \rangle$

$\overline{ST}$, where $S = \langle 3, -2 \rangle$ and $T = \langle 4, -7 \rangle$

A. Only $\overline{LP}$ is equal to $\overline{MN}$.
B. Only $\overline{QR}$ is equal to $\overline{MN}$.
C. Only $\overline{ST}$ is equal to $\overline{MN}$.
D. None of these three vectors are equal to $\overline{MN}$.

7. Identify which of the following is a negative number.

A. i^{32}
B. i^{25}
C. i^{50}
D. i^{75}

8. Assuming that $i^x = i^y$, which of the following alternatives is or are always true?

I. x is equal to y.

II. x plus y is equal to an even number.

III. $x - y$ is a multiple of 4.

A. Only I is true.

B. Only III is true.

C. Only I and III are true.

D. Only II and III are true.

9. Indicate the value of $f(-8)$ for $f(x) = -5x^3 - 5\sqrt[3]{x}$.

A. 2570

B. 2560

C. -2560

D. -2570

10. Identify the graph that matches the following equation: $y = |x^2 - 4x + 2|$

A.

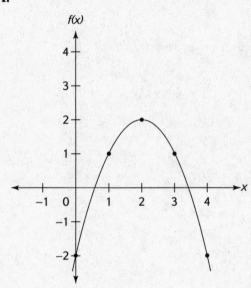

C.

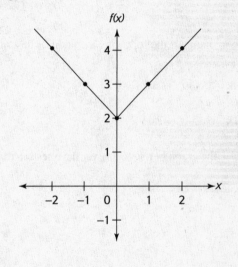

B.

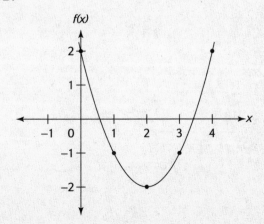

D.

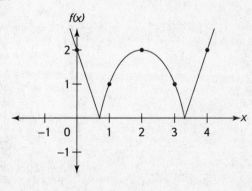

GO ON TO THE NEXT PAGE

11. Find the statement that is equivalent to the following statement: "If $0 < x < 1$, then $\sqrt{x}$ is irrational."

  A.   If $\sqrt{x}$ is rational, then $0 < x < 1$.
  B.   If $\sqrt{x}$ is rational, then $x \leq 0$, or $x \geq 1$.
  C.   If $0 < x < 1$, then $\sqrt{x}$ is rational.
  D.   If $\sqrt{x}$ is rational, then $0 < x < 1$.

12. Use the graph below to answer the question that follows.

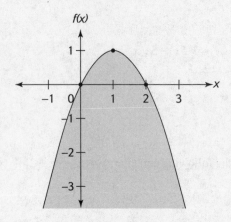

Which one of the following inequalities describes the shaded region shown in the graph?

  A. $y \leq -x^2 - 2x$
  B. $y > -x^2 + 2x$
  C. $y \leq -x^2 + 2x$
  D. $y \leq -x^2 + 2x + 2$

13. Use the graph below to answer the question that follows.

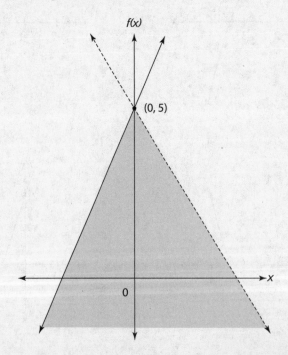

Which of the following systems of inequalities represents the shaded region above?

A. $y - 2x \leq 5$
    $y + x < 5$
B. $y - 2x \leq 5$
    $y + x \leq 5$
C. $y - 2x \geq 5$
    $y + x < 5$
D. $y - 2x < 5$
    $y + x > 5$

14. Assuming that r_1 and r_2 are the roots of the equation $x^2 - 2x - 1 = 0$, and that $r_1 > r_2$, what is $r_1 - r_2$?

A. $-2\sqrt{2}$
B. $2\sqrt{2}$
C. -2
D. 2

15. Use the graph of the function below to answer the question that follows.

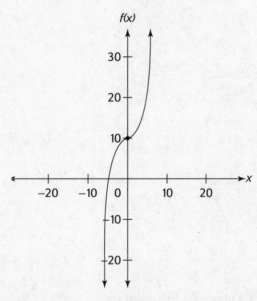

Above is the graph of $f(x) = 2x^3 + 10$. If this function is translated 3 units in the positive direction on the x-axis, which one of the following functions would represent the resulting translation?

A. $g(x) = 6x^3 + 30$
B. $g(x) = 2x^3 + 18x^2 + 54x + 64$
C. $g(x) = 2x + 13$
D. $g(x) = 2x^3 - 18x^2 + 54x - 44$

GO ON TO THE NEXT PAGE

16. What is $f(f(x))$ for $f(x) = x + \frac{1}{x}$?

    A. $\dfrac{x^2 + 1}{x}$

    B. $x^2 + \dfrac{1}{x^2}$

    C. $\dfrac{x^2 + 1}{x} + \dfrac{x}{x^2 + 1}$

    D. $x + \dfrac{1}{x}$

17. Identify the domain of $f(x) = \dfrac{(x-2)^3}{(x+2)^2}$ out of the following alternatives.

    A. $\{x \mid x \neq -2\}$

    B. $\{x \mid x \neq 2\}$

    C. $\{x \mid -2 < x < 2\}$

    D. All real numbers

18. Which of the following sets of numbers is considered a non-ordered field?

    A. the complex numbers

    B. the integers

    C. the rational numbers

    D. the natural numbers

19. Which pair of vectors is perpendicular?

    A. $\langle -2, 1 \rangle, \langle 1, -2 \rangle$

    B. $\langle -2, 1 \rangle, \langle -1, -2 \rangle$

    C. $\langle 2, -1 \rangle, \langle -1, 2 \rangle$

    D. $\langle -2, -1 \rangle, \langle -1, -2 \rangle$

20. Find the length of the vector <-1, 3, 2>.

    A. $\sqrt{14}$

    B. $\sqrt{6}$

    C. 2

    D. 14

21. Find the values of x and y in the following matrix equation.

$$\begin{bmatrix} -3 & 6x \\ y & 5 \end{bmatrix} + 3\begin{bmatrix} 4 & -y \\ 2x & 2 \end{bmatrix} = \begin{bmatrix} 9 & 5 \\ 17 & 11 \end{bmatrix}$$

    A. $x = \frac{1}{3}; y = -1$

    B. $x = 1; y = 15$

    C. $x = 3; y = \frac{7}{3}$

    D. $x = \frac{7}{3}; y = 3$

22. When the equation $x^2 + 5x + c = 0$ has only one solution, what would be the value of c?

A. 3.75
B. 6.25
C. –2.25
D. –6.25

23. Given that $A = \begin{bmatrix} 1 & 2 & 4 \\ 2 & 6 & 0 \end{bmatrix}$ and $B = \begin{bmatrix} 4 & 1 & 4 & 3 \\ 0 & -1 & 3 & 1 \\ 2 & 7 & 5 & 2 \end{bmatrix}$, which of the following responses is equal to AB?

A. $\begin{bmatrix} 13 & 14 & 19 & 13 \\ 14 & 13 & 20 & 14 \end{bmatrix}$

B. $\begin{bmatrix} 13 & 14 \\ 14 & 13 \\ 19 & 20 \\ 13 & 14 \end{bmatrix}$

C. $\begin{bmatrix} 12 & 8 \\ 27 & -4 \\ 30 & 26 \\ 13 & 12 \end{bmatrix}$

D. $\begin{bmatrix} 12 & 27 & 30 & 13 \\ 8 & -4 & 26 & 12 \end{bmatrix}$

24. If a and b and c are vectors and d is a scalar, which of the following statements are true?

A. $a \times b = b \times a$
B. $d(a \times b) = a \times (db)$
C. $a \cdot (b \times c) = (a \cdot b) \times (a \cdot c)$
D. $a \times (b \times c) = (a \times b) \times (a \times c)$

25. Which one of the following pair of factors does not have a Greatest Common Factor (GCF) equal to 6?

A. 24, 6
B. 42, 150
C. 54, 18
D. 18, 30

26. Find the Greatest Common Factor (GCF) of the following pair of algebraic expressions: $20x^2y$, and $50xy^2$.

A. xy
B. 10
C. $100x^2y^2$
D. $10xy$

GO ON TO THE NEXT PAGE

27. Indicate which one of the following statements is true.

    A.   An integer n is divisible by 6 if and only if it is divisible by 3.

    B.   A number k divides the sum of three consecutive integers n, $n + 1$, and $n + 2$ if and only if it divides the middle integer $n + 1$.

    C.   If r and s are integers, then $r|s$ if and only if $r^2|s^2$.

    D.   For all integers a, b, and c, $a|(b + c)$ if and only if $a|b$ and $a|c$.

28. The Euclidean Algorithm is used to produce a sequence $N_1 > N_2 > N_3 > N_4 > N_5 = 0$ of positive integers where $N_t = q_{t+1}N_{t+1} + N_{t+2}$, $t = 1, 2, 3$. The quotients are $q_2 = 3$, $q_3 = 2$, and $q_4 = 2$. Which of the following is correct?

    A.   GCF $(N_1, N_2) = {}^-2N_1 + 6N_2$

    B.   GCF $(N_1, N_2) = 2N_1 + 7N_2$

    C.   GCF $(N_1, N_2) = {}^-2N_1 - 6N_2$

    D.   GCF $(N_1, N_2) = {}^-2N_1 + 7N_2$

29. Indicate which one of the following statements is true.

    A.   An integer n is odd if and only if $n^2 + 2n$ is odd.

    B.   A number is irrational if and only if its square is irrational.

    C.   A number is rational if and only if its square is rational.

    D.   A number n is odd if and only if $n(n + 1)$ is even.

30. What is the number of prime numbers of the form $|n^2 - 6n + 5|$ where n is an integer?

    A.   1

    B.   2

    C.   0

    D.   3

Constructed-Response Question: Use extra lined paper to answer this question.

31. Complete the exercise that follows.

Indicate whether the following quadratic polynomial is reducible or irreducible:

$$f(x) = x^2 - \sqrt{2}$$

GO ON TO THE NEXT PAGE

Constructed-Response Question: Use extra lined paper to answer this question.

32. Complete the exercise that follows.

If $a, b, \ldots, e$ are real numbers and $a \neq 0$, and $az + by = c$ has the same solution set as $ax + dy = e$, then they are the same equation. Explain why this statement is true.

Constructed-Response Question: Use extra lined paper to answer this question.

33. Complete the exercise that follows.

Create a four equations and four unknowns system having the following sets:

A. a one-parameter solution set,

B. a two-parameter solution set, and

C. a three-parameter solution set.

GO ON TO THE NEXT PAGE

Constructed-Response Question: Use extra lined paper to answer this question.

34. Complete the exercise that follows.

Prove the divisibility rule for 3: If the sum of the digits of a number is divisible by 3, then the number is divisible by 3.

Practice CSET: Mathematics Subtest II

Continue the test. Remember to read and follow the instructions carefully.

The set of multiple-choice questions and constructed-response questions presented in this Practice CSET: Mathematics Test I are similar to the questions you will see on the **Mathematics Subtest II: Geometry; Probability and Statistics**. This subtest includes the same amount of items you will find on the actual CSET: Mathematics test. We have included an answer key and explanation for each item's possible responses; however, we recommend and encourage you to respond to the items without looking at these sections of this book. You should record your responses on a separate sheet of paper and review your answers with the provided responses afterward.

As you complete this subsection of the practice exam, you should consider the guidelines given by the Department of Education regarding the use of calculators for this test: A calculator will be needed and **will be allowed only for Mathematics Subtest II: Geometry; Probability and Statistics**. You must bring your own graphing calculator to the test administration, and it must be one of the approved models listed in the current version of the CSET registration bulletin. Since the approved calculator brands and models are subject to change, the list of approved graphing calculators will be updated as necessary. Test administration staff will clear the memory of your calculator before and after the test. Be sure you back up the memory on your calculator, including applications, to an external device before arriving at the test site.

35. What is the approximate volume of the circular cone illustrated here in cubic centimeters?

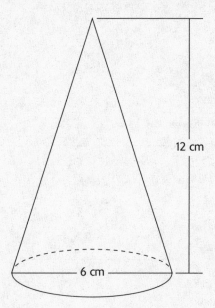

A. 113 cubic centimeters
B. 452 cubic centimeters
C. 339 cubic centimeters
D. 103 cubic centimeters

36. What is the approximate surface area of a cylinder that has a diameter of 15 cm and a height of 35 cm (see the following figure)?

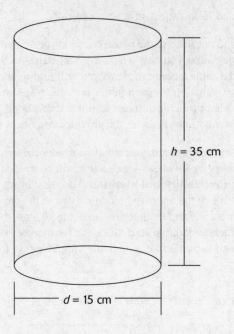

$h = 35$ cm

$d = 15$ cm

    A.   1825 cm^2
    B.   2002 cm^2
    C.   4710 cm^2
    D.   4003 cm^2

37. In the figure below, which of the following is false?

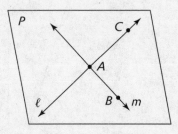

    A.   Lines ℓ and m intersect at point A.
    B.   Points A, B, and C are coplanar.
    C.   Points A, B, and C are non-collinear.
    D.   There is more than one plane that contains lines ℓ and m.

38. ∠HUT is both equal to ∠SOT and corresponds to it with respect to transversal $\overline{OT}$. $\overline{UH}$ intersects $\overline{ST}$ at H. What relation does $\overline{UH}$ have to $\overline{OS}$?

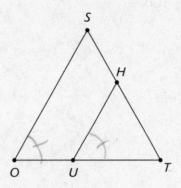

A. $\overline{UH} \perp \overline{OS}$
B. $\overline{UH}$ intersects $\overline{OS}$
C. $\overline{UH} \mathbin{/\!/} \overline{OS}$
D. $\overline{UH} = \overline{OS}$

39. In the figure below, if line segments *PC* and *AB* are parallel, which angles are equal?

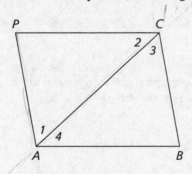

A. Angles 3 and 1 are equal.
B. Angles 3 and 4 are equal.
C. Angles 2 and 4 are equal.
D. Angles 2 and 1 are equal.

40. What is the value of *n* in the figure below?

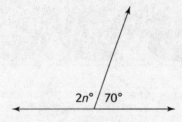

A. 45
B. 55
C. 75
D. 90

GO ON TO THE NEXT PAGE

41. According to the definition of congruent polygons, how many pairs of parts must be equal if two triangles are congruent?

    A. six
    B. five
    C. three
    D. nine

42. Which of the following statements is false?

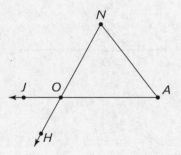

    A. $\angle JON > \angle NAO$
    B. $\angle JON > \angle ONA$
    C. $\angle JON = \angle HOA$
    D. $\angle JON = \angle HOJ$

43. Assume that you have an isosceles right triangle, with legs equal to 6 units, that is rotated around on one of its legs to generate a right circular cone. Find the volume of this cone.

    A. 216π
    B. 144π
    C. 72π
    D. $48\sqrt{2}\,\pi$

44. Three identical tennis balls are placed inside a cylindrical can, like in the figure below. The radius of the can equals the radius of the balls, and the balls just touch the bottom and top of the can. What percent of the volume of the can do the balls occupy?

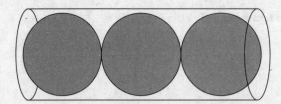

    A. 67%
    B. 75%
    C. 50%
    D. 44%

45. Given that line m is tangent to the circle whose center is at $(3, 2)$, and the point of tangency is $(6, 6)$, identify the slope of this line.

A. $-\dfrac{3}{4}$

B. $-\dfrac{4}{3}$

C. $\dfrac{3}{4}$

D. $\dfrac{4}{3}$

46. What happens to the volume of a sphere if its radius is doubled?

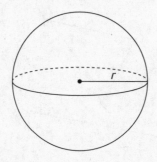

A. The volume is multiplied by 2.

B. The volume is multiplied by 3.

C. The volume is multiplied by 8.

D. The volume is multiplied by 4.

47. In $\triangle ABC$, $\overrightarrow{BD}$ bisects $\angle ABC$. Which of the following statements about the figure below matches the Angle Bisector Theorem?

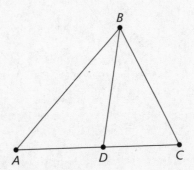

A. If $\overline{BD}$ is between $\overline{BC}$ and $\overline{AB}$, then $m(\angle ABD) + m(\angle DBC) = m(\angle ABC)$.

B. If $\overline{BD}$ bisects $\angle ABC$, then $m(\angle ABD) = m(\angle DBC)$.

C. If the $m\left(\overline{BA}\right) > m\left(\overline{BD}\right) > m\left(\overline{BC}\right)$, then $\overline{BC}$ is between $\overline{BA}$ and $\overline{BC}$.

D. If $\overline{BD}$ bisects $\angle ABC$ and divides $\overline{AC}$ into segments, then $\dfrac{AD}{DC} = \dfrac{AB}{BC}$.

48. If two angles are vertical angles, they are equal. Which one of the following statements is true?

A. This is a definition.

B. This is a theorem.

C. This is a postulate.

D. This is a conundrum.

GO ON TO THE NEXT PAGE

49. If two sides and the angle opposite one of them in a triangle are equal to the corresponding parts of another triangle, then it follows that the triangles are congruent.

    A. This statement could never be true.

    B. This statement is always true.

    C. This statement could be true if the hypotenuse and a leg of one right triangle are equal to the corresponding part of another right triangle.

    D. This statement could be true if the corresponding angles are right angles.

50. In the figure below, $\triangle QRS$ is the reflection of $\triangle XYZ$ through line m_1, and $\triangle LMO$ is the reflection of $\triangle QRS$ through m_2. Line m_1 is parallel to line m_2. Through what transformation is $\triangle LMO$ the image of $\triangle XYZ$?

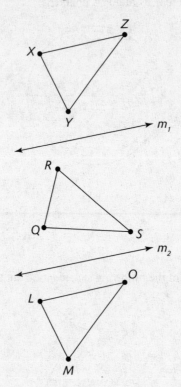

    A. a translation

    B. a reflection

    C. a rotation

    D. a translation and a rotation

Use the following figure for questions 51 and 52.

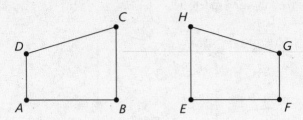

51. Using the previous figure, what transformation seems to relate *ABCD* and *EFGH*?

    A. a translation

    B. a reflection

    C. a rotation

    D. a translation and a rotation

52. Using the previous figure, which point of *EFGH* seems to be the image of *A?*

    A. point *E*

    B. point *F*

    C. point *G*

    D. point *H*

53. Based on the figure below involving two equilateral triangles, which one of the following statements is false?

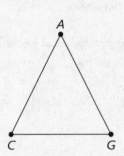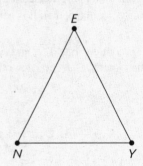

    A. $\overline{CA} = \overline{AG} = \overline{GC}$, and $\overline{NE} = \overline{EY} = \overline{YN}$.

    B. $\dfrac{\overline{CA}}{\overline{NE}} = \dfrac{\overline{AG}}{\overline{EY}} = \dfrac{\overline{GC}}{\overline{YN}}$.

    C. The corresponding angles of the two triangles are equal.

    D. The two triangles are not similar.

GO ON TO THE NEXT PAGE

54. In the figure below, lines *s* and *m* intersect plane *A* in point *P*. Lines *n* and *o* lie in plane *A*. Based on this information, which one of the following statements is false?

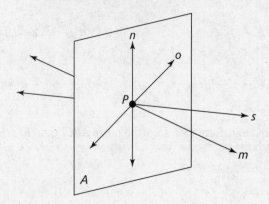

- **A.**   If *s* ⊥ *n*, then it follows that *s* ⊥ *A*.
- **B.**   If *s* ⊥ *A*, then it follows that *s* ⊥ *o*.
- **C.**   Lines *n* and *o* can both be perpendicular *s*.
- **D.**   If *m* is not perpendicular *A*, then *m* can be perpendicular *o*.

55. Indicate which one of the following statements is false.

- **A.**   If two planes intersect, then their intersection is a line.
- **B.**   If a line intersects a plane that does not contain it, then the line and plane intersect in exactly one point.
- **C.**   If three planes intersect, then their intersection is a single point.
- **D.**   If a line does not intersect a plane, then it is parallel to the plane.

56. In the figure below, plane *P* contains line $\overline{XN}$, and line $\overline{XN}$ is perpendicular to plane *R*. Plane *R* contains line $\overline{XT}$. What relationship do planes *R* and *P* have to each other?

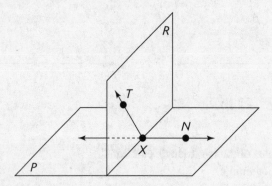

- **A.**   They are complementary planes.
- **B.**   They are oblique planes.
- **C.**   They are parallel planes.
- **D.**   They are perpendicular planes.

57. A box contains four yellow square tiles, six red square tiles, three blue square tiles, and eight orange square tiles. If one square tile is drawn randomly from the box, what is the probability that it will be either yellow or orange?

    A. $\frac{2}{3}$

    B. $\frac{4}{7}$

    C. $\frac{1}{3}$

    D. $\frac{4}{13}$

58. If two fair dice are rolled, find the probability that the sum of the number of dots on the top faces will be 7.

    A. $\frac{1}{12}$

    B. $\frac{1}{9}$

    C. $\frac{1}{6}$

    D. $\frac{1}{2}$

59. At the same time, a number cube is rolled (with numbers 1, 2, 3, 4, 5, and 6), and a coin (head or tail) is tossed. What is the probability of rolling a prime number, and tossing a head?

    A. $\frac{1}{3}$

    B. $\frac{1}{4}$

    C. $\frac{1}{2}$

    D. 1

60. A pizza place is offering a large three-topping pizza for \$15.95 each. They have 10 toppings from which to select. How many different three-topping pizzas are available?

    A. 120

    B. 720

    C. 240

    D. 180

61. A survey of 1,188 students at a high school was taken to find how they get to school each day. The results are shown in the following table.

How Students Get to School Each Day by Grade Level					
	Take a Bus	**Walk**	**Adult Drivers**	**Other**	**Total**
10th Grade	139	123	76	85	423
11th Grade	47	140	113	89	389
12th Grade	158	143	41	34	376
Total	344	406	230	208	1188

GO ON TO THE NEXT PAGE

Which of the following statements can be verified using the information in the previous table?

    A. At this high school, fewer 11th graders use different forms of transportation than 12th graders, because fewer students attend 11th grade.

    B. At this high school, the number of 11th graders who take the bus is greater than the number of 10th graders who walk to school.

    C. At this high school, more students in all grade levels take the bus to get to school than any of the other types of transportation.

    D. At this high school, the number of 12th graders who take the bus is greater than the number of 11th graders who walk to school.

62. Mike made the following table based on the number of hours he worked per day last month. Find the median number of hours he worked last month.

Number of Hours	Tally	Frequency
7	⁄⁄⁄⁄ ⁄⁄⁄⁄ //	12
8	///	3
9	//	2
10	⁄⁄⁄⁄ //	7

    A. 7 hours
    B. 8 hours
    C. 7.5 hours
    D. 2.5 hours

63. Find the mean for the data set given in the following table. Round your answer to the closest hundredth.

Number of Hours	Frequency
1	23
2	13
3	2
4	7

    A. 20.75 hours
    B. 2.5 hours
    C. 11.25 hours
    D. 1.84 hours

64. Robert had seven test scores, rejected the lowest and highest of these scores, and used the remaining five to do some statistical analyses. Which of the following statistics will remain unaffected by rejecting the lowest and highest test scores?

    A. range
    B. standard deviation
    C. mean
    D. median

Constructed-Response Question: Use extra lined paper to answer this question.

65. Complete the exercise that follows.

In the figure below, construct a line through E that is perpendicular to line a. Label this line as s. After that, construct a line through point E that is perpendicular to line s. Label this new line as t.

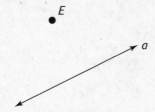

What relation does line t have to line a? Explain your answer.

GO ON TO THE NEXT PAGE

Constructed-Response Question: Use extra lined paper to answer this question.

---

66. Complete the exercise that follows.

Find the volume of a square pyramid with a base area of 36 square units and four faces that are equivalent triangles. Show your work.

Constructed-Response Question: Use extra lined paper to answer this question.

67. **Complete the exercise that follows.**

In the figure below, you are given two straight lines: line *KL* and line *MP*. These two lines intersect at point *Q*. ∠*LQM* is 20° greater than 5 times this same number and ∠*KQP* is 60° greater than 3 times this same number.

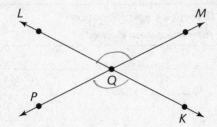

Use the information above to answer the following questions. Show your work and justify your answers.

A. What is the unknown fixed quantity?
B. What is the measure of ∠*LQM*?
C. What is the measure of ∠*MQK*?

GO ON TO THE NEXT PAGE

Constructed-Response Question: Use extra lined paper to answer this question.

68. Complete the exercise that follows.

The following table presents the speed of a newspaper printer and its corresponding percent of defective copies produced by this machine.

Speed of the Newspaper Printer (rpm)	% Defective Copies Produced by the Newspaper Printer
50	1.5
75	1.9
60	2.0
65	1.5
90	3.0
70	2.5
55	1.0
45	1.2
80	1.7
70	2.0

Using the information provided in the previous table, compute the regression equation where X is equal to the speed of newspaper printer measured in revolutions per minute (rpm), and Y is equal to the percentage of defective copies produced by the newspaper printer at the specified rates. Explain your results based on the regression formula. Show your work in the space provided.

Practice CSET: Mathematics Subtest III

Continue the test. Remember to read and follow the instructions carefully.

The set of multiple-choice questions and constructed-response questions presented in this Practice CSET: Mathematics Test I are similar to the questions you will see on the **Subtest III: Calculus; History of Mathematics**. This subtest includes the same amount of items you will find on the actual CSET: Mathematics test. We have included an answer key and explanation for each item's possible responses; however, we recommend and encourage you to respond to the items without looking at these sections of this book. You should record your responses on a separate sheet of paper and review your answers with the provided responses afterward.

Note: The use of calculators is not allowed for the CSET: Mathematics Subtest III.

69. What are the solutions to $\tan\left(x - \frac{\pi}{3}\right) = \frac{1}{\sqrt{3}}$ where $0 \le x \le 2\pi$?

   A. $\frac{\pi}{3}, \frac{4\pi}{3}$

   B. $\frac{2\pi}{3}, \frac{5\pi}{3}$

   C. $\frac{\pi}{2}, \frac{3\pi}{2}$

   D. $\frac{\pi}{6}, \frac{7\pi}{6}$

70. Let $f(x) = \begin{cases} x & \text{if } x < 0 \\ x^2 & \text{if } 0 \le x > 2. \\ x+2 & \text{if } x \ge 2 \end{cases}$

Find $\lim_{x \to 2^+} f(x)$.

   A. 0
   B. 4
   C. does not exist
   D. 5

71. The Intermediate Value Theorem can be used to show there is a root for the equation $x^3 + x - 3 = 0$ for which of the following intervals?

   A. $(-1, 0)$
   B. $(1, 2)$
   C. $(2, 3)$
   D. $(0, 1)$

72. Find all values of x in the interval $[0, 2\pi]$ that satisfy the equation $2\sin^2 x - \sqrt{3}\sin x = 0$.

   A. $\left\{0, \frac{\pi}{3}\right\}$

   B. $\left\{\frac{\pi}{6}, \frac{\pi}{2}, \frac{5\pi}{6}, \frac{3\pi}{2}\right\}$

   C. $\left\{0, \frac{\pi}{3}, \frac{2\pi}{3}, \pi, 2\pi\right\}$

   D. $\left\{0, \frac{\pi}{3}, \pi, \frac{5\pi}{3}, 2\pi\right\}$

GO ON TO THE NEXT PAGE

73. Find an equation of a line tangent to the curve $f(x) = 3x^4 - 2x^2 + 4x - 7$ at the point $(1, -2)$.

    A. $y = 12x$

    B. $y = x + 32$

    C. $y = 12x - 14$

    D. $y = 14x - 12$

74. Which of the following can be derived directly from $\sin^2 x + \cos^2 x = 1$?

    A. $\sin 2x = 2\sin x \cos x$

    B. $1 + \tan^2 x = \sec^2 x$

    C. $\cos^2 x = \dfrac{1 + \cos 2x}{2}$

    D. $\cos^2 x = \cos^2 x - \sin^2 x$

75. If the functions $f(x)$ and $g(x)$ are continuous at a and c if $g(a)$ is not equal to 0, which of the following may not be continuous at a?

    A. $f(x)g(x)$

    B. $f(x) + g(x)$

    C. $\dfrac{f(x)}{g(x)}$

    D. $cf(x)$

76. Which of the following equations matches the graph given below?

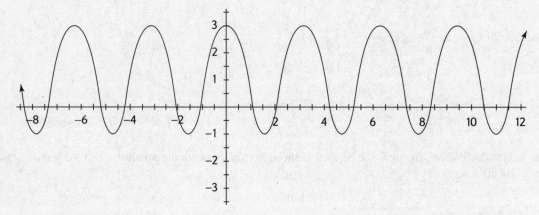

    A. $f(x) = 4\cos(2x) + 1$

    B. $f(x) = 2\cos(2x) + 1$

    C. $f(x) = 4\cos\left(\dfrac{x}{2}\right) + 1$

    D. $f(x) = 2\cos\left(\dfrac{x}{2}\right) + 1$

77. Find $\displaystyle\lim_{x \to 0} \dfrac{\tan x}{x + \sin x}$.

    A. 0

    B. ∞

    C. $\dfrac{1}{2}$

    D. $-\dfrac{1}{2}$

78. The rate of change of atmospheric pressure P with respect to altitude h is proportional to P, provided that the temperature is constant. At 15°C, the pressure is 101.3 kPa at sea level and 87.14 kPa at $h = 1000$ m. Find the pressure at an altitude of 3000 m.

   A.   4.17 kPa
   B.   64.43 kPa
   C.   20.33 kPa
   D.   4.92 kPa

79. A ladder 13 feet long rests against the side of a house. The bottom of the ladder slides away from the house at a rate of 0.5 ft/s. How fast is the top of the ladder sliding down the wall when the bottom of the ladder is 5 feet from the house?

   A. $\frac{5}{24}$ ft/s

   B. $\frac{5}{12}$ ft/s

   C. $-\frac{5}{24}$ ft/s

   D. $-\frac{5}{12}$ ft/s

80. Find $\left(\frac{\sqrt{3}}{2} + \frac{\sqrt{3}}{2}i\right)^3$.

   A. $-\frac{3\sqrt{3}}{2} + \frac{3\sqrt{3}}{2}i$

   B. $\frac{3\sqrt{3}}{4} - \frac{3\sqrt{3}}{4}i$

   C. $\frac{3\sqrt{3}}{2} - \frac{3\sqrt{3}}{2}i$

   D. $-\frac{3\sqrt{3}}{4} + \frac{3\sqrt{3}}{4}i$

81. Find the derivative of the function $g(x) = \int_{-2}^{x} \sqrt{1 + 3t^2}\, dt$.

   A. $g'(x) = \sqrt{13}$
   B. $g'(x) = \sqrt{1 + 3x^2} - \sqrt{13}$
   C. $g'(x) = \sqrt{1 + 3x^2}$
   D. $g'(x) = \sqrt{13} - \sqrt{1 + 3x^2}$

82. Express the number $2.\overline{4}$ as a rational number.

   A. $\frac{4}{9}$

   B. $2\frac{4}{9}$

   C. $2\frac{2}{5}$

   D. $2\frac{11}{25}$

GO ON TO THE NEXT PAGE

83. Find all values of c that satisfy the Mean Value Theorem for $f(x) = x^3 - 2x^2$ on the interval $[0, 3]$.

   A. $\dfrac{2+\sqrt{13}}{3}, \dfrac{2-\sqrt{13}}{3}$

   B. $\dfrac{2+\sqrt{13}}{3}$

   C. $\dfrac{2-\sqrt{13}}{3}$

   D. No solution

84. Which of the following is the derivative of $f(x) = \dfrac{3x-2}{2x+1}$?

   A. $\displaystyle\lim_{x \to a} \dfrac{\dfrac{3x-2}{2x+1} - \dfrac{3a-2}{2a-1}}{x-a}$

   B. $\displaystyle\lim_{x \to a} \dfrac{\dfrac{3a-2}{2a-1} - \dfrac{3x-2}{2x+1}}{x-a}$

   C. $\displaystyle\lim_{a \to 0} \dfrac{\dfrac{3x-2}{2x+1} - \dfrac{3a-2}{2a-1}}{x-a}$

   D. $\displaystyle\lim_{a \to 0} \dfrac{\dfrac{3a-2}{2a-1} - \dfrac{3x-2}{2x+1}}{x-a}$

85. Given the function $f(x) = x^3 - x^2 - 8x = 12$, find all maximum and minimum points.

   A. maximum at $(2, 0)$ and minimum at $\left(-\dfrac{4}{3}, \dfrac{628}{27}\right)$

   B. minimum at $(2, 0)$ and maximum at $\left(-\dfrac{4}{3}, \dfrac{628}{27}\right)$

   C. minimum at $(2, 0)$ and maximum at $\left(-\dfrac{4}{3}, 0\right)$

   D. maximum at $(2, 0)$ and minimum at $\left(-\dfrac{4}{3}, 0\right)$

86. Find the volume of the solid obtained by rotating the region bound by the curves $y = x^3 + 1$, $x = 1$, and $y = 0$ about the x-axis.

   A. $\dfrac{23\pi}{7}$

   B. $\dfrac{16\pi}{7}$

   C. 2π

   D. $\dfrac{19\pi}{7}$

87. Which of the following is equivalent to $(\sin x + \cos x)^2$?

   A. $\sin^2 x + \cos^2 x$

   B. $\cos 2x$

   C. $1 + \sin 2x$

   D. $1 - \sin 2x$

88. For what values of r is the series $\sum_{n=1}^{\infty} 3\left(\dfrac{r}{2}\right)^{n-1}$ convergent?

    A. $r < 1$

    B. $r < 2$

    C. $-1 < r < 1$

    D. $-2 < r < 2$

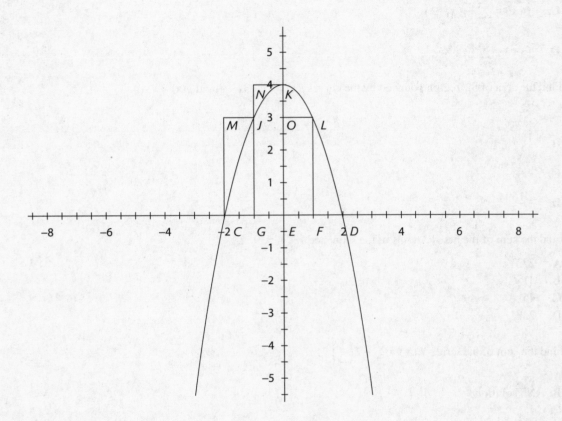

89. Given the function $f(x) = -x^2 + 4$ on the interval $[-2, 2]$. The partitions are shown in the graph provided. Find the area under the curve with a Riemann Sum.

    A. 10

    B. 4

    C. 3

    D. 14

90. Find $\lim\limits_{x \to -2} \dfrac{x^2 + 5x + 6}{x^2 - x + 6}$.

    A. ∞

    B. $\dfrac{1}{5}$

    C. 0

    D. $-\dfrac{1}{5}$

GO ON TO THE NEXT PAGE

91. Find the Taylor series for $f(x) = e^x$ at $a = 2$.

    A. $f(x) = \sum_{n=0}^{\infty} \dfrac{x^n}{n!}$

    B. $f(x) = \sum_{n=0}^{\infty} \dfrac{(x-2)^n}{n!}$

    C. $f(x) = \sum_{n=0}^{\infty} \dfrac{e^2}{n!}(x-2)^n$

    D. $f(x) = \sum_{n=0}^{\infty} \dfrac{e^2}{n!} x^n$

92. Find the area of the region bounded by the curves $f(x) = x^2 - 3x - 4$ and $g(x) = x - 4$.

    A. $\dfrac{32}{3}$

    B. $\dfrac{160}{3}$

    C. $-\dfrac{32}{3}$

    D. $-\dfrac{160}{3}$

93. Find the sum of the first 12 terms of the sequence –3, 1, 5, 9, ...

    A. 273
    B. 41
    C. 45
    D. 228

94. Find the sum of the series $f(x) = \sum_{n=1}^{\infty} -2\left(\dfrac{1}{2}\right)^{n-1}$.

    A. –4
    B. No solution
    C. 4
    D. $-\dfrac{4}{3}$

95. Although there is debate as to who invented calculus, which of the following mathematicians was partially credited with the development of calculus as we know it?

    A. Omar Khayyam
    B. Pythagoras
    C. Gottfried Wilhelm Liebniz
    D. Blaise Pascal

96. Which of the following mathematicians is credited with approximating π as $\dfrac{22}{7}$ by considering the perimeters of 96-sided polygons inscribed in and circumscribed about circles?

    A. Leonhard Euler
    B. Archimedes
    C. Euclid
    D. Rene Descartes

97. The Babylonian system of mathematics used what base system?

    A. Binary

    B. Hexadecimal

    C. Base Ten

    D. Sexagesimal

98. Hindu mathematicians first developed what procedure for ensuring the accuracy of hand calculations of sums, differences, products, and quotients?

    A. Casting out Nines

    B. Pythagorean Theorem

    C. Napier's Bones

    D. Abacus

GO ON TO THE NEXT PAGE

Constructed-Response Question: Use extra lined paper to answer this question.

---

99. Complete the exercise that follows.

Use the definition of continuity and the properties of limits to show that the function $f(x) = x^3 - 2x^2 + 4x - 2$ is continuous at $a = 2$.

Constructed-Response Question: Use extra lined paper to answer this question.

100. Complete the exercise that follows.

Angle addition formulas are given in the box below.

$$\sin(x+y) = \sin x \cos y + \cos x \sin y$$
$$\cos(x+y) = \cos x \cos y - \sin x \sin y$$
$$\tan(x+y) = \frac{\tan x + \tan y}{1 - \tan x \tan y}$$

Use the angle addition formulas and other trigonometric identities to derive the half-angle formulas for $\sin x$ and $\cos x$ as given below.

$$\sin x = \pm \sqrt{\frac{1 - \cos 2x}{2}}$$
$$\cos x = \pm \sqrt{\frac{1 + \cos 2x}{2}}$$

GO ON TO THE NEXT PAGE

Constructed-Response Question: Use extra lined paper to answer this question.

101. Complete the exercise that follows.

Use the definition of a derivative to find the derivative of $f(x) = 5x^2 - 2x + 3$.

102. Complete the exercise that follows.

Use the figure below to prove the Pythagorean Theorem.

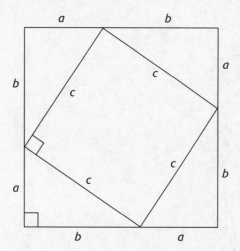

Answer Key for Practice CSET: Mathematics Test I

1. C
2. D
3. A
4. B
5. D
6. C
7. C
8. D
9. A
10. D
11. B
12. C
13. A
14. B
15. D
16. C
17. A
18. A
19. B
20. A
21. D
22. B
23. D
24. B
25. C
26. D
27. C
28. D
29. A
30. B

31. Written or Constructed Response Question. Yes, the given quadratic polynomial is reducible. See solution section for details.

32. Written or Constructed Response Question. You get the same equations. See solution section for details.

33. Written or Constructed Response Question. You can get different possibilities. Answer will vary. See solution section for details.

34. Written or Constructed Response Question. See solution section for details.

35. A

36. B

37. D

38. C

39. C

40. B

41. A

42. D

43. C

44. A

45. A

46. C

47. D

48. B

49. C

50. A

51. B

52. B

53. D

54. A

55. C

56. D

57. B

58. C

59. B

60. A

61. D

62. C

63. D

64. D

65. Written or Constructed Response Question. See solution section for details.

66. Written or Constructed Response Question. $V = 36\sqrt{2}$ cubic units. See solution section for details.

67. Written or Constructed Response Question. The unknown value is 20. See solution section for details.

68. Written or Constructed Response Question. See solution section for details.

69. C

70. D

71. B

72. C

73. C

74. B

75. C

76. B

77. C

78. B

79. C

80. D

81. C

82. B

83. B

84. A

85. A

86. B

87. C

88. D

89. A

90. D

91. C

92. A

93. D

94. A

95. C

96. B

97. D

98. A

99. Written or Constructed Response Question. See solution section for details.

100. Written or Constructed Response Question. See solution section for details.

101. Written or Constructed Response Question. See solution section for details.

102. Written or Constructed Response Question. See solution section for details.

Solutions for Practice CSET: Mathematics Test I

Use these answers and explanations to help you understand possible solutions and improve your test-taking ability. Remember that you are recommended and encouraged to complete the test before looking at the possible solutions and explanations. Record your answers and responses on a separate piece of paper and then compare them with the response provided here. You should not take more that one practice exam per day. You need some wait time before taking and reviewing the other practice exams (at least one day). You might have used a different path for your solution. This is okay; if you get to the same answer and the procedures you used are mathematically accurate, you don't need to have the same solution process. It is good to also learn other ways to solve the problem. Also, you might want to check the domain given in parentheses for each item. This will give an idea of your strengths and weaknesses for different topics and where you might need extra practice or review.

Some of the multiple-choice questions have been identified as **ENHANCED.** This term is used to indicate that these items are complex multiple-choice questions, which require 2–3 minutes each to complete. Enhanced multiple-choice questions will not be identified on the actual CSET: Mathematics Test. No calculators are allowed for the CSET: Mathematics Subtests I and II. Graphing calculators are allowed for CSET: Mathematics Subtest II.

Practice CSET: Mathematics Subset I

This Subtest involves Algebra (items 1–24, and 31–33) and Number Theory (items 25–30, and 34).

Algebra

1. The best choice for this item is **C. (SMR 1.1 Algebraic Structures)**

We know that the values of the power i repeat indefinitely in groups of four (i^a, i^b, i^c, i^d), and in some order (i, -1, $-i$, and 1). This implies that the sum is equal to the following:

$i + -1 + -i + 1 = i + -1 + -i + 1$

$$= (i + -i) + (-1 + 1)$$

$$= 0 + 0 = 0$$

2. The best choice for this item is **D. (SMR 1.2 Polynomial Equations and Inequalities)** You need to solve the equation $\sqrt{4n} + 9 = 5$:

$\sqrt{4n} + 9 - -9 = 5 + -9$ Subtract -9 from both sides of the equation.

$\sqrt{4n} + 9 - -9 = 5 + -9$ $9 - -9 = 0$, and $5 + -9 = -4$

$\sqrt{4n} = -4$ Simplify.

We know that by definition a square root cannot be negative; this equation has no solution.

3. The best choice for this item is **A. (SMR 1.1 Algebraic Structures) (ENHANCED)**

The vector $z = 2 - 4i$ has a slope of $\frac{-4}{2} = -2$. If you multiply z by i, you would obtain the vector $w = 2i - 4i^2 = 4 + 2i$. The slope of this vector is $\frac{2}{4} = \frac{1}{2}$. These slopes are negative reciprocals, so the vectors are perpendicular.

If one was to plot the vector beginning at the origin, the original vector z is in quadrant four. The new vector w is in quadrant one. This is a counterclockwise rotation of 90 degrees. The magnitude of the vector did not change, only the direction.

4. The best choice for this item is **B. (SMR 1.3 Functions) (ENHANCED)**

You should look carefully at the graph and notice that it passes through $(2, 0)$. So, $x = 2$ and $y = 0$ must satisfy the equation. In this case, you will need to test each of the four equations to see which one could work:

A. $y = 2x^2 + 4$; if $x = 2$ and $y = 0$, then by substitution $0 = 2(2^2) + 4$, and solve. So, if $0 \neq 8$, then this equation does not work.

B. $y = x^2 - 4x + 4$; if $x = 2$ and $y = 0$, then by substitution $0 = 2^2 - 4(2) + 4$, and solve. So, $0 = 0$, then this equation could be a possible match. You could try other points in the graph to make sure you are correct. For example, you could try or might have selected other ordered pairs like $(0, 4)$ or $(1, 1)$. These will also work, except that $(0, 4)$ also work for the equation in alternative **C.** This equation is the right choice because it is the only one that has the right ordered pairs and represents a parabola.

Also, by looking at the graph, you may notice that this graph is a parabola shifted to the right 2 units. This makes the equation $y = (x - 2)^2 = x^2 - 4x + 4$.

C. $y = x^2 + 4x + 4$; if $x = 2$ and $y = 0$, then by substitution $0 = (2^2) + 4(2) + 4$, and solve. So, $0 \neq 16$, then this equation does not work.

D. $y = x^2$; if $x = 2$ and $y = 0$, then by substitution $0 = 2^2$, and solve. So, $0 \neq 4$; this equation does not work.

5. The best choice for this item is **D.** (**SMR 1.3 Functions**)

Substitute 9 for x in the equation and solve:

$$
\begin{aligned}
-3\sqrt{x} - 3\left(x^3\right) &= -3\sqrt{9} - 3\left(9^3\right) \\
&= -3(3) - 3(729) \\
&= -9 - 2187 \\
&= -2196
\end{aligned}
$$

6. The best choice for this item is **C.** (**SMR 1.4 Linear Algebra**) (**ENHANCED**)

The vector's ordered pair is determined by subtracting the coordinates of the endpoint from the corresponding coordinates of the tip. In this case, the tip of $\overrightarrow{MN}$ is the point corresponding to the second letter of the notation, which is N. The endpoint is the point corresponding to the first letter of the notation, which is M. Also, notice that the vectors involved in this problem do not lie at the origin.

First, you need to find the order pair that represents $\overrightarrow{MN}$:

$$\overrightarrow{MN} = <3 - 2, -4 - 1> = <1, -5>$$

Then find the ordered pair that represents each of the vectors:

$$\overrightarrow{QR} = (-3 - -4, 10 - 5) = (1, 5)$$
$$\overrightarrow{LP} = (2 - 1, 3 - -1) = (1, 4)$$
$$\overrightarrow{ST} = (4 - 3, -7 - -2) = (1, -5)$$

You should see that only $\overrightarrow{ST}$ is equal to $\overrightarrow{MN}$.

7. The best choice for this item is **C.** (**SMR 1.1 Algebraic Structures**)

A. Since 32 is a multiple of 4, $i^{32} = 1$.
B. When 25 is divided by 4, the remainder is 1; so $i^{25} = i$.
C. When 50 is divided by 4, the remainder is 2; so $i^{50} = -1$.
D. When 75 is divided by 4, the remainder is 3; so $i^{75} = -i$. In this case, only, i^{50} is a negative number.

8. The best choice for this item is **D.** (**SMR 1.1 Algebra**)

You can take a look at each one of the alternatives and evaluate the validity of each one:

I. x is equal to y is not necessarily true because you could have $i^4 = i^8$, which then means that $x = 4$ and $y = 8$, and $x \neq y$.

II. x plus y is equal to an even number must be true because if x is odd and y is even, then i^x equals i or -1, and i^y is equal to 1 or -1, which implies that $i^x \neq i^y$. The same can be said if x is even and y is odd. This implies that x and y both must be even or odd. In either case, $x + y$ is equal to an even number, and alternative II is true.

III. $x - y$ is a multiple of 4 is also true because $i^y = i^x \Rightarrow i^y/i^x = 1 \Rightarrow i^{y-x} = 1 \Rightarrow y - x$ is a multiple of 4. This makes alternative III also true.

In this case, only alternatives II and III are true.

9. The best choice for this item is **A**. (SMR 1.3 **Functions**)

Substitute –8 for x in the equation and solve:

$$-5\left(x^3\right) - 5\sqrt[3]{x} = -5\left(-8^3\right) - 5\sqrt[3]{-8}$$
$$= -5\left(-512\right) - 5\left(\sqrt[3]{-2^3}\right)$$
$$= 2560 - 5\left(-2\right)$$
$$= 2560 - -10$$
$$= 2570$$

10. This best choice for this item is **D**. (SMR 1.3 **Functions**)

You need to find the solution to this question without using a graphing calculator. By definition, the absolute values of an equation will only provide positive numbers, never negative numbers. So, look at the alternatives you have, and you should notice that alternatives **A** and **B** can be eliminated because they include negative numbers. You only have alternatives **C** and **D** left. Use any number for x in the equation. For example, if $x = 2$, then $y = \left|2^2 - 4\left(2\right) + 2\right| = \left|4 - 8 + 2\right| = \left|-2\right| = 2$. So, (2, 2) must be on the graph. This point is on alternative **D** but not on **C**.

11. The best choice for this item is **B**. (SMR 1.1 **Algebraic Structures**)

The initial statement ("If $0 < x < 1$, then $\sqrt{x}$ is irrational.") is false because we can find examples in which the statement is not true. For example, $\sqrt{\dfrac{16}{25}} = \dfrac{4}{5}$ is between 0 and 1, but it is a rational number, not an irrational number. All the given alternatives are false, but the only one that is equivalent to the initial statement is alternative **B** (If $\sqrt{x}$ is rational, then $0 < x < 1$.), which is the contrapositive of the initial statement:

p:	$0 < x < 1$	q:	$\sqrt{x}$ is irrational.
$\sim p$:	$x \leq 0$, or $x \geq 1$	$\sim q$:	$\sqrt{x}$ is irrational.

The alternative that matches this contrapositive is **B**.

12. The best answer for this item is **C**. (SMR 1.2 **Polynomials Equations and Inequalities**) (ENHANCED)

Substituting different points for the different equations [like (1, 1), (0, 0) and (2, 0)], we can see that only $y = -x^2 + 2x$ works, which is the equation of the solid line. The solid line indicates that points on the boundary are included as solutions to the inequality. Substituting a point in the shaded region [(1, 0) for example] shows that the inequality is $y + -x^2 - 2x \leq 0$ (because by substitution: $0 + -1^2 - 2(1) \leq 0; -1 \leq 0$).

A closer look at the alternatives that we have might help in eliminating some of them:

Alternative **A**, $y \leq -x^2 - 2x$, does not work because it does not match the given shading. The shading for this graph would go up instead of down.

Alternative **B**, $y > -x^2 + 2x$, does not include numbers on the boundary, and its graph would need to be represented using a dotted line. The given graph uses a solid line. Also, the shaded area in the given graph includes values under the curve (less than), not values over the curve (greater than) as a solution of the inequality.

Alternative **D**, $y \leq -x^2 + 2x + 2$, represents a whole different situation and is not part of the solution.

13. The best answer for this item is **A**. (SMR 1.2 **Polynomial Equations and Inequalities**) (ENHANCED)

The equation of the solid line is $y = 2x + 5$, or in standard form $y - 2x = 5$. Substituting a point in the shaded region [(0, 4) for example] shows that the inequality is $y - 2x \leq 5$ (because by substitution: $4 - 2(4) \leq 5; -4 \leq 5$). The dotted line is given by $y + x = 5$. Substituting for (0, 4) gives the inequality $y + x \leq 5$ (because by substitution: $4 + 2 \leq 5; 6 \leq 5$). The dotted line indicates that points on the boundary are not solutions to the inequality.

14. The best choice for this item is **B.** (**SMR 1.2 Polynomials Equations and Inequalities**) (ENHANCED)

In this question, you can use the Quadratic Formula and find r_1 and r_2 for this equation. We have that $a = 1$, $b = -2$, and $c = -1$. By substituting in the Quadratic Formula, we have the following:

$$x = \frac{2 \pm \sqrt{4 - (-4)}}{2} \qquad \text{Substitute the values.}$$

$$= \frac{2 \pm \sqrt{8}}{2} \qquad \text{Solve.}$$

$$= \frac{2 \pm 2\sqrt{2}}{2} \qquad \sqrt{8} \text{ is } \sqrt{2^3} \text{ or } 2\sqrt{2}.$$

$$= \frac{2\left(1 \pm \sqrt{2}\right)}{2} \qquad \text{Factor out the 2 and simplify by dividing 2 by 2 = 1.}$$

$$= 1 \pm \sqrt{2} \qquad \text{Two possible solutions: } r_1 = 1 + \sqrt{2} \text{ and } r_2 = 1 - \sqrt{2}.$$

Then, we need to subtract r_2 from r_1:

$$r_1 - r_2 = \left(1 + \sqrt{2}\right) - \left(1 - \sqrt{2}\right)$$

$$= 1 + \sqrt{2} + -1 + \sqrt{2}$$

$$= 2\sqrt{2}$$

15. The best choice for this item is **D.** (**SMR 1.2 Polynomials Equations and Inequalities**)

$f(x - a)$ represents a translation of $f(x) = 2x^3 + 10$ by a units in the positive direction on the x-axis. In this case, a is equal to 3. So, $f(x - 3) = g(x) = 2(x - 3)^3 + 10$, which represents a translation by 3 units in the positive direction on the x-axis.

$$f(x - 3) = g(x)$$

$$= 2(x - 3)^3 + 10 \qquad \text{Substitution.}$$

$$= 2(x^3 - 9x^2 + 27x - 27) + 10 \qquad \text{Cubing the binomial.}$$

$$= 2x^3 - 18x^2 + 54x - 54 + 10 \qquad \text{Multiply by 2.}$$

$$= 2x^3 - 18x^2 + 54x - 44 \qquad \text{Simplify.}$$

16. The best choice for this item is **C.** (**SMR 1.3 Functions**) (ENHANCED)

In this case, we have that $f(x) = x + \frac{1}{x}$. So, $f(f(x))$ is equal to $f(x) + \frac{1}{f(x)}$. We need solve this equation.

$$f\left(f(x)\right) = f(x) + \frac{1}{f(x)} \qquad \text{Substitute } f(x) \text{ for } x.$$

$$= \left(x + \frac{1}{x}\right) + \frac{1}{x + \frac{1}{x}} \qquad \text{Substitute } x + \frac{1}{x} \text{ for } f(x).$$

$$= \frac{x^2 + 1}{x} + \frac{1}{\frac{x^2 + 1}{x}} \qquad \text{Find common denominator: } x + \frac{1}{x} = \frac{x^2 + 1}{x}$$

$$= \frac{x^2 + 1}{x} + \frac{x}{x^2 + 1} \qquad \text{Simplify: } \frac{1}{\frac{x^2 + 1}{x}} = 1 \div \frac{x^2 + 1}{x} = 1 \cdot \frac{x}{x^2 + 1} = \frac{x}{x^2 + 1}.$$

17. The best choice for this item is **A.** (**SMR 1.3 Functions**)

In this function, the denominator must not be equal to zero because division by zero is undefined. The denominator is equal to zero when $x = -2$. This is $(x + 2)^2 = (-2 + 2)^2 = (0)^2 = 0$. So, $x \neq 0$ is the restriction needed for the domain of this function.

18. The best choice for this item is **A**. (**SMR 1.1 Algebraic Structures**)

Of the given response choices, only complex and rational numbers are fields. Integers and natural numbers are not fields. Rational numbers are an ordered field, and complex numbers are a non-ordered field. So, response choice **A** is the correct response.

19. The best choice for this item is **B**. (**SMR 1.4 Linear Algebra**)

In order for the vectors to be perpendicular, the dot product must be zero. Examining each pair gives the following:

A. dot product = $(-2)(1) + (1)(-2) = -2 + -2 = -4$

B. dot product = $(-2)(-1) + (1)(-2) = 2 + -2 = 0$

C. dot product = $(2)(-1) + (-1)(2) = -2 + -2 = -4$

D. dot product = $(-2)(-1) + (-1)(-2) = 2 + 2 = 4$

The only one the dot product of which is zero is Choice **B**.

20. The best choice for this item is **A**. (**SMR 1.4 Linear Algebra**)

The length of a vector $\langle x, y, z \rangle$ is $\sqrt{x^2 + y^2 + z^2}$. For this vector, the length is $\sqrt{(-1)^2 + (3)^2 + (2)^2} = \sqrt{1 + 9 + 4} = \sqrt{14}$.

21. The best choice for this item is **D**. (**SMR 1.4 Linear Algebra**)

Adding the right hand side together gives you $\begin{bmatrix} -3 + 12 & 6x - 3y \\ y + 6x & 5 + 6 \end{bmatrix}$. Therefore, we can set up a system of equations $\begin{cases} 6x - 3y = 5 \\ y + 6x = 17 \end{cases}$. We can multiply the second equation by -1 and add it to the first to eliminate the

x variable. Then we have:

$\begin{cases} 6x - 3y = 5 \\ -6x - y = -17 \end{cases} \Rightarrow -4y = -12$. Therefore, $y = 3$. Substituting back into the original equations gives

$3 + 6x = 17$

$6x = 14$

$x = \dfrac{14}{6} = \dfrac{7}{3}$

22. The best choice for this item is **B**. (**SMR 1.2 Polynomials Equations and Inequalities**) (ENHANCED)

Since the given quadratic equation $(x^2 + 5x + c = 0)$ has only one solution, its discriminant is equal to zero. Using substitution of values ($b = 5$, and $a = 1$), we have the following:

$0 = b^2 - 4ac$	
$0 = 5^2 - 4(1)c$	Substitution of the values for b and a.
$0 = 25 - 4c$	Solve.
$0 + 4c = 25 - 4c + 4c$	Add $4c$ on both sides of the equation.
$4c = 25$	Solve.
$4c \div 4 = 25 \div 4$	Divide by 4 on both sides of the equation.
$c = 6.25$	Solve.

23. The best choice for this item is **D**. (SMR 1.4 Linear Algebra) (ENHANCED)

Given that A is a 2-by-3 matrix, and B is a 3-by-4 matrix, the resulting product AB is a 2-by-4 matrix. This means that responses **B** and **C** are not possible answers. We are left with responses **A** or **D**. AB is equal to the product of A and B:

$$AB = \begin{bmatrix} 1 & 2 & 4 \\ 2 & 6 & 0 \end{bmatrix} \begin{bmatrix} 4 & 1 & 4 & 3 \\ 0 & -1 & 3 & 1 \\ 2 & 7 & 5 & 2 \end{bmatrix}$$

$$= \begin{bmatrix} 1\cdot4+2\cdot0+4\cdot2 & 1\cdot1+2(-1)+4\cdot7 & 1\cdot4+2\cdot3+4\cdot5 & 1\cdot3+2\cdot1+4\cdot2 \\ 2\cdot4+6\cdot0+0\cdot2 & 2\cdot1+6\cdot(-1)+0\cdot7 & 2\cdot4+6\cdot3+0\cdot5 & 2\cdot3+6\cdot1+0\cdot2 \end{bmatrix}$$

$$= \begin{bmatrix} 4+0+8 & 1+-2+28 & 4+6+20 & 3+2+8 \\ 8+0+0 & 2-6+0 & 8+18+0 & 6+6+0 \end{bmatrix}$$

$$= \begin{bmatrix} 12 & 27 & 30 & 13 \\ 8 & -4 & 26 & 12 \end{bmatrix}$$

24. The best choice for this item is **B**. (SMR 1.4 Linear Algebra)

The only statement that is true is **B**. Statement **A** should be $a \times b = -b \times a$. Statement **C** should be $a \cdot (b \times c) = (a \times b) \cdot c$. Statement **D** should be $a \times (b \times c) = (a \cdot c)b - (a \cdot b)c$.

Number Theory

25. The best choice for this item is **C**. (SMR 3.1 Natural Numbers)

One way to solve this problem is by using prime factorization. Find the prime factorization of each pair of numbers and then use these prime factorizations to find the GCF. Look at the common prime factors within each pair (shown with boxes for each pair below).

A. $24 = \boxed{2} \cdot 2 \cdot 2 \cdot \boxed{3}$, and $6 = \boxed{2} \cdot \boxed{3}$ GCF $= 2 \cdot 3 = 6$ Yes

B. $42 = \boxed{2} \cdot \boxed{3} \cdot 7$, and $150 = \boxed{2} \cdot \boxed{3} \cdot 5 \cdot 5$ GCF $= 2 \cdot 3 = 6$ Yes

C. $54 = \boxed{2} \cdot \boxed{3} \cdot \boxed{3} \cdot 3$, and $18 = \boxed{2} \cdot \boxed{3} \cdot \boxed{3}$ GCF $= 2 \cdot 3 \cdot 3 = 18$ No

D. $18 = \boxed{2} \cdot \boxed{3} \cdot 3$, and $30 = \boxed{2} \cdot \boxed{3} \cdot 5$ GCF $= 2 \cdot 3 = 6$ Yes

26. The best choice for this item is **D**. (SMR 3.1 Natural Numbers)

Look at the common factors within this pair of expressions (shown with boxes below).

$20x^2y = \boxed{2} \cdot 2 \cdot \boxed{5} \cdot \boxed{x} \cdot x \cdot \boxed{y}$

$50xy^2 = \boxed{2} \cdot \boxed{5} \cdot 5 \cdot \boxed{x} \cdot \boxed{y} \cdot y$

GCF $= 2 \cdot 5 \cdot x \cdot y = 10xy$

27. The best choice for this item is **C**. (SMR 3.1 Natural Numbers) (ENHANCED)

One way to respond to this item is by evaluating each of the alternatives as being true or false:

A. An integer n is divisible by 6 if and only if it is divisible by 3: This alternative is false because it is not enough for a number to be divisible by 3 in order for it to be divisible by 6. The number needs to also be divisible by 2. A number may be divisible by 3 and still not be divisible by 6. For example, 21 is divisible by 3, but is not divisible by 6.

B. A number k divides the sum of three consecutive integers n, $n + 1$, and $n + 2$, if and only if it divides the middle integer $n + 1$: This alternative is false because it does not both work in both directions. For example, 39 divides the sum of three consecutive numbers ($25 + 26 + 27 = 78$), but 39 does not divide the middle integer of these three consecutive integers (25, 26, and 27).

C. If r and s are integers, then $r\,|\,s$ if and only if $r^2\,|\,s^2$. This is always true. If a number is divisible by another number, then the square of this number will be divisible by square of the other number; and if the square of a number that is divisible by the square of another number, the number will also be divisible by the other number. If $r\,|\,s$, then $s = xr$, where x is any integer; and $s^2 = (xr)^2$ or x^2r^2, which implies that $r^2\,|\,s^2$. Also, if $r^2\,|\,s^2$, then $s^2 = xr^2$, where x is any integer; this implies that $r\,|\,s$. For example, $5\,|\,25$ if $25\,|\,625$, and $25\,|\,625$ if $5\,|\,25$. Or $3\,|\,15$ if $9\,|\,225$, and $9\,|\,225$ if $3\,|\,15$.

D. For all integers a, b, and c, $a\,|\,(b+c)$ if and only if $a\,|\,b$ and $a\,|\,c$. This alternative is false because it not always true. For example, $5\,|\,(12+3)$, but $5 \nmid 12$ and $5 \nmid 3$.

28. The best choice for this item is **D. (SMR 3.1 Natural Numbers) (ENHANCED)**

We provide a brief introduction to the Euclidean Algorithm before we address the response to this item. The Euclidean Algorithm is a method used to find the greatest common factors of a pair of numbers. As an example, consider computing the GCF of 1071 and 1029, which is 21, with this algorithm:

1071	1029	**Step 1:**	We start by putting the larger number on the left, and the smaller on the right.
1029	42	**Step 2:**	The remainder of 1071 divided by 1029 is 42, which is put on the right, and the divisor 1029 is put on the left.
42	21	**Step 3:**	We repeat Step 2, dividing 1029 by 42, and get 21 as remainder.
21	0	**Step 4:**	We stop here since the remainder is 0. So, 21 is the GCF of these numbers.

Going back to the problem at hand, we have the following possible response. From the given conditions that $N_1 > N_2 > N_3 > N_4 > N_5 = 0$; $N_t = q_{t+1}N_{t+1} + N_{t+2}$, $t = 1, 2, 3$; and the quotients are $q_2 = 3$, $q_3 = 2$, and $q_4 = 2$, we have the following:

$$N_1 = q_{1+1}N_{1+1} + N_{1+2} = q_2N_2 + N_3 = 3N_2 + N_3$$

$$N_2 = q_{2+1}N_{2+1} + N_{2+2} = q_3N_3 + N_4 = 2N_3 + N_4$$

$$N_3 = q_{3+1}N_{3+1} + N_{3+2} = q_4N_4 + N_5 = 2N_4 + 0$$

$$GCF = N_4$$

$$N_5 = 0$$

From this information, we have the following relationships:

$$N_1 = 3N_2 + N_3; \text{ so, } N_3 = N_1 - 3N_2$$

$$N_2 = 2N_3 + N_4; \text{ so, } N_4 = N_2 - 2N_3$$

Substituting for N_3 in $N_4 = N_2 - 2N_3$, we get the following:

$$N_4 = N_2 - 2(N_1 - 3N_2) = N_2 - 2N_1 + 6N_2 = -2N_1 + 7N_2$$

29. The best choice for this item is **A. (SMR 3.1 Natural Numbers)**

A. An integer n is odd if and only if $n^2 + 2n$ is odd: This statement is always true. If n is even, then $n^2 + 2n$ is an even, too; the square of an even number is even plus an even number ($2n$) is still even. If n is odd, then $n^2 + 2n$ is odd, too; the square of an odd number is odd plus an even number ($2n$) is still odd. Conversely, $n^2 + 2n$ is odd only if n is odd.

B. A number is irrational if and only if its square is irrational: This is not always true. The square of an irrational number may result in a rational number. For example, $\sqrt{2}$ is an irrational number, and $\left(\sqrt{2}\right)^2 = 2$, which is a rational number.

C. A number is rational if and only if its square is rational: The square of an irrational number may also result in a rational number, as the case with $\sqrt{2}$ presented earlier.

D. A number n is odd if and only if $n(n + 1)$ is even: This is false because this statement will always result in an even number. For example, $3(3 + 1) = 3(4) = 12$, or $4(4 + 1) = 4(5) = 20$.

30. This best choice for this item is **B. (SMR 3.1 Natural Numbers) (ENHANCED)**

The number of prime numbers of the form $\left|n^2 - 6n + 5\right|$ where n is an integer is 2. You may check this by substituting values in the expression.

If $n = 0$, then $\left|(0)^2 - 6(0) + 5\right| = 5.$ This is one of the prime numbers of this form.

If $n = 1$, then $\left|(1)^2 - 6(1) + 5\right| = 0.$ Zero is not a prime number.

If $n = 2$, then $\left|(2)^2 - 6(2) + 5\right| = 3.$ This is the other of the prime numbers of this form.

If $n = 3$, then $\left|(3)^2 - 6(3) + 5\right| = 14.$ 14 is not a prime number.

If $n = -1$, then $\left|(-1)^2 - 6(-1) + 5\right| = 12.$ 12 is not a prime number.

If $n = -2$, then $\left|(-2)^2 - 6(-2) + 5\right| = 21.$ 21 is not a prime number.

If $n = -4$, then $\left|(-4)^2 - 6(-4) + 5\right| = 12.$ 12 is not a prime number.

Algebra

31. Written or Constructed Response Question. **(SMR SMR 1.2 Polynomial Equations and Inequalities)**

The polynomial has two real roots, and then it is reducible. The two roots are located at the following positions:

$x = -\sqrt{\sqrt{2}} = -\sqrt[4]{2}$, and $x = \sqrt{\sqrt{2}} = \sqrt[4]{2}$.

The polynomial graph for $f(x) = x^2 - \sqrt{2}$ is the following:

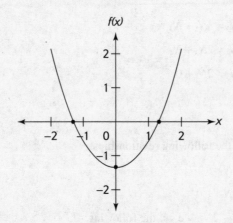

32. Written or Constructed Response Question. **(SMR 1.4 Linear Algebra)**

When $a \neq 0$, the solution of the first equation is $\left\{(x, y)\,\middle|\, x = \dfrac{(c - by)}{a}\right\}$. Using $y = 0$, you get the solution

$(\frac{c}{a}, 0)$. Remember that you are assuming that the second equation has the same solution set as the first equation. So, you may substitute this value into the second equation and get that $a\left(\dfrac{c}{a}\right) + d \cdot 0 = e$, and

$c = e$. Using $y = 1$ in $x = \dfrac{(c - by)}{a}$, you get that $a\left(\dfrac{(c - b)}{a}\right) + d \cdot 1 = e$, and $b = d$. This means that they are the same equation.

In the case of $a = 0$, the equations can be different and still have the same solution set.

For example, $0x + 3y = 6$, and $0x + 6y = 12$.

33. Written or Constructed Response Question. (**SMR 1.4 Linear Algebra**)

A. This is a possible answer for this section of the question:

$$x + y - z + w = 0$$
$$y - z = 0$$
$$2z + 2w = 0$$
$$z + w = 0$$

B. This is a possible answer for this section of the question:

$$x + y - z + w = 0$$
$$w = 0$$
$$w = 0$$
$$w = 0$$

C. This is a possible answer for this section of the question:

$$x + y - z + w = 0$$
$$x + y - z + w = 0$$
$$x + y - z + w = 0$$
$$x + y - z + w = 0$$

Number Theory

34. Written or Constructed Response Question. (**SMR 3.1 Natural Numbers**)

Suppose that a number n is three digits and can be written as $100a + 10b + c$. This can be written as $(99 + 1)a + (9 + 1)b + c = 99a + a + 9b + b + c = 99a + 9b + a + b + c = 3(33a + 3b) + (a + b + c)$. Since the first term has a common factor of 3, it is divisible by 3. In order for the entire number to be divisible by 3, $a + b + c$ must be divisible by 3. This is the sum of the digits. This can be extended to any number of digits.

Practice CSET: Mathematics Subset II

This Subtest involves Geometry (items 35–56, and 65–67) and Probability and Statistics (items 57–64, and 68).

Geometry

35. The best choice for this item is **A**. (SMR 2.3 **Three-Dimensional Geometry**)

The formula for finding the volume of a circular cone is the following: $V = \frac{1}{3}\pi^2 h$. You can use 3.14 for the approximate value of π (other values could be used as approximation of π). For the value of the radius of the circular base of the cone, you need to divide the given diameter (6 cm) by 2 to find the radius, which yields 3 cm for the radius. The height is equal to 12 cm. Using these values for the formula, we have the following:

$\frac{1}{3}\left(3.14\left(3^2\right)(12)\right) \approx 113$ cubic centimeters

36. The best choice for this item is **B**. (SMR 2.3 **Three-Dimensional Geometry**) (ENHANCED)

You need to use the Surface Area formula for this problem: $2\pi rh + 2\pi r^2$. Since the diameter of this cylinder is 15 cm, the radius (r) is equal to $\frac{1}{2}$ of that (7.5 cm). This is because $d = 2r$ or $\frac{1}{2}d = r$ (divide by 2 for each side of the equality). Let $\pi \approx 3.14$. Substitute the values in the formula and solve:

$2\pi rh + 2\pi r^2 = 2(3.14)(7.5)(35) + 2(3.14)(7.5)^2$

$\qquad\qquad = 1648.5 + 353.25$

$\qquad\qquad = 2001.75 \approx 2002$ cm^2

37. The best choice for this item is **D**. (SMR 2.3 **Three-Dimensional Geometry**)

Check whether each statement is true or false.

A. Lines ℓ and m intersect at point A: Yes, the two lines intersect at point A.

B. Points A, B, and C are coplanar: Yes, A, B, and C are in the same plane.

C. Points A, B, and C are non-collinear: Yes, A, B, and C are not in the same line.

D. There is more than one plane that contains lines ℓ and m: No, there is only one plane that contains these two lines.

38. The best choice for this item is **C**. (SMR 2.1 **Parallelism**)

$\overline{UH} \| \overline{OS}$ because the two angles are equal corresponding angles formed by lines ℓ and m and transversal line segment UH, $\overline{UH}$.

39. The best choice for this item is **C**. (SMR 2.1 **Parallelism**)

If two parallel lines are cut by a transversal, then the corresponding angles are equal, and the alternate interior angles are equal.

40. The best choice for this item is **B**. (SMR 2.2 **Plane Euclidean Geometry**)

Since we are dealing with supplementary angles, we have that $2a° = 180° - 70°$, then $2a° = 110°$, and $a° = 55°$.

41. The best choice for this item is **A**. (SMR 2.2 **Plane Euclidean Geometry**)

By definition, two polygons are equal if and only if there is a correspondence between their vertices such that all of their corresponding sides and angles are equal. For example, a triangle ABC below could be flipped over vertically and slid over triangle FDE. Vertex A would fall over F, B over E, and C over D. The corresponding six equal parts are the following:

Line segment AB = line segment FE; line segment AC = line segment FD; line segment BC = line segment ED; $\angle A = \angle F$, $\angle B = \angle E$, and $\angle C = \angle D$.

42. The best choice for this item is **D**. (**SMR 2.2 Plane Euclidean Geometry**)

Check each alternative to see which one is true or false:

A. $\angle JON > \angle NOA$:   True. An exterior angle of a triangle is greater than either remote interior angle.

B. $\angle JON > \angle JOH$:   True. An exterior angle of a triangle is greater than either remote interior angle.

C. $\angle JON = \angle HOA$:   True. These are opposite angles, and opposite angles have the same measure.

D. $\angle JON = \angle AON$:   False. These are supplementary angles that are not equal. They are not right angles.

43. The best choice for this item is **C**. (**SMR 2.2 Plane Euclidean Geometry**)

The formula for the volume of a right circular cone is equal to $\frac{1}{3}\pi^2 h = \frac{1}{3}\pi(6^2)(6) = \frac{1}{3}\pi(216) = 72\pi$.

44. The best choice for this item is **A**. (**SMR 2.2 Plane Euclidean Geometry**) (ENHANCED)

Let the radius of the tennis ball be equal to the one unit.

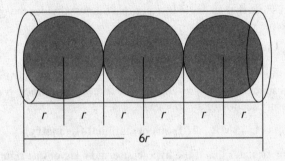

Then the height of the can is equal to six units, and the diameter is equal to two units. The volume of the ball or sphere is equal to $\frac{4}{3}\pi^3 = \frac{4}{3}\pi(1^3) = \frac{4}{3}\pi$ cubic units. So the volume of the three balls in the can is equal to $3 \cdot \frac{4}{3}\pi = 4\pi$ (the 3s cancel out each other). The volume of the can or right circular cylinder is equal to $\pi r^2 h = \pi(1^2)(6) = 6\pi$ cubic units. The balls take a portion of this volume: $\frac{4\pi}{6\pi} = \frac{2}{3}$ (simplify the fraction, and the πs cancel out each other) $\approx 67\%$ of the can.

45. The best choice for this item is **A**. (**SMR 2.2 Plane Euclidean Geometry**) (ENHANCED)

You should start by drawing a rough sketch of the situation presented in the problem.

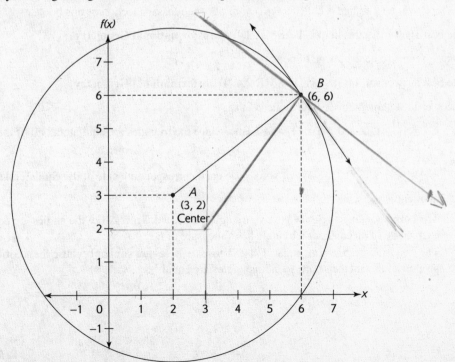

Then notice that line segment *AB,* joining (3, 2) and (6, 6) is a radius of the circle. A line tangent to a circle is perpendicular to the radius drawn to the point of contact, in this case (6, 6). This implies that this radius is perpendicular to line *m*. Also, we need to find the slope of segment *AB,* which is $\frac{6-3}{6-2} = \frac{3}{4}$. When two non-vertical lines are perpendicular, the product of their slope is –1. So, the slope of line *m* is $\frac{4}{3}$.

46. The best choice for this item is **C. (SMR 2.3 Three-Dimensional Geometry)**

Volume of the sphere is equal to $\frac{4}{3}\pi r^3$. If we double the radius, we have $\frac{4}{3}\pi(2r)^3 = \frac{4}{3}\pi(8r^3)$.

Then we can divide this volume by the original volume to see how many times it multiplied: $\dfrac{\frac{4}{3}\pi(8r^3)}{\left(\frac{4}{3}\pi^3\right)} = 8$.

The volume is multiplied by 8 when the radius is doubled.

47. The best choice for this item is **D. (2.2 Plane Euclidean Geometry)**

The angle bisector theorem states that an angle bisector in a triangle divides the opposite side into segments that have the same ratio as the other two sides.

48. The best choice for this item is **B. (2.1 Parallelism)**

This is a *theorem.* A theorem is a statement that is proved by reasoning deductively from already accepted statements. A *postulate* is a statement that is assumed to be true without proof. A *definition* is a description of a term or idea. See the glossary section of this book.

49. The best choice for this item is **C. (SMR 2.4 Transformational Geometry)**

The H.L. Congruence Theorem states that if the hypotenuse and a leg of one right triangle are equal to the corresponding parts of another right triangle, then the triangles are congruent.

50. This best choice for this item is **A. (SMR 2.4 Transformational Geometry)**

A translation can be thought of as the result of sliding without turning a figure from one position to another. A translation is the result of two successive reflections in parallel mirrors. By definition, a transformation is a translation if and only if it is the composite of two successive reflections through parallel lines. A translation is compared to a "sliding" motion.

51. The best choice for this item is **B. (SMR 2.4 Transformational Geometry)**

The transformation that seems to relate to *ABCD* and *EFGH* is a reflection. A transformation that flips the plane or shape over a fixed line is called a *reflection.* See the glossary section of this book.

52. The best answer for this item is **B. (SMR 2.4 Transformational Geometry)**

Point *F* seems to be the image of point *A.*

53. The best answer for this item is **D. (SMR 2.4 Transformational Geometry)**

Check each statement to see which one is false:

A. $\overline{CA} = \overline{AG} = \overline{GC}$, and $\overline{NE} = \overline{EY} = \overline{YN}$: True. Since the triangles are equilateral, all of their respective sides are equal.

B. $\dfrac{\overline{CA}}{\overline{NE}} = \dfrac{\overline{AG}}{\overline{EY}} = \dfrac{\overline{GC}}{\overline{YN}}$: True. When you divide each corresponding side of the equilateral triangles, the quotient is the same.

C. The corresponding angles of the two triangles are equal: True. All of the angles are equal to 60° because each angle of an equilateral triangle has a measure of 60°.

D. The two triangles are not similar: False. These triangles are similar because their corresponding sides are proportional, and their corresponding angles are equal.

54. The best choice for this item is **A. (SMR 2.3 Three-Dimensional Geometry)**

Check each statement to see which one is true or false:

A. If $s \perp n$, then it follows that $s \perp A$: False.
B. If $s \perp A$, then it follows that $s \perp o$: True.
C. Lines n and o can both be perpendicular s: True.
D. If m is not perpendicular A, then m can be perpendicular o: True.

55. The best choice for this item is **C. (SMR 2.3 Three-Dimensional Geometry)**

It is a good idea to think about an example to test whether a statement is false. Check each statement to see which one is true or false:

A. If two planes intersect, then their intersection is a line: True.
B. If a line intersects a plane that does not contain it, then the line and plane intersect in exactly one point: True.
C. If three planes intersect, then their intersection is a single point: False. The three planes might intersect in a line. For example, in the following figure, planes X, Y, and Z intersect in line m.

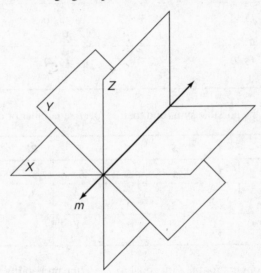

D. If a line does not intersect a plane, then it is parallel to the plane: True.

56. The best choice for this item is **D. (SMR 2.3 Three-Dimensional Geometry)**

By definition, two planes are perpendicular if and only if one plane contains a line that is perpendicular to the other plane. The two planes described in this problem meet this condition. Two planes are parallel if and only if they do not intersect each other. These two planes do intersect each other. The term oblique is used to refer to a line and plane, or two planes that intersect without being perpendicular to each other. This is not the case here. A line and plane or two planes are oblique if and only if they are neither parallel nor perpendicular.

Probability and Statistics

57. The best choice for this item is **B. (SMR 4.1 Probability) (ENHANCED)**

The probability that an event will happen is somewhere between 0 and 1. A box contains the following amounts of square tiles: 4 yellow, 6 red, 3 blue, and 8 orange. The total number of square tiles is $4 + 6 + 3 + 8 = 21$. If one square tile is drawn from the box, the probability for each of these two independent events is the following: $P(\text{yellow}) = \frac{4}{21}$, and $P(\text{orange}) = \frac{8}{21}$. So, $P(\text{yellow or orange}) = = \frac{4}{21} + \frac{8}{21} = \frac{12}{21} = \frac{4}{7}$.

58. The best choice for this item is **C. (SMR 4.1 Probability)** (ENHANCED)

The possible combinations for the two dice are $6 \times 6 = 36$. These possible combinations are shown in the table below, including ordered pairs and sums for dice combinations.

	1	2	3	4	5	6
1	(1, 1) 2	(1, 2) 3	(1, 3) 4	(1, 4) 5	(1, 5) 6	(1, 6) 7
2	(2, 1) 3	(2, 2) 4	(2, 3) 5	(2, 4) 6	(2, 5) 7	(2, 6) 8
3	(3, 1) 4	(3, 2) 5	(3, 3) 6	(3, 4) 7	(3, 5) 8	(3, 6) 9
4	(4, 1) 5	(4, 2) 6	(4, 3) 7	(4, 4) 8	(4, 5) 9	(4, 6) 10
5	(5, 1) 6	(5, 2) 7	(5, 3) 8	(5, 4) 9	(5, 5) 10	(5, 6) 11
6	(6, 1) 7	(6, 2) 8	(6, 3) 9	(6, 4) 10	(6, 5) 11	(6, 6) 12

The following table includes the possible sums and their respective number of combinations and probabilities.

Sums	2	3	4	5	6	7	8	9	10	11	12
# of combinations	1	2	3	4	5	6	5	4	3	2	1
Probabilities	$\frac{1}{36}$	$\frac{2}{36}$	$\frac{1}{18}$	$\frac{3}{36}$	$\frac{1}{12}$	$\frac{4}{36}$	$\frac{1}{8}$	$\frac{5}{36}$	$\frac{6}{36}$	$\frac{1}{6}$	$\frac{5}{36}$
		$\frac{4}{36}$	$\frac{3}{36}$	$\frac{1}{12}$		$\frac{2}{36}$			$\frac{1}{12}$	$\frac{1}{36}$	

Six of the possible combinations are for the sum equal to 7. So, the probability is $\frac{6}{36} = \frac{1}{6}$.

59. The best choice for this item is **B. (SMR 4.1 Probability)**

Since these are two independent events, you need to multiply the probability of rolling a prime number by the probability of tossing a head. The probability of rolling a prime number is the same as the

$P\left(2, 3, \text{ or } 5\right) = \frac{1}{6} + \frac{1}{6} + \frac{1}{6} = \frac{3}{6} = \frac{1}{2}$. The probability of tossing a head is $\frac{1}{2}$. Then, P(prime and head) $= \frac{1}{2} \cdot \frac{1}{2} = \frac{1}{4}$.

60. The best choice for this item is **A. (SMR 4.1 Probability)**

This problem is about finding possible combinations. An arrangement, or listing of objects in which order is not important, is called a combination. Permutation and combinations are related. You can find the number of combinations of objects in a given situation by dividing the number of permutations for the entire set by the number of ways each smaller set can be arranged. In this case, we have a permutation of 10 toppings taken 3 at a time, and 3! ways to select the three toppings:

$\frac{10 \cdot 9 \cdot 8}{3!} = \frac{720}{3 \cdot 2 \cdot 1} = \frac{720}{6} = 120$

61. The best choice for this item is **D. (SMR 4.2 Statistics)**

One way to find the best choice for this item is by analyzing each alternative.

A. At this high school, fewer 11th graders use different forms of transportation than 12th graders, because fewer students attend 11th grade: This one indicates that there are more 12th graders than 11th graders attending this high school, but this is not true. There are more 11th graders (389) than 12th graders (376).

B. At this high school, the number of 11th graders who take the bus is greater than the number of 10th graders who walk to school: This one indicates that more 11th graders take the bus than 10th graders who walk to school, but this is not true. The number of 11th graders who take the bus is 47, and the number of 10th graders who walk to school is 123, which indicates that there are more 10th graders walking than 11th graders taking the bus.

C. At this high school, more students in all grade levels take the bus to get to school than any of the other types of transportation: This one indicates that more students take the bus than students who use any of the other types of transportation. This is not true because fewer students (344) take the bus than students who walk to school (406). More students walk to school that any of the other types of transportation.

D. At this high school, the number of 12th graders who take the bus is greater than the number of 11th graders who walk to school: This item indicates that more 12th graders (158) take the bus than 11th graders who walk to school (140). This is true and is the only alternative that can be verified by the information provided in the table.

62. The best choice for this item is **C.** (**SMR 4.2 Statistics**) (ENHANCED)

The median is a measure of central tendency of data. The median of a set of data is the middle number of the ordered data, or the mean of the middle two numbers:

7, 7, 7, 7, 7, 7, 7, 7, 7, 7, 7, $\boxed{7, 8,}$ 8, 8, 9, 9, 10, 10, 10, 10, 10, 10, 10

The median divides the data in half. In this case, the middle of the data is the between the 12th and 13th number because we have 24 numbers: $(7 + 8) \div 2 = 7.5$. The median number of hours that Mike worked last month is 7.5 hours.

63. The best choice for this item is **D.** (**SMR 4.2 Statistics**) (ENHANCED)

To find the mean, multiply each number of hour by its frequency, add the products, and divide the sum by the total frequency (45): $(23 \cdot 1 + 13 \cdot 2 + 2 \cdot 3 + 7 \cdot 4) \div 45 = 83 \div 45 \approx 1.84$ (to the closest hundredth). The mean is 1.84 hours.

64. The best choice for this item is **D.** (**SMR 4.2 Statistics**)

The median is the only one that will remain the same because the middle of the sample will still be the same after rejecting the lowest and highest score. The other measures of central tendency might not remain the same.

Geometry

65. Written or Constructed Response Question. (**SMR 2.1 Parallelism**)

The drawing should be similar to the following figure.

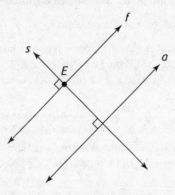

In a plane, two lines that are perpendicular to a third line are also parallel to each other.

66. Written or Constructed Response Question. (**SMR 2.3 Three-Dimensional Geometry**)

You should start by sketching the pyramid:

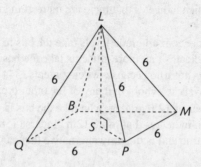

The area of the base is $6 \cdot 6$ or 36 square units. The area of each triangular face is an equilateral triangle, and each edge of the pyramid is 6 units. Then, the height of the triangles (line segment LS) can be found by using the Pythagorean Theorem and appropriate line segments: $c^2 = a^2 + b^2$ or $(LP)^2 = (LS)^2 + (SP)^2$. We know LP is 6 units

and SP is $\frac{1}{2}$ of BP. Then, $m(BP)$ is equal to $\sqrt{6^2 + 6^2} = \sqrt{2 \cdot 2 \cdot 2 \cdot 3 \cdot 3} = 2 \cdot 3\sqrt{2} = 6\sqrt{2}$.

So, $m(BP) = \frac{1}{2}\left(6\sqrt{2}\right)$ or $3\sqrt{2}$ cubic units.

Using this information, we have the following:

$$(LP)^2 = (LS)^2 + (SP)^2$$
$$(6)^2 = (LS)^2 + \left(3\sqrt{2}\right)^2$$
$$36 = (LS)^2 + 18$$
$$36 - 18 = (LS)^2 + 18 - 18$$
$$18 = (LS)^2$$
$$\sqrt{18} = LS$$
$$\sqrt{2 \cdot 3 \cdot 3} = LS$$
$$3\sqrt{2} = LS$$

So, the volume of the pyramid is $\frac{1}{3}Bh = \frac{1}{3}(36)\left(3\sqrt{2}\right) = 36\sqrt{2}$.

67. Written or Constructed Response Question. (**2.2 Euclidean Geometry**)

These are the possible solutions to each part of the problem.

A. Angles LQM and KQP are vertical angles that are congruent and their measures are equal. So, letting x be the fixed quantity we need to find, $\angle LQM = 5x + 20$, and $\angle KQP = 3x + 60$. Using these equalities, since we know that $\angle LQM = \angle KQP$, then $5x + 20 = 3x + 60$; $5x - 3x = 60 - 20$; $2x = 40$; $x = 20$. Then the unknown value that we are looking for is 20.

B. The measure of $\angle LQM$ is equal to $(5x + 20)°$. So, we have that the measure of $\angle LQM$ is equal to $5(20°) + 20° = 100° + 20° = 120°$. The measure of $\angle LQM$ is equal to $120°$.

C. Given that straight lines KL and MP intersect at point Q, $\angle MQK$ and $\angle MQK$ are supplementary angles, which sum is equal to $180°$. So $m(\angle MQK) + m(\angle MQK) = 180°$. Since $\angle MQK = 120°$, it follows that $\angle MQK = 180° - 120° = 60°$.

Probability and Statistics

68. Written or Constructed Response Question. (**SMR 4.2 Statistics.**)

X (rpm)	Y (%)	XY	X²
50	1.5	75.0	2,500
75	1.9	142.5	5,625
60	2.0	120.0	3,600
65	1.5	97.5	4,225
90	3.0	270.0	8,100
70	2.5	175.0	4,900
55	1.0	55.0	3,025
45	1.2	54.0	2,025
80	1.7	136.0	6,400
70	2.0	140.0	4,900
Total: 660	18.3	1,265.0	45,300

$$\overline{X} = \sum \frac{X}{n} \qquad \overline{Y} = \sum \frac{Y}{n}$$

$$= \frac{660}{10} \qquad\qquad = \frac{18.3}{10}$$

$$= 66 \qquad\qquad\quad = 1.83$$

$$b = \frac{XY - n\overline{X}\,\overline{Y}}{\sum X^2 - n\overline{X}^2}$$

$$= \frac{1265 - 10\,(66)(1.83)}{45,300 - 10\,(66)^2}$$

$$= \frac{1265 - 1207.8}{45,300 - 43,560}$$

$$= \frac{52.2}{1740} = 0.033$$

$$a = \frac{\sum Y - b \sum X}{n}$$

$$= \frac{18.3 - 0.033\,(660)}{10}$$

$$= \frac{18.3 - 21.78}{10}$$

$$= \frac{-3.48}{10} = -0.348$$

This implies that the regression equation $Y = a + bX$ is equal to $-0.348 + 0.33X$. In this formula, the value of b is the slope of the line. In this case, $b = 0.033$ and implies that for every unit increase in rpm, the percentage of defective printouts produced by the newspaper printer increases by 0.033 percent. This also implies a positive relationship between speed of the printer (X) and the percentage of defective printouts produced by the printer (Y). In other words, as the rpm increases so does the percentage of defective printouts produced by the printer. The value of a, which is the same as the y-intercept, indicates that, at the point where $X = 0$, the regression line crosses the y-axis at -0.348.

Practice CSET: Mathematics Subset III

This Subtest involves Calculus (items 69–94, and 99–101) and History of Mathematics (items 95–98, and 102).

Calculus

69. The best choice for this item is **C**. (SMR 5.1 Trigonometry)

We know that $\tan\left(\dfrac{\pi}{6}\right) = \dfrac{1}{\sqrt{3}}$. Therefore, $x - \dfrac{\pi}{3} = \dfrac{\pi}{6}$. This gives $x = \dfrac{\pi}{6} + \dfrac{\pi}{3} = \dfrac{3\pi}{6} = \dfrac{\pi}{2}$. We are looking at the interval $0 \le x \le 2\pi$, so we also need to consider that $\tan\left(\dfrac{7\pi}{6}\right) = \dfrac{1}{\sqrt{3}}$. This gives $x - \dfrac{\pi}{3} = \dfrac{7\pi}{6}$, so $x = \dfrac{7\pi}{6} + \dfrac{\pi}{3} = \dfrac{9\pi}{6} = \dfrac{3\pi}{2}$. This gives two possible solutions in the desired interval, $\dfrac{\pi}{2}, \dfrac{3\pi}{2}$.

70. This best choice for this item is **D**. (SMR 5.2 Limits and Continuity)

The $\lim\limits_{x \to 2^+} f(x)$ is the value of $f(x)$ as x approaches 2 from the right. This is from the direction of values of x which are greater than 2. The function when x is greater than 2 is defined as the value of $x + 3$. At the point when $x = 2$, the value from the left is equal to 5.

71. The best choice for this item is **B**. (SMR 5.2 Limits and Continuity) (ENHANCED)

The Intermediate Value Theorem states that:

Suppose that f is continuous on the closed interval $[a, b]$ and let N be any number strictly between $f(a)$ and $f(b)$. Then there exists a number c in (a, b) such that $f(c) = N$.

In order to use the Intermediate Value Theorem to show there is a root, let $f(x) = x^3 + x - 3$ and let $N = 0$. If $f(a)<0$ and $f(b)>0$ or $f(a)>0$ and $f(b)<0$, then there is a value c that is a root of $f(x)$ between a and b. Evaluate $f(x)$ at each endpoint. The only interval in which $f(a)<0$ and $f(b)>0$ is Choice **B**. $f(1)=-1$ and $f(2)=7$, so there is a value of c in the interval $(1, 2)$ where $f(c)=0$.

72. The best answer for this item is **C**. (SMR 5.1 Trigonometry)

If you factor out the common factor of $\sin x$, the equation becomes $\sin x \left(2\sin x - \sqrt{3}\right) = 0$. This means either $\sin x = 0$ or $2\sin x - \sqrt{3} = 0$. In order for $\sin x$ to be 0, x must be 0. Since we are between 0 and 2π, x can also be π or 2π. In order for $2\sin x - \sqrt{3} = 0$, then $\sin x = \dfrac{\sqrt{3}}{2}$. This occurs at $x = \dfrac{\pi}{3}$. The sine function is also positive in quadrant II, so x can also be $\dfrac{2\pi}{3}$. This gives five possible answers: $\left\{0, \dfrac{\pi}{3}, \dfrac{2\pi}{3}, \pi, 2\pi\right\}$. If you chose **A**, you neglected to consider the other quadrants in which the value of sine is the same. If you chose **B**, you reversed sine and cosine functions. If you chose **D**, you used quadrant IV instead of quadrant II as the other place sine is positive.

73. The best answer for this item is **C**. (SMR 5.3 Derivatives and Applications)

The slope of the tangent line is found by evaluating $f'(x)$ when $x = 1$. Taking the first derivative gives $f'(x) = 12x^3 - 4x + 4$. Substituting $x = 1$ into $f'(x)$ gives $f'(x) = 12(1)^3 - 4(1) + 4 = 12 - 4 + 4 = 12$. The slope of the tangent line is 12. The point the line goes through is $(1, -2)$. Using the point and the slope, the equation of the line is $(y - (-2)) = 12(x - 1)$. Solving for y gives:

$$y + 2 = 12x - 12$$

$$y = 12x - 14$$

74. The best choice for this item is **B**. (SMR 5.1 Trigonometry)

From the equation $\sin^2 x + \cos^2 x = 1$, if you divide both sides by $\sin^2 x$, the equation becomes $1 + \cot^2 x = \csc^2 x$. Similarly, if you divide both sides by $\cos^2 x$, the equation becomes $\tan^2 x + 1 = \sec^2 x$. This is equivalent to Choice **B**. Choices **A** and **D** are derived from angle addition formulas, and Choice **C** is a half-angle formula that is also derived from angle addition formulas.

75. The best choice for this item is **C**. (**SMR 5.2 Limits and Continuity**)

In order to be continuous, the limit has to exist at a. Since $f(x)$ and $g(x)$ are continuous at a, then $\lim_{x \to a} f(x) = f(a)$ and $\lim_{x \to a} g(x) = g(a)$. Therefore, using the laws of limits, $\lim_{x \to a} f(x) g(x) = \lim_{x \to a} f(x) \lim_{x \to a} g(x) = f(a) g(a)$. Similarly, $\lim_{x \to a} f(x) + g(x) = f(a) + g(a)$ and $\lim_{x \to a} cf(x) = cf(a)$.

For Choice **C**, if $\lim_{x \to a} g(x) = 0$, then $\lim_{x \to a} \dfrac{f(x)}{g(x)} = \dfrac{\lim_{x \to a} f(x)}{\lim_{x \to a} g(x)} = \dfrac{f(a)}{0} = \infty$.

Therefore, Choice **C** is only continuous if we know that $g(a) \neq 0$.

76. The best choice for this item is **B**. (**SMR 5.1 Trigonometry**)

The general form for this curve is $f(x) = A\cos(Bx + C) + D$. The horizontal axis is at $y = 1$, so the graph is shifted up 1 unit. This gives $D = 1$. There is no horizontal shift, so $C = 0$. The amplitude is the distance from the horizontal axis to the highest point on the curve. This can also be seen as half the distance from the highest peak to the lowest peak. In this curve, that is 2 units, so $A = 2$. The period of the curve is π. The value of B is $\dfrac{2\pi}{period}$, so $B = \dfrac{2\pi}{\pi} = 2$. Therefore, the function is $f(x) = 2\cos(2x) + 1$.

77. The best choice for this item is **C**. (**SMR 5.3 Derivatives and Applications**) (ENHANCED)

If you plug 0 into the function, the outcome is $\dfrac{0}{0}$. Therefore, you can use L'Hôpital's Rule. Then

$$\lim_{x \to 0} \frac{\tan x}{x + \sin x} = \lim_{x \to 0} \frac{\sec^2 x}{1 + \cos x} = \frac{(1)^2}{1 + 1} = \frac{1}{2}.$$

78. The best choice for this item is **B**. (**SMR 5.3 Derivatives and Applications**) (ENHANCED)

Since the rate of change of atmospheric pressure P with respect to the altitude h is proportional to P, the equation will be $\dfrac{dP}{dh} = kP$. This is a separable differential equation that is equivalent to $\dfrac{dP}{P} = kdh$. Integrating both sides gives $\ln P = kh + C$. Using the information in the problem, when $h = 0$, $P = 101.3$ and when $h = 1000$, $P = 87.14$. This gives two equations: $\ln(101.3) = k(0) + C$ and $\ln(87.14) = k(1000) + C$. Solving the first equation gives the value of C to be $\ln(101.3)$. Using this information in the second equation gives $\ln(87.14) = k(1000) + \ln(101.3)$. Solving this for k gives $k = \dfrac{\ln(0.86)}{1000} = -0.00015057$. This makes the equation for the problem become $\ln P = \left(\dfrac{\ln(0.86)}{1000}\right)h + \ln(101.3)$. The question asks to find P when $h = 3000$ m, so substituting into the equation gives $\ln P = \left(\dfrac{\ln(0.86)}{1000}\right)(3000) + \ln(101.3) = 64.43$ kPa. Therefore, $P = e^{4.166} = 64.43$.

79. The best choice for this item is **C**. (**SMR 5.3 Derivatives and Applications**) (ENHANCED)

A picture of this problem might look like the following figure.

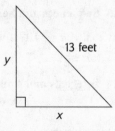

This figure leads us to the equation $x^2 + y^2 = 13^2$. Differentiating this with respect to time gives $2x\dfrac{dx}{dt} + 2y\dfrac{dy}{dt} = 0$. We are looking for $\dfrac{dy}{dt}$, so we can solve this equation for $\dfrac{dy}{dt}$.

$$2y\frac{dy}{dt} = -2x\frac{dx}{dt}$$

$$\frac{dy}{dt} = -\frac{2x}{2y}\frac{dx}{dt}$$

$$\frac{dy}{dt} = -\frac{x}{y}\frac{dx}{dt}$$

We are given that $\frac{dx}{dt} = 0.5$ and $x = 5$. When $x = 5$, we can use the original equation to find y.

$$(5)^2 + y^2 = 13^2$$

$$25 + y^2 = 169$$

$$y^2 = 144$$

$$y = 12$$

Plugging this into the equation gives:

$$\frac{dy}{dt} = -\frac{5}{12}\left(\frac{1}{2}\right) = -\frac{5}{24}$$

80. The best choice for this item is **D. (SMR 5.1 Trigonometry) (ENHANCED)**

To find $\left(\frac{\sqrt{3}}{2} + \frac{\sqrt{3}}{2}i\right)^3$, we can use De Moivre's Theorem. First, we need to find a polar representation for $\left(\frac{\sqrt{3}}{2} + \frac{\sqrt{3}}{2}i\right)$. This is equivalent to $\frac{\sqrt{3}}{2}(1 + i)$. We need to find the magnitude and direction for the complex number $1 + i$. The magnitude is $r = |z| = \sqrt{1+1} = \sqrt{2}$. The angle is found with $\tan\theta = \frac{1}{1}$. This gives $\theta = \frac{\pi}{4}$. So, the polar form of $1 + i$ is $\sqrt{2}\left(\cos\frac{\pi}{4} + i\sin\frac{\pi}{4}\right)$. Then we can write $\frac{\sqrt{3}}{2}(1 + i)$ as $\frac{\sqrt{3}}{2}\left(\sqrt{2}\left(\cos\frac{\pi}{4} + i\sin\frac{\pi}{4}\right)\right) = \frac{\sqrt{6}}{2}\left(\cos\frac{\pi}{4} + i\sin\frac{\pi}{4}\right)$. To find $\left(\frac{\sqrt{6}}{2}\left(\cos\frac{\pi}{4} + i\sin\frac{\pi}{4}\right)\right)^3$, we use De Moivre's Theorem, which states that $(r(\cos\theta + i\sin\theta))^n = r^n(\cos n\theta + i\sin n\theta)$. So $\left(\frac{\sqrt{6}}{2}\left(\cos\frac{\pi}{4} + i\sin\frac{\pi}{4}\right)\right)^3 = \left(\frac{\sqrt{6}}{2}\right)^3\left(\cos\frac{3\pi}{4} + i\sin\frac{3\pi}{4}\right) = \frac{6\sqrt{6}}{8}\left(-\frac{1}{\sqrt{2}} + i\frac{1}{\sqrt{2}}\right) = \frac{-3\sqrt{3}}{4} + \frac{3\sqrt{3}}{4}i$.

81. The best choice for this item is **C. (SMR 5.4 Integrals and Applications)**

The Fundamental Theorem of Calculus states that:

If f is continuous on $[a, b]$, then the function g defined by $g(x) = \int_a^x f(t)\,dt$ where $a \le x \le b$ is continuous on $[a, b]$ and differentiable on (a, b) and $g'(x) = f(x)$. Since $f(t) = \sqrt{1 + 3t^2}$ is continuous and differentiable for all real numbers, the Fundamental Theorem of Calculus states that $g'(x) = f(x) = \sqrt{1 + 3x^2}$.

82. The best choice for this item is **B. (SMR 5.5 Sequences and Series)**

If we define the number, $n = 2.\overline{4}$, we can say that $10n = 24.\overline{4}$. If we subtract these two numbers, we get $10n - n = 24.\overline{4} - 2.\overline{4}$. This leads to $9n = 22$, so $n = \frac{22}{9} = 2\frac{4}{9}$.

83. The best choice for this item is **B. (SMR 5.4 Integrals and Applications) (ENHANCED)**

The Mean Value Theorem states that:

If f is a function that satisfies the following hypotheses:

1. f is continuous on the closed interval $[a, b]$.

2. f is differentiable on the open interval (a, b).

Then there is a number c in (a, b) such that $f'(c) = \frac{f(b) - f(a)}{b - a}$.

For this problem, $f(x) = x^3 - 2x^2$, $a = 0$ and $b = 3$. Since f is a polynomial, it is continuous and differentiable on $[0,3]$. We want to find the values of c that satisfy the Mean Value Theorem: $f'(x) = 3x^2 - 4x$. So, we have

$$3c^2 - 4c = \frac{\left(3^3 - 2(3)^2\right) - 0}{3 - 0} = \frac{27 - 18}{3} = 3.$$ Therefore, $3c^2 - 4c - 3 = 0$. This is not factorable, so use the quadratic formula:

$$x = \frac{-b \pm \sqrt{b^2 - 4ac}}{2a} = \frac{4 \pm \sqrt{(-4)^2 - 4(3)(-3)}}{2(3)} = \frac{4 \pm \sqrt{16 + 36}}{6} = \frac{4 \pm \sqrt{52}}{6} = \frac{4 \pm 2\sqrt{13}}{6} = \frac{2 \pm \sqrt{13}}{3}.$$

These values of c will satisfy the Mean Value Theorem, but only $c = \dfrac{2 \pm \sqrt{13}}{3}$ is in the interval $[0, 3]$.

84. The best choice for this item is **A.** (**SMR 5.3 Derivatives and Applications**)

The limit definition of a derivative can be written as $f'(x) = \lim\limits_{x \to a} \dfrac{f(x) - f(a)}{x - a}$. For this function, this becomes

$$\lim_{x \to a} \frac{\dfrac{3x - 2}{2x + 1} - \dfrac{3a - 2}{2a - 1}}{x - a}.$$

85. The best choice for this item is **A.** (**SMR 5.3 Derivatives and Applications**) (ENHANCED)

To find the maximum and minimum points, first the derivative needs to be found. For this function, the derivative is $f'(x) = 3x^2 - 2x - 8$. The first derivative gives the slope of the tangent line to the curve. The maximum and minimum points are where the slope of the tangent line is zero. Therefore, we need to solve $3x^2 - 2x - 8 = 0$. First, factor the left hand side. $(3x + 4)(x - 2) = 0$. This gives $x = \dfrac{-4}{3}$ or $x = 2$. To determine which is a maximum and which is a minimum, we need to look at the value of the derivative for x values below $x = \dfrac{-4}{3}$, between $x = \dfrac{-4}{3}$ and $x = 2$, and greater than $x = 2$. When $x = < -\dfrac{4}{3}$, the value of $f'(x)$ is positive. Between $x = \dfrac{-4}{3}$ and $x = 2$, the value of $f'(x)$ is negative. When $x > 2$, the value of $f'(x)$ is positive. At $x = \dfrac{-4}{3}$, there is a maximum, and at $x = 2$ there is a minimum. To find the coordinates of the points, substitute the x values into the original function. This gives

$$f\left(-\frac{4}{3}\right) = \left(-\frac{4}{3}\right)^3 - \left(-\frac{4}{3}\right)^2 - 8\left(-\frac{4}{3}\right) + 12 = -\frac{64}{27} - \frac{16}{9} + \frac{32}{3} + 12 = \frac{64 - 48 + 288 + 324}{27} = \frac{628}{27}$$

$f(2) = (2)^3 - (2)^2 - 8(2) + 12 = 8 - 4 - 16 + 12 = 0$. So there is a maximum at $(2, 0)$ and a minimum at $\left(-\dfrac{4}{3}, \dfrac{628}{27}\right)$.

86. The best choice for this item is **B.** (**SMR 5.4 Integrals and Applications**) (ENHANCED)

First, it is often helpful to graph the functions to have a picture of the region that is being rotated.

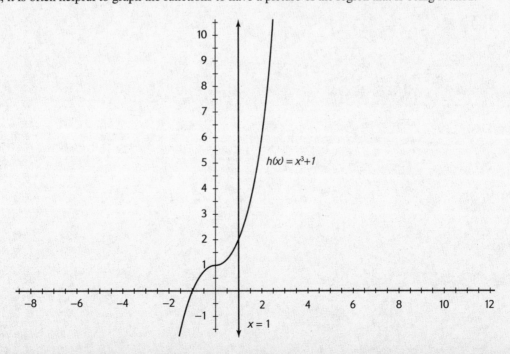

Once this is determined, we need to look at a slice of the region revolved about, in this case, the x-axis. The slice, or disk, would have a radius of y and the height of the disk would be dx. Use the volume of a cylinder formula to determine the volume of the disk. This gives $Disk = \pi r^2 h = \pi y^2 dx$. To find the volume of the entire region, we need to integrate this volume over the region. This gives $V = \int_{-1}^{1} \pi y^2 \, dx$. In order to find this, we need to replace y with what it is equal to from the original function. This gives

$$V = \int_{-1}^{1} \pi \left(x^3 + 1\right)^2 dx = \pi \int_{-1}^{1} x^6 + 2x^3 + 1 = \pi \left(\frac{x^7}{7} + \frac{2x^4}{4} + x\right)\Bigg|_{-1}^{1}$$

$$= \pi \left(\left(\frac{1}{7} + \frac{1}{2} + 1\right) - \left(-\frac{1}{7} + \frac{1}{2} - 1\right)\right) = \pi \left(\frac{2}{7} + 2\right) = \frac{16\pi}{7}.$$

87. The best choice for this item is **C. (SMR 5.3 Derivatives and Applications)**

Applying algebra rules to $(\sin x + \cos x)^2$ gives $\sin^2 x + 2\sin x \cos x + \cos^2 x$. Using the trigonometric identities $\sin^2 x + \cos^2 x = 1$ and $\sin 2x = 2 \sin x \cos x$, this can be written as $1 + \sin 2x$.

88. The best choice for this item is **D. (SMR 5.5 Sequences and Series)**

This is an infinite geometric series. Infinite geometric series are convergent if $|ratio| < 1$. Therefore, we need $\left|\frac{r}{2}\right| < 1$. This gives $-1 < \frac{r}{2} < 1$. Solving for r gives $-2 < r < 2$.

89. The best choice for this item is **A. (SMR 5.4 Integrals and Applications)**

The Reimann Sum is the sum of the rectangles when the area under the curve is partitioned. There are three rectangles. The dimensions of these rectangles are 1×3, 1×4, and 1×3. These areas total 10 units^2.

90. This best choice for this item is **D. (SMR 5.2 Limits and Continuity)**

When -2 is substituted into the function, the limit is evaluated at $\frac{0}{0}$. The trinomials can be factored, so the limit becomes $\lim_{x \to -2} \frac{x^2 + 5x + 6}{x^2 - x + 6} = \lim_{x \to -2} \frac{(x+2)(x+3)}{(x+2)(x-3)} = \lim_{x \to -2} \frac{(x+3)}{(x-3)} = \frac{-2+3}{-2-3} = -\frac{1}{5}$.

91. The best choice for this item is **C. (SMR 5.5 Sequences and Series) (ENHANCED)**

The Taylor series is defined as $f(x) = \sum_{n=0}^{\infty} \frac{f^{(n)}(a)}{n!}(x-a)^n$. Here, $f(x) = e^x$. $f^{(n)}(x) = e^x$ as well. Since $a = 2$, $f^{(n)}(2) = e^2$. The Taylor Series will then be $f(x) = \sum_{n=0}^{\infty} \frac{e^2}{n!}(x-2)^n$.

92. The best answer for this item is **A**. (**SMR 5.4 Integrals and Applications**)

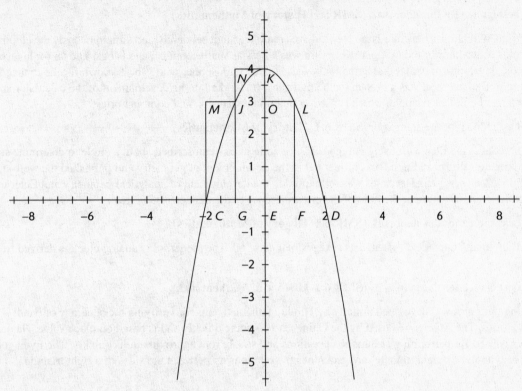

The curves intersect at the points $(0, -4)$ and $(4, 0)$. The area between the curves is $\int_0^4 (x-4) - (x^2 - 3x - 4)\, dx$. This leads to

$$\int_0^4 (-x^2 + 4x)\, dx = \left(-\frac{x^3}{3} + \frac{4x^2}{2} \right)\Bigg|_0^4 = \left(-\frac{4^3}{3} + 2(4)^2 \right) - \left(-\frac{0}{3} + 2(0) \right) = -\frac{64}{3} + 32 = -\frac{64}{3} + \frac{96}{3} = \frac{32}{3}.$$

93. The best answer for this item is **D**. (**SMR 5.5 Sequences and Series**) (ENHANCED)

Since there is a common difference of 4, this is an arithmetic sequence. The sum of an arithmetic sequence is found with the formula $S_n = \dfrac{n(a_1 + a_n)}{2}$. We are looking for the sum of the first 12 terms, so $n = 12$. We need to find the twelfth term of the sequence using the formula $a_n = a_1 + d(n-1)$. $a_1 = -3$; $d = 4$; $n = 12$, so $a_{12} = -3 + 4(12-1) = -3 + 4(11) = -3 + 44 = 41$. Then the sum of the first 12 terms is $S_{12} = \dfrac{12(-3+41)}{2} = \dfrac{12(38)}{2} = 228$.

94. The best choice for this item is **A**. (**SMR 5.5 Sequences and Series**)

The series is geometric. The series converges because $|r| = \left|\dfrac{1}{2}\right| < 1$. The sum of the series is $\sum_{n=1}^{\infty} ar^{n-1} = \dfrac{a}{1-r}$.

For this series, $a = -2$ and $r = \dfrac{1}{2}$. Therefore, $\sum_{n=1}^{\infty} -2\left(\dfrac{1}{2}\right)^{n-1} = \dfrac{-2}{1-\frac{1}{2}} = \dfrac{-2}{\frac{1}{2}} = -2\left(\dfrac{2}{1}\right) = -4.$

History of Mathematics

95. The best choice for this item is **C**. (**SMR 6.1 History of Mathematics**)

Gottfried Wilhelm Liebniz and Issac Newton are credited as independently and simultaneously developing Calculus as we know it today. Omar Khayyam was a Persian mathematician and is best known for his work with the development of algebra. Pythagoras was a Greek philosopher who is best known for the Pythagorean Theorem. Blaise Pascal was a French mathematician who worked in the development of the calculator and is well known for the Pascal Triangle, which is used in binomial expansion and combinatorics.

96. The best choice for this item is **B**. (**SMR 6.1 History of Mathematics**)

Archimedes is credited with using polygons inscribed in and circumscribed about a circle to determine an approximate value of π. Euclid was influential in the development of geometry and published the well-known Euclid's *Elements*. Rene Descartes was influential in the development of analytical geometry and Euler used the Greek letter, π, to represent the ratio of the circumference to the diameter of a circle.

97. The best choice for this item is **D**. (**SMR 6.1 History of Mathematics**)

The Babylonian numerical system was sexagesimal, base 60. The modern-day analog clock is derived from this system.

98. The best choice for this item is **A**. (**SMR 6.1 History of Mathematics**)

Casting out nines was developed initially by Hindu mathematicians for verifying the accuracy of hand calculations. The Abacus was used by the Chinese to compute quickly and is based on place value. Napier's Bones is used for performing arithmetic operations and square root approximations quickly. The Pythagorean Theorem applies to right triangles and examines the relationship between the sides of a right triangle.

Calculus

99. Written or Constructed Response Question. (**SMR 5.2 Limits and Continuity**.)(5.2.b)

Solution:

In order to be continuous at a number, $\lim_{x \to a} f(x) = f(a)$. So, we need to show that $\lim_{x \to 2} x^3 - 2x^2 + 4x - 2 = f(2)$. The value of the function at $a = 2$ is $f(2) = 2^3 - 2(2)^2 + 4(2) - 2 = 8 - 8 + 8 - 2 = 6$. Then, using the properties of limits,

$$\lim_{x \to 2} x^3 - 2x^2 + 4x - 2 = \lim_{x \to 2} x^3 - \lim_{x \to 2} 2x^2 + \lim_{x \to 2} 4x - \lim_{x \to 2} 2$$
$$= \lim_{x \to 2} x^3 - 2\lim_{x \to 2} x^2 + 4\lim_{x \to 2} x - \lim_{x \to 2} 2$$
$$= 2^3 - 2(2)^2 + 4(2) - 2$$
$$= 8 - 8 + 8 - 2$$
$$= 6 = f(2).$$

Therefore, since $\lim_{x \to 2} f(x) = f(2)$, the function $f(x)$ is continuous at $a = 2$.

100. Written or Constructed Response Question. (**SMR 5.1 Trigonometry**)

Starting from the cosine angle addition formula, $\cos(x + y) = \cos x \cos y - \sin x \sin y$, if you substitute x for y, then the formula becomes $\cos(x + x) = \cos x \cos x - \sin x \sin x$

$$\cos(2x) = \cos^2 x - \sin^2 x$$

Using the Pythagorean Identity that $\sin^2 x = 1 - \cos^2 x$, then $\cos(2x)$ becomes $\cos(2x) = \cos^2 x - (1 - \cos^2 x) = 2\cos^2 x - 1$. Solving this for $\cos x$ gives

$$\cos(2x) = 2\cos^2 x - 1$$
$$2\cos^2 x = 1 + \cos(2x)$$
$$\cos^2 x = \frac{1 + \cos(2x)}{2}$$
$$\cos x = \pm \sqrt{\frac{1 + \cos(2x)}{2}}.$$

Similarly, $\cos(2x)$ can also be written as $\cos(2x) = (1 - \sin^2 x) - \sin 2x = 1 - 2\sin^2 x$. Again, solving for $\sin x$ gives

$$1 - 2\sin^2 x = \cos(2x)$$
$$2\sin^2 x = 1 - \cos(2x)$$
$$\sin^2 x = \frac{1 - \cos(2x)}{2}$$
$$\sin x = \pm\sqrt{\frac{1 - \cos(2x)}{2}}.$$

101. Written or Constructed Response Question. (**SMR 5.3 Derivatives and Applications**)

The definition of the derivative states that $f'(x) = \lim\limits_{h \to 0} \dfrac{f(x+h) - f(x)}{h}$.

For this function

$$f'(x) = \lim_{h \to 0} \frac{\left(5(x+h)^2 - 2(x+h) + 3\right) - \left(5x^2 - 2x + 3\right)}{h}$$

$$= \lim_{h \to 0} \frac{\left(5(x^2 + 2xh + h^2) - 2x - 2h + 3\right) - 5x^2 + 2x - 3}{h} = \lim_{h \to 0} \frac{5x^2 + 10xh + 5h^2 - 2x - 2h - 3 - 5x^2 + 2x - 3}{h}$$

$$= \lim_{h \to 0} \frac{10xh + 5h^2 - 2h}{h} = \lim_{h \to 0} \frac{h(10x + 5h - 2)}{h} = \lim_{h \to 0} 10x + 5h - 2 = 10x - 2$$

So $f'(x) = 10x - 2$.

History of Mathematics

102. Written or Constructed Response Question. (**SMR 6.1 History of Mathematics**)

Since there is no overlap and no gaps, the sum of the four triangles and the smaller square is equal to the area of the larger square. The large square has an area of $(a + b)^2$. Each of the four triangles has an area of $\frac{1}{2}ab$, and the interior square has an area of c^2. Therefore,

$$(a + b)^2 = 4\left(\frac{1}{2}ab\right) + c^2$$
$$a^2 + 2ab + b^2 = 2ab + c^2$$
$$a^2 + b^2 = c^2.$$

Since a and b are the legs of a right triangle and c is the hypotenuse of the same right triangle, this proves the Pythagorean Theorem.

Practice CSET: Mathematics Test II

Remember to read and follow the instructions carefully.

The set of multiple-choice questions and constructed-response questions presented in this Practice CSET: Mathematics Test II are similar to the questions you will see on the **Mathematics Subtest I: Algebra; Number Theory**. This subtest includes the same amount of items you will find on the actual CSET: Mathematics test. We have included an answer key and explanation for each item's possible responses; however, we recommend and encourage you to respond to the items without looking at these sections of this book. You should record your responses on a separate sheet of paper and review your answers with the provided responses afterward.

Note: The use of calculators is not allowed for the CSET: Mathematics Subtest I.

Practice CSET: Mathematics Subtest I

1. Which of the following cannot be shown on a number line?

   A. the natural numbers
   B. the rational numbers
   C. the integers
   D. the complex numbers

2. Which of the following is the solution of the equation $x^2 - 4x + 13 = 0$?

   A. $\pm 5i$
   B. $2 \pm 3i$
   C. $\pm 6i$
   D. $3 \pm 2i$

3. Find the alternative that is equal to $(i + 1)^2$.

   A. $2i$
   B. $-2i$
   C. 2
   D. -2

GO ON TO THE NEXT PAGE

4. Which of the following possible values is not in the range of the function g below?

$$g(x) = \frac{g^2 - 16}{g^2 + 9}$$

    A. -1

    B. 1

    C. 0

    D. -0.5

5. For which of the values of x is $f(x) = \sqrt{x}$ undefined under the set of real numbers?

    A. 25

    B. 7

    C. -25

    D. 0

6. Which pair of vectors is perpendicular?

    A. $\langle -5, -3 \rangle, \langle -3, -5 \rangle$

    B. $\langle 5, -3 \rangle, \langle -3, 5 \rangle$

    C. $\langle -5, 3 \rangle, \langle 3, -5 \rangle$

    D. $\langle -5, 3 \rangle, \langle -3, -5 \rangle$

7. Which of the following set of numbers would you use to solve the equation $x^2 = -9$?

    A. real numbers

    B. complex numbers

    C. rational numbers

    D. natural numbers

8. Let a and b be real numbers; identify the alternative that is equal to $(a + bi)(a - bi)$.

    A. $a^2 - b^2$

    B. $a^2 + 2abi - b^2$

    C. $a^2 + b^2$

    D. $a^2 - 2abi + b^2$

9. Identify the graph that is not the graph of a function.

A.

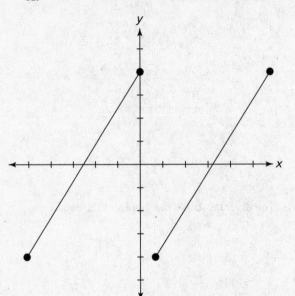

C.

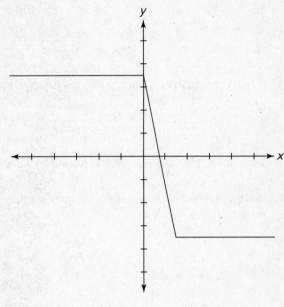

B.

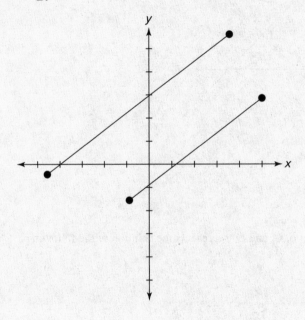

D.

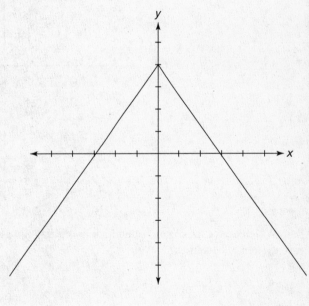

GO ON TO THE NEXT PAGE

10. Identify the alternative that is not the equation of a function.

   A. $x = 5$

   B. $y = \dfrac{|x|}{x}$

   C. $y = x$

   D. $y = 5$

11. Identify the alternative that represents a complex number.

   A. $-\sqrt{16}$

   B. -1

   C. $\sqrt{-16}$

   D.   None of the above represents a complex number.

12. Use the diagram below to answer the question that follows. The diagram shows the graphs of the equations $y - x = -1$, and $x + y = 4$.

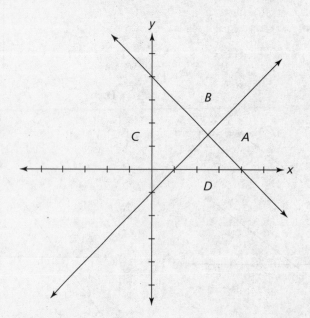

Which one of the regions (identified in the diagram as *A, B, C,* and *D*) represents the solution of the following system of equalities?

$$y - x \le -1$$
$$x + y \le 4$$

   A.   region *A*

   B.   region *B*

   C.   region *C*

   D.   region *D*

13. Let a and b be real numbers, and $ai^2 = bi^4$. Which of the following alternative is true?

    Alternative I: $a = b$

    Alternative II: $a = -b$

    Alternative III: $|a| = |b|$

A. Alternatives II and III only

B. Alternatives I and II only

C. Alternatives I and III only

D. Alternatives I, II, and III

14. If i^2 is -1, what is the value of $i^{27} - (-i)^{27}$?

A. $2i$

B. $-2i$

C. 0

D. -2

15. Solve the equation $\sqrt{2n} + 5 = 3$.

A. 32

B. 4

C. 16

D. This equation has no solution.

16. Let $f(x)$ be equal to $x^2 - 1$ and $g(x)$ equal to $x^2 + 1$. Identify the alternative that shows the following relation:

$(f \circ g)(x) - (g \circ f)(x)$

A. $4x^2$

B. $x^4 - 1$

C. $4x^2 - 2$

D. -2

17. Which of the following is not a logarithmic property?

A. $\log_b M N = \log_b M + \log_b N$

B. $\log_b b^x = x$

C. $\log_b M^p = p \log_b N$

D. $\log_b \dfrac{M}{N} = \log_b M - \log_b N$

18. If $\log_{10} 3 = 0.4771$ and $\log_{10} 4 = 0.6021$, what is the $\log_{10} 12$?

A. 1.0792

B. 0.1250

C. 0.2873

D. 1.2620

GO ON TO THE NEXT PAGE

19. Are the following vectors equal to $\overrightarrow{MN}$ if $M = \langle 5, -4 \rangle$ and $N = \langle -8, 3 \rangle$?

$\overrightarrow{QR}$, where $Q = \langle -4, 5 \rangle$ and $R = \langle 3, -8 \rangle$

$\overrightarrow{LP}$, where $L = \langle -5, 4 \rangle$ and $P = \langle -3, 8 \rangle$

$\overrightarrow{ST}$, where $S = \langle 5, -3 \rangle$ and $T = \langle -8, 4 \rangle$

A. Only $\overrightarrow{LP}$ is equal to $\overrightarrow{MN}$.

B. Only $\overrightarrow{QR}$ is equal to $\overrightarrow{MN}$.

C. Only $\overrightarrow{ST}$ is equal to $\overrightarrow{MN}$.

D. None of these three vectors are equal to $\overrightarrow{MN}$.

20. Given that $A = \begin{bmatrix} 4 & 5 & 9 \\ 0 & 5 & 2 \end{bmatrix}$ and $B = \begin{bmatrix} 2 & 4 & -8 & 8 \\ 1 & -7 & 5 & 7 \\ 0 & -5 & 3 & 8 \end{bmatrix}$, which of the following responses is equal to AB?

A. $\begin{bmatrix} 13 & -64 & 20 & 139 \\ 5 & -45 & 31 & 51 \end{bmatrix}$

B. $\begin{bmatrix} 21 & 10 \\ 3 & 9 \\ 18 & 7 \\ 41 & 30 \end{bmatrix}$

C. $\begin{bmatrix} 21 & 3 & 18 & 41 \\ 10 & 9 & 7 & 30 \end{bmatrix}$

D. $\begin{bmatrix} 13 & 5 \\ -64 & -45 \\ 20 & 31 \\ 139 & 51 \end{bmatrix}$

21. Let s and t represent vectors and c represent a real constant. Which of the following does not represent one of the multiplicative properties of vectors?

A. $c(st) = (cs)t$

B. $0 \cdot s = s$

C. $1 \cdot s = s$

D. $s \cdot s = |s|^2$

22. If $|k + 3| < 2$, which of the following alternatives is true?

Alternative I: k is a negative number

Alternative II: $k + 3 < 2$

Alternative III: $-k - 3 < -2$

A. Alternatives I and II only

B. Alternative III only

C. Alternative II only

D. Alternative I only

23. Find the values of x and y in the following matrix equation.

$$3\begin{bmatrix} -4 & 5x \\ y & 4 \end{bmatrix} + 5\begin{bmatrix} -2 & -y \\ 3x & 3 \end{bmatrix} = \begin{bmatrix} 5 & 8 \\ 6 & -9 \end{bmatrix}$$

    A. $x = -\dfrac{7}{15}; \ y = -3$

    B. $x = \dfrac{28}{15}; \ y = 4$

    C. $x = \dfrac{1}{4}; \ y = \dfrac{7}{20}$

    D. $x = \dfrac{7}{20}, \ y = \dfrac{1}{4}$

24. Find the length of the vector $\langle 5, -9, -12 \rangle$.

    A. 250

    B. $\sqrt{200}$

    C. 200

    D. $\sqrt{250}$

25. Which is the sum of the prime factors of 120?

    A. 7

    B. 14

    C. 10

    D. 8

26. Indicate the alternative that represents the smallest whole number that has a remainder of 1 when it is divided by 2, 3, 4, 5, 6 and 7.

    A. 421

    B. 211

    C. 141

    D. 61

27. If $(x^a)(x^b) = \dfrac{x^c}{x^d}$, how would you define d in terms of a, b and c?

    A. $a + b - c$

    B. $c - a - b$

    C. $c - ab$

    D. $ab - c$

28. Which one of the following pair of factors does not have a Least Common Multiple (LCM) equal to 120?

    A. 30, 40

    B. 8, 15

    C. 30, 80

    D. 20, 24

GO ON TO THE NEXT PAGE

29. Which of the following statements about operations with odd and even number is false?

    A. The product of an odd number multiplied by an odd number is always an even number.
    B. The sum of an even number plus an odd is always equal to an odd number.
    C. The product of an even number multiplied by an odd number is always an even number.
    D. The sum of an odd number and an odd number is always equal to an even number.

30. Which of the following is the Least Common Multiple (LCM) of the following set of algebraic expressions? $5abd$, $45a^3b$, and $60abd^2$.

    A. $60abd$
    B. $5ab$
    C. $180abd$
    D. $180a^3bd^2$

Constructed-Response Question: Use extra lined paper to answer this question.

31. Complete the exercise that follows.

Simplify the following mathematical expression and show each step of your work.

$$\dfrac{\dfrac{1}{x-1} - \dfrac{1}{x-2}}{\dfrac{1}{x-2} - \dfrac{1}{x-3}}$$

GO ON TO THE NEXT PAGE

Constructed-Response Question: Use extra lined paper to answer this question.

32. Complete the exercise that follows.

If a, b, and c are rational numbers with $a \neq 0$, $ax^2 + bx + c = 0$, and r_1 and r_2 are two roots, then use the quadratic formula to find the following:

A. the sum of the roots,

B. the product of the roots, and

C. a quadratic equation for which the sum of the roots is 5 and the product of the roots is 5.

Constructed-Response Question: Use extra lined paper to answer this question.

33. Complete the exercise that follows.

Solve the following system of equations and use a graph to explain your answer:

$$\begin{cases} y = -x^2 + 7x - 5 \\ y - 2x = 2 \end{cases}$$

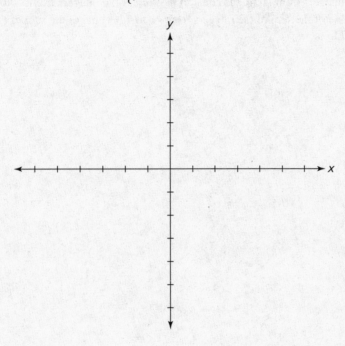

GO ON TO THE NEXT PAGE

Constructed-Response Question: Use extra lined paper to answer this question.

---

34. Complete the exercise that follows.

For each of the following statements, indicate whether it is a true or false statement and explain why you think it is true or false.

A. The product of the integers from –6 to 7 is equal to the product of the integers from –7 to 6.

B. The sum of the integers from –6 to 7 is equal to the sum of the integers from –7 to 6.

C. The absolute value of the sum of the integers from –6 to 7 is equal to the sum of the absolute value of the integers from –7 to 6.

Practice CSET: Mathematics Subtest II

Continue the test. Remember to read and follow the instructions carefully.

The set of multiple-choice questions and constructed-response questions presented in this Practice CSET: Mathematics Test II are similar to the questions you will see on the **Mathematics Subtest II: Geometry; Probability and Statistics**. This subtest includes the same amount of items you will find on the actual CSET: Mathematics test. We have included an answer key and explanation for each item's possible responses; however, we recommend and encourage you to respond to the items without looking at these sections of this book. You should record your responses on a separate sheet of paper and review your answers with the provided responses afterward.

As you complete this subsection of the practice exam, you should consider the guidelines given by the Department of Education regarding the use of calculators for this test: A calculator will be needed and **will be only allowed for Mathematics Subtest II: Geometry; Probability and Statistics**. You must bring your own graphing calculator to the test administration, and it must be one of the approved models listed in the current version of the CSET registration bulletin. Since the approved calculator brands and models are subject to change, the list of approved graphing calculators will be updated as necessary (check the following site for updates of approved calculators: www.cset.nesinc.com/CS12_testselection.asp#graph). Test administration staff will clear the memory of your calculator before and after the test. Be sure you back up the memory on your calculator, including applications, to an external device before arriving at the test site.

35. A packing company is designing a box to package 36 cans. They need to decide what dimensions they want to use for the box. For example, they can use a box that is 1 can high, 6 cans wide, and 6 cans long, or $1 \cdot 6 \cdot 6$ for 36 cans.

    How many different total ways can the packing company arrange the 36 cans and make the boxes?

    A. 20
    B. 10
    C. 18
    D. 9

36. Find the approximate surface area of the circular cone illustrated in square centimeters.

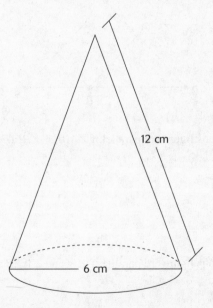

    A. 113.04 square centimeters
    B. 339.12 square centimeters
    C. 141.3 square centimeters
    D. 122.46 square centimeters

GO ON TO THE NEXT PAGE

37. Find the volume in cubic centimeters of the pyramid with a square base illustrated in the following figure.

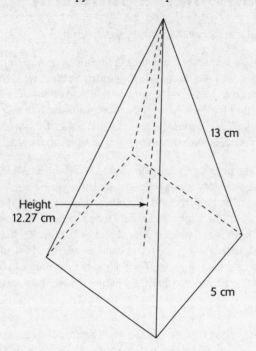

13 cm

Height
12.27 cm

5 cm

  A. 108.33 cm³
  B. 106.25 cm³
  C. 318.75 cm³
  D. 797.55 cm³

Note: Use the following figure for questions 38, 39, and 40.

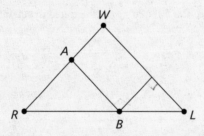

38. Which line segments in the previous figure are parallel if ∠ABE = ∠BEL?

  A. $\overline{AB}$ and $\overline{WL}$
  B. $\overline{RW}$ and $\overline{BE}$
  C. $\overline{RW}$ and $\overline{RL}$
  D. $\overline{AB}$ and $\overline{BE}$

39. Which line segments in the previous figure are parallel if ∠W and ∠WEB are supplementary?

  A. $\overline{AB}$ and $\overline{WE}$
  B. $\overline{AW}$ and $\overline{BE}$
  C. $\overline{WL}$ and $\overline{AB}$
  D. $\overline{AB}$ and $\overline{BE}$

40. Which line segments in the previous figure are parallel if $\angle R = \angle EBL$?

    A. $\overline{WL}$ and $\overline{AB}$

    B. $\overline{AB}$ and $\overline{WE}$

    C. $\overline{AW}$ and $\overline{AB}$

    D. $\overline{RA}$ and $\overline{BE}$

41. Use the following figure for this problem. Given that $\overline{AB}$ is parallel to $\overline{DC}$, which of the following alternatives is equal to the sum of angles x and y?

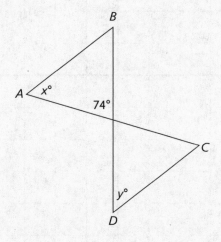

    A. 106°

    B. 90°

    C. 74°

    D. 47°

42. In the following figure, $\overline{MN}$ is parallel to $\overline{YZ}$, and $\angle XYZ = 90°$. What is the length of $\overline{XN}$?

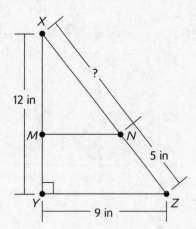

    A. 15 in.

    B. 3 in.

    C. 7 in.

    D. 10 in.

GO ON TO THE NEXT PAGE

43. What is the distance between points *M* and *N* on the following graph?

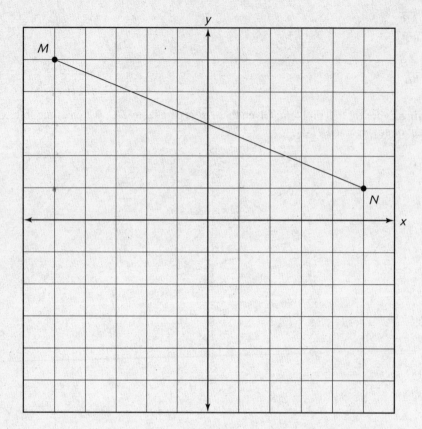

    A. $2\sqrt{29}$
    B. $4\sqrt{29}$
    C. 58
    D. 29

44. Using the following figure, where $\overrightarrow{AG}$ is perpendicular to $\overrightarrow{EF}$, and the measure of ∠*ACB* is equal to 30°, what is the measure of ∠*BCF*?

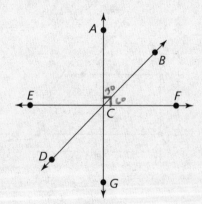

    A. 60°
    B. 30°
    C. 90°
    D. 150°

45. The diameter of a bicycle wheel is 35 inches long. About how far does this bicycle wheel travel in 120 revolutions of the wheel? Use 3.14 for π.

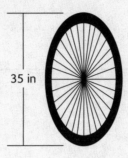

35 in

A. 1,099 ft.
B. 13,188 ft.
C. 2,198 ft.
D. 26,376 ft.

46. Two similar cylinders have a ratio of 2:3 for their radii and heights. What is the ratio for their volumes?

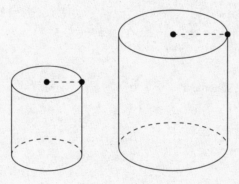

A. 4:6
B. 2:3
C. 8:27
D. 6:6

47. To the nearest hundredth of a centimeter, what is the area of the following figure?

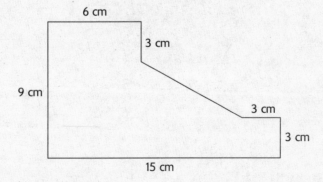

6 cm
3 cm
9 cm
3 cm
3 cm
15 cm

A. 99 cm²
B. 81 cm²
C. 135 cm²
D. 90 cm²

GO ON TO THE NEXT PAGE

48. As described by the following illustration, Alexandra is adding 5 meters to the length and 5 meters to the width of her 40-meter by 30-meter rectangular room. Which of the following expressions best represents the area of room that will be added to the garden?

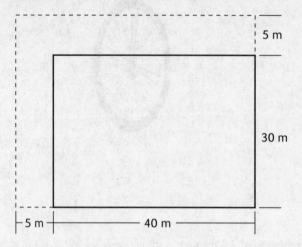

A. $(30 + 5)(40 + 5)$

B. $(30 - 5)(40 - 5)$

C. $(30 + 5)(40 + 5) - (30)(40)$

D. $(30 - 5)(40 - 5) - (30)(40)$

49. Which of the following is a true statement?

A. All trapezoids are similar.

B. All rhombi are similar.

C. All squares are similar.

D. All triangles are similar.

50. A ball has a diameter of 35 cm. If this ball is cut in half, what is the area (to the nearest square centimeter) of the cross section?

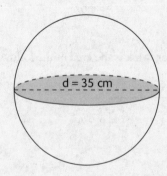

A. 962 cm^2

B. 3846 cm^2

C. 306 cm^2

D. 1225 cm^2

51. The figure below shows a line *l* with points *B* and *C*, and a point, *A*, not on the line. We can draw exactly one plane, *P*, that contains points *A*, *B*, and *C*. Which of the following sentences justify this statement?

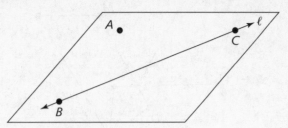

A. Three noncollinear points do not determine a plane.

B. Three collinear points determine a plane.

C. Two collinear points determine a plane.

D. Three noncollinear points determine a plane.

52. Which of the following statements describes the point-line relation illustrated by the following figure?

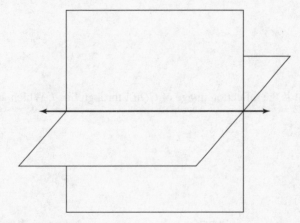

A. Two planes that do not intersect.

B. Two planes that intersect in a line.

C. A line that contains only one plane.

D. A line that intersects a two planes in two different points.

GO ON TO THE NEXT PAGE

Note: Use the following figure to answer questions 53 and 54.

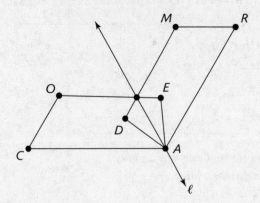

53. In the figure above, *RMDA* is the reflection image of *COEA* through line *l*. Which point is the reflection of point *O*?

    A. *D*

    B. *M*

    C. *E*

    D. *A*

54. In the figure above, *RMDA* is the reflection image of *COEA* through line *l*. Which angle is the reflection of ∠*CAE*?

    A. ∠*MRA*

    B. ∠*EAC*

    C. ∠*DAR*

    D. ∠*COE*

55. In the figure below, *IJKL* is an image of *ABCD* under a certain transformation. What transformation seems to relate *ABCD* and *IJKL*?

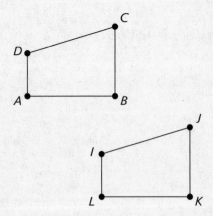

    A. a translation and a reflection

    B. a rotation

    C. a translation

    D. a reflection

56. In the figure below, $\triangle P'A'L'$ is an image of $\triangle PAL$ under a certain transformation. Which of the following is true about this situation?

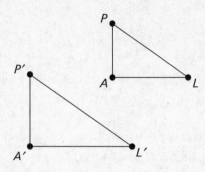

- **A.** It appears to be an isometry.
- **B.** It appears to preserve distance.
- **C.** The two triangles appear to be congruent.
- **D.** It appears to preserve collinearity.

57. There are two boxes of books in Peter's room. One box contains 2 biography books, 3 children's books, 2 self-help books, and 1 romance book. The other box contains 4 biography books, 1 children's book, 2 self-help books, and 3 romance books. If Peter randomly selects one book from each box, what is the probability that both books are biography books?

- **A.** $\dfrac{1}{10}$
- **B.** $\dfrac{1}{3}$
- **C.** $\dfrac{2}{81}$
- **D.** $\dfrac{9}{20}$

58. A bowl contains 5 blue marbles, 11 red marbles, 15 green marbles, and 7 yellow marbles. The red marbles and yellow marbles are the only ones that have a plastic cover for each marble. What is the probability that you will randomly select a marble that has a plastic cover for it from the bowl?

- **A.** $\dfrac{7}{38}$
- **B.** $\dfrac{11}{38}$
- **C.** $\dfrac{1}{2}$
- **D.** $\dfrac{9}{19}$

59. If you roll two six-sided dice at the same time with the numbers 1, 2, 3, 4, 5, and 6 for each die, what is the probability of rolling 5 and 6?

- **A.** $\dfrac{1}{2}$
- **B.** $\dfrac{1}{6}$
- **C.** $\dfrac{1}{18}$
- **D.** $\dfrac{1}{36}$

GO ON TO THE NEXT PAGE

60. You have two bags of marbles. The first bag has two red, one yellow, and two green. The second bag has two blue, two black, and one purple. What is the probability that you will draw a yellow marble from the first bag and a purple marble from the second bag?

A. $\frac{1}{50}$

B. $\frac{1}{5}$

C. $\frac{1}{25}$

D. $\frac{2}{25}$

Note: Use the following data set for items 61, 62, 63, and 64.

The students in a class received the following scores in a test worth 25 points:

12, 13, 10, 14, 23, 12, 13, 22, 12, 12, 10, 11, 15, 20, 10, 12, 10, 15, 22, 23

61. What is the mean of the data set?

A. 12
B. 14.55
C. 12.5
D. 291

62. What is the median of the data set?

A. 12.5
B. 14
C. 13
D. 12

63. What is the mode of the data set?

A. 10
B. 12
C. 2
D. 10 and 12

64. What is the range of the data set?

A. 4
B. 14
C. 12
D. 13

Constructed-Response Question: Use extra lined paper to answer this question.

65. Complete the exercise that follows.

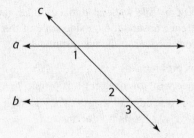

Given lines *a* and *b* with transversal *c*, ∠1 and ∠2 are supplementary angles. Prove that lines *a* and *b* are parallel lines.

GO ON TO THE NEXT PAGE

Constructed-Response Question: Use extra lined paper to answer this question.

66. Complete the exercise that follows.

Suppose that you want to build a 400-cm wide walk around a circular garden. The circular garden has a diameter of 132 cm. You also want to build a fence around the outside edge of the walk with an opening of about 50 cm to get in and out the garden. Express your answer to the nearest meter.

A. Make a drawing describing this problem.
B. About how many meters of fence will you need for this project?
C. If you put the fence around the inside edge of the garden, you save $375. Given this scenario, about how much does one meter of fencing cost? Explain your answer.

Constructed-Response Question: Use extra lined paper to answer this question.

67. Complete the exercise that follows.

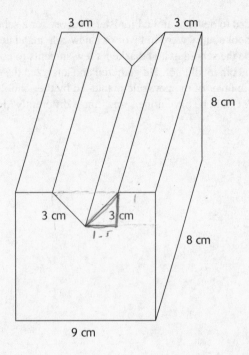

Find the volume of the solid figure illustrated here, rounding to the nearest cubic centimeter.

Constructed-Response Question: Use extra lined paper to answer this question.

68. Complete the exercise that follows.

At a local school, Carlos decided to develop and administer a survey for a school project. He wanted to know whether the students in the school county were in favor of a new rule mandated by the school board. At the end of the school day, he stood outside the school exit and asked a few students to complete the survey as they went out. Some students participated, and others did not. He gathered and analyzed the data and concluded that the students in the school county were not in favor of the new rule mandated by the school board. Did Carlos interpret the results of the survey correctly? Could he have done some things differently? Explain your answer.

Practice CSET: Mathematics Subtest III

Continue the test. Remember to read and follow the instructions carefully.

The set of multiple-choice questions and constructed-response questions presented in this Practice CSET: Mathematics Test II are similar to the questions you will see on the **Subtest III: Calculus; History of Mathematics**. This subtest includes the same amount of items you will find on the actual CSET: Mathematics test. We have included an answer key and explanation for each item's possible responses; however, we recommend and encourage you to respond to the items without looking at these sections of this book. You should record your responses on a separate sheet of paper and review your answers with the provided responses afterward.

Note: The use of calculators is not allowed for the CSET: Mathematics Subtest III.

69. Let $f(x) = \begin{cases} x - 3 & if & x < -4 \\ 2x + 1 & if & -4 \le x < 4 \\ x^2 & if & x \ge 4 \end{cases}$.

Find $\lim\limits_{x \to 4} f(x)$.

A. 16
B. 9
C. does not exist
D. 1

70. Find all values of x in the interval $[0, 2\pi]$ which satisfy the equation $2\cos^2 x + \cos x - 1 = 0$.

A. $\left\{ \dfrac{\pi}{3}, \pi, \dfrac{5\pi}{3} \right\}$

B. $\left\{ 0, \dfrac{\pi}{3}, \dfrac{2\pi}{3}, \pi \right\}$

C. $\left\{ \dfrac{\pi}{6}, \pi, \dfrac{11\pi}{6} \right\}$

D. $\left\{ 0, \dfrac{\pi}{3}, \pi, \dfrac{5\pi}{3}, 2\pi \right\}$

71. What are the solutions to $\sin\left(x + \dfrac{\pi}{4}\right) = \dfrac{\sqrt{3}}{2}$ where $0 \le x \le 2\pi$?

A. $\dfrac{\pi}{12}, \dfrac{5\pi}{12}$

B. $\dfrac{7\pi}{12}, \dfrac{23\pi}{12}$

C. $\dfrac{\pi}{12}, \dfrac{17\pi}{12}$

D. $0, \dfrac{\pi}{2}$

GO ON TO THE NEXT PAGE

72. What is the slope of the line tangent to the curve $f(x) = 2x^3 + x^2 - 5x - 7$ when $x = -2$?

    A.   −9

    B.   15

    C.   −15

    D.   −22

73. Which of the following functions is **not** continuous on the interval $(-\infty, \infty)$?

    A. $f(x) = \sqrt[3]{2x - 5}$

    B. $f(x) = \dfrac{2x - 4}{x + 7}$

    C. $f(x) = 3x^2 + 2x - 5$

    D. $f(x) = \dfrac{3x + 7}{2}$

74. Find $\lim\limits_{x \to 1} \dfrac{\ln x}{2x - 2}$.

    A. $\dfrac{1}{2}$

    B. ∞

    C.   0

    D. $-\dfrac{1}{2}$

75. The Intermediate Value Theorem can be used to show there is a root in the interval $(-2,3)$ for which of the following equations?

    A. $y = x^2 - 4x + 5$

    B. $y = 2x^2 - x + 1$

    C. $y = -x^2 + 2x - 3$

    D. $y = -x^2 + 2x - 5$

76. Which of the following graphs represents $f(x) = 3 \sin\left(\dfrac{x}{2}\right) - 1$?

A.

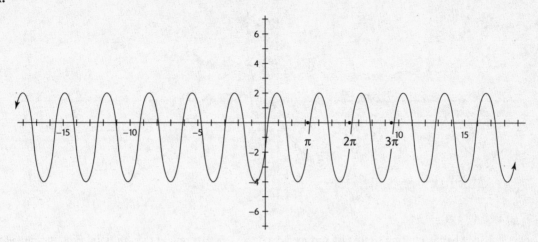

B.

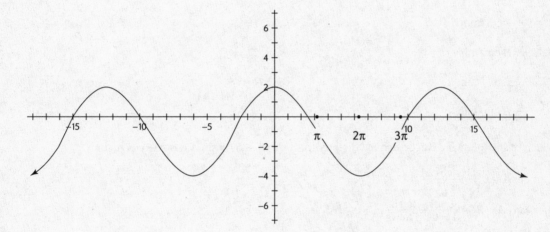

C.

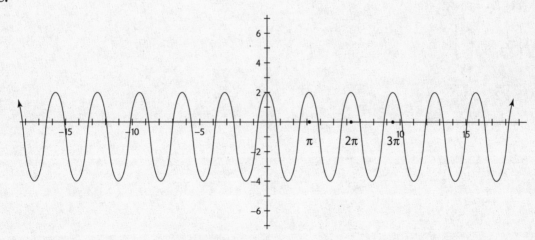

GO ON TO THE NEXT PAGE

D.

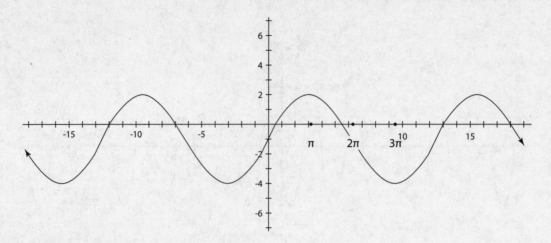

77. A spherical snowball is melting so that its surface area decreases at a rate of 0.5 cm²/min. Find the rate at which the diameter decreases when the diameter is 10 cm.

    A. $\dfrac{1}{40\pi}$ cm/min

    B. $\dfrac{1}{80}\pi$ cm/min

    C. $\dfrac{1}{80\pi}$ cm/min

    D. $\dfrac{1}{40}\pi$ cm/min

78. Which of the following can be derived directly from $\sin(A+B) = \sin A \cos B + \cos A \sin B$?

    A. $\cos A = \pm\sqrt{\dfrac{1+\cos 2A}{2}}$

    B. $\tan(A+B) = \dfrac{\tan A + \tan B}{1 - \tan A \tan B}$

    C. $\sin 2A = 2\sin A \cos A$

    D. $\cos 2A = \cos^2 A - \sin^2 A$

79. Find $\left(\dfrac{1}{\sqrt{2}} + \dfrac{1}{\sqrt{2}}i\right)^5$.

    A. $-\dfrac{1}{\sqrt{2}} + \dfrac{1}{\sqrt{2}}i$

    B. $-\dfrac{1}{\sqrt{2}} - \dfrac{1}{\sqrt{2}}i$

    C. $\dfrac{1}{\sqrt{2}} - \dfrac{1}{\sqrt{2}}i$

    D. $\dfrac{1}{\sqrt{2}} + \dfrac{1}{\sqrt{2}}i$

80. A bacteria culture begins with 500 bacteria. After 3 hours, the population is 2000 bacteria. Assuming the culture grows at a rate proportional to its size, find the population after 6 hours.

    A. 3500 bacteria
    B. 4000 bacteria
    C. 8000 bacteria
    D. 8500 bacteria

81. Express the number $1.\overline{32}$ as a rational number.

    A. $\dfrac{32}{99}$

    B. $1\dfrac{8}{25}$

    C. $1\dfrac{34}{99}$

    D. $1\dfrac{32}{99}$

82. Given the function $f(x) = x^4 - x^3 - 9x^2 + 12x + 6$. Find the interval(s) on which $f(x)$ is concave up.

    A. $\left(-1, \dfrac{3}{2}\right)$

    B. $\left(-\infty, \dfrac{3}{2}\right)$ and $(-1, \infty)$

    C. $(-\infty, -1)$ and $\left(\dfrac{3}{2}, \infty\right)$

    D. $(-1, -13)$

83. Find the volume of the solid obtained by rotating the region bound by the curves $y = -x^2 + 4$ and $y = 0$ about the y-axis.

    A. $\dfrac{2\pi}{3}$

    B. 7π

    C. 8π

    D. $\dfrac{22\pi}{3}$

84. Find the derivative of the function $g(x) = \displaystyle\int_x^4 (2t - 5)\, dt$.

    A. $g'(x) = -2x + 5$
    B. $g'(x) = 2x - 5$
    C. $g'(x) = 3$
    D. $g'(x) = -2x + 8$

85. Given the function $f(x) = x^2$ on the interval $[-2, 1]$ with partitions at $\{-2, -1.5, -1, -0.5, 0, 0.5, 1\}$. Find the Riemann Sum if the left endpoint of each subinterval is used.

    A. $\dfrac{35}{8}$

    B. $\dfrac{19}{8}$

    C. $\dfrac{29}{8}$

    D. $\dfrac{31}{8}$

GO ON TO THE NEXT PAGE

86. Find the Taylor series for $f(x) = x\cos x$ at $a = 0$.

A. $f(x) = \sum_{n=0}^{\infty} (-1)^n \dfrac{x^{2n+1}}{(2n)!}$

B. $f(x) = \sum_{n=0}^{\infty} (-1)^n \dfrac{x^{2n+1}}{(2n+1)!}$

C. $f(x) = \sum_{n=0}^{\infty} (-1)^n \dfrac{x^{2n}}{(2n)!}$

D. $f(x) = \sum_{n=0}^{\infty} (-1)^n \dfrac{x^{2n+2}}{(2n+1)!}$

87. Which of the following series is convergent for $-2 < r < 2$?

A. $\sum_{n=1}^{\infty} 4(2r)^{n-1}$

B. $\sum_{n=1}^{\infty} 3(4r)^{n-1}$

C. $\sum_{n=1}^{\infty} -2\left(\dfrac{r}{2}\right)^{n-1}$

D. $\sum_{n=1}^{\infty} -2(r)^{n-1}$

88. Find $\lim\limits_{x \to 2} \dfrac{2x^2 - x - 6}{3x^2 - 7x + 2}$.

A. $\dfrac{7}{5}$

B. -3

C. $\dfrac{1}{7}$

D. 0

89. Find all values of c that satisfy the Mean Value Theorem for $f(x) = x^2 + 2x - 5$ on the interval $[0, 2]$.

A. 1

B. -3

C. 0

D. No solution

90. Which of the following is equivalent to $1 + \sqrt{3}\,i$?

A. $2\left(\cos\left(\dfrac{\pi}{3}\right) - i\sin\left(\dfrac{\pi}{3}\right)\right)$

B. $2\left(\cos\left(\dfrac{\pi}{3}\right) + i\sin\left(\dfrac{\pi}{3}\right)\right)$

C. $2\left(\cos\left(\dfrac{\pi}{6}\right) + i\sin\left(\dfrac{\pi}{6}\right)\right)$

D. $2\left(\cos\left(\dfrac{\pi}{6}\right) - i\sin\left(\dfrac{\pi}{6}\right)\right)$

91. If the derivative of $f(x)$ can be represented by $\lim\limits_{h \to 0} \dfrac{3(x+h)^2 - 3(x+h) - 3x^2 + 2x}{h}$, which of the following represents $f(x)$?

  A. $f(x) = -3x^2 + 2x$
  B. $f(x) = 3x^2 - 2x$
  C. $f(x) = 3(x+h)^2 - 3(x+h)$
  D. $f(x) = 3x^2$

92. Find the sum of the series $\sum\limits_{n=1}^{11} 3n + 2$.

  A. 40
  B. 220
  C. 165
  D. 222

93. Find the area of the region bounded by the curves $f(x) = x^2 - 4$ and $g(x) = 2x - 1$.

  A. $-\dfrac{32}{3}$
  B. $\dfrac{22}{3}$
  C. $\dfrac{32}{3}$
  D. $-\dfrac{22}{3}$

94. Find the sum of the first 7 terms of the sequence $\dfrac{4}{3}, \dfrac{2}{3}, \dfrac{1}{3}, \dfrac{1}{6} \cdots$

  A. $\dfrac{127}{48}$
  B. $\dfrac{8}{3}$
  C. $\dfrac{85}{32}$
  D. $\dfrac{508}{3}$

95. Which of the following people groups had a numeration system which involved place value?

  A. Babylonians
  B. Egyptians
  C. Greeks
  D. Romans

96. The Sieve of Eratosthenes can be used to identify which of the following?

  A. Pythagorean Triples
  B. Greatest common factor
  C. Prime numbers
  D. Least common multiples

97. Sofia Kovalevskaya was known for her contributions to which area of mathematics?

  A. Differential equations
  B. Algebra
  C. Geometry
  D. Number theory

GO ON TO THE NEXT PAGE

98. The Bridges of Konigsburg was a problem-inspired work in the field of topology by what famous mathematician?

    A. Pythagoras

    B. Leonhard Euler

    C. Isaac Newton

    D. Euclid

Constructed-Response Question: Use extra lined paper to answer this question.

99. Complete the exercise that follows.

Use the formal (precise) definition of a limit to show $\lim_{x \to 2} (2x + 4) = 8$.

GO ON TO THE NEXT PAGE

Constructed-Response Question: Use extra lined paper to answer this question.

100. Complete the exercise that follows.

The main Pythagorean Identity is given as $\sin^2 x + \cos^2 x = 1$. Use this to prove the other two Pythagorean Identities, namely $1 + \tan^2 x = \sec^2 x$ and $1 + \cot^2 x = \csc^2 x$.

Constructed-Response Question: Use extra lined paper to answer this question.

101. Complete the exercise that follows.

Use the definition of a derivative to show the following:

If $F(x) = f(x)g(x)$, $f'(x)$, and $g'(x)$ both exist, then $F'(x) = f(x)g'(x) - g(x)f'(x)$.

GO ON TO THE NEXT PAGE

Constructed-Response Question: Use extra lined paper to answer this question.

102. Complete the exercise that follows.

Use the figure below to prove the Pythagorean Theorem.

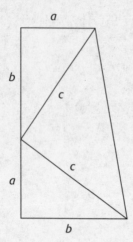

Answer Key for Practice CSET: Mathematics Test II

1. D
2. B
3. A
4. B
5. C
6. D
7. B
8. C
9. B
10. A
11. C
12. D
13. A
14. B
15. D
16. C
17. C
18. A
19. C
20. A
21. B
22. A
23. D
24. D
25. C
26. A
27. B
28. C
29. A
30. D
31. Written or Constructed-Response Question. See solution section for details.
32. Written or Constructed-Response Question. See solution section for details.
33. Written or Constructed-Response Question. See solution section for details.
34. Written or Constructed-Response Question. See solution section for details.
35. B

36. C

37. B

38. A

39. B

40. D

41. A

42. D

43. A

44. A

45. A

46. C

47. D

48. C

49. C

50. A

51. D

52. B

53. B

54. C

55. C

56. D

57. A

58. D

59. C

60. C

61. B

62. A

63. B

64. D

65. Written or Constructed-Response Question. See solution section for details.

66. Written or Constructed-Response Question. See solution section for details.

67. Written or Constructed-Response Question. See solution section for details.

68. Written or Constructed-Response Question. See solution section for details.

69. C

70. A

71. A

72. B

73. B

74. A

75. D

76. D

77. A

78. C

79. B

80. C

81. D

82. C

83. C

84. A

85. D

86. A

87. C

88. A

89. A

90. B

91. B

92. B

93. C

94. A

95. A

96. C

97. A

98. B

99. Written or Constructed-Response Question. See solution section for details.

100. Written or Constructed-Response Question. See solution section for details.

101. Written or Constructed-Response Question. See solution section for details.

102. Written or Constructed-Response Question. See solution section for details.

Solutions for Practice CSET: Mathematics Test II

Use these answers and explanations to help you understand possible solutions and improve your test-taking ability. Remember that you are recommended and encouraged to complete the test before looking at the possible solutions and explanations. Record your answers and responses on a separate piece of paper and then compare them with the response provided here. You should not take more that one practice exam per day. You need some wait time before taking and reviewing the other practice exams (at least one day). You might have used a different path for your solution. This is okay; if you get to the same answer and the procedures you used are mathematically accurate, you don't need to have the same solution process. It is good to also learn other ways to solve the problem. Also, you might want to check the domain given in parentheses for each item. This will give an idea of your strengths and weaknesses for different topics and where you might need extra practice or review.

Some of the multiple-choice questions have been identified as **ENHANCED**. This term is used to indicate that these items are complex multiple-choice questions, which require 2–3 minutes each to complete. Enhanced multiple-choice question will not be identified on the actual CSET: Mathematics test. No calculators are allowed for the CSET: Mathematics Subtests I and III. Graphing calculators are allowed for CSET: Mathematics Subtest II.

Practice CSET: Mathematics Subset I

This Subtest involves algebra (items 1–24, and 31–33) and number theory (items 25–30, and 34).

Algebra

1. The best choice for this item is **D.** (SMR 1.1. **Algebraic Structures**)

   Complex numbers cannot be shown of a number line. They require a two-dimensional number plane. The other numbers (rational, integers, and natural numbers) can be shown on a number line.

2. The best choice for this item is **B.** (SMR 1.2 **Polynomial Equations and Inequalities**) (ENHANCED)

   You can find the solution to the equation $x^2 - 4x + 13 = 0$ by using the quadratic formula:

   $$\frac{-b \pm \sqrt{b^2 - 4ac}}{2a} = \frac{-(-4) \pm \sqrt{4^2 - 4(1)(13)}}{2(1)}$$
   Substitute: $a = 1$, $b = -4$, and $c = 13$.

   $$= \frac{4 \pm \sqrt{16 - 52}}{2}$$
   Multiply.

   $$= = \frac{4 \pm \sqrt{-36}}{2}$$
   Subtract: $16 - 52 = -36$.

   $$= = \frac{4 \pm 6i}{2}$$
   $\sqrt{-36} = \sqrt{-1} \cdot \sqrt{36} = i \cdot 6 = 6i$.

   $$= 2 \pm 3i$$
   Divide by 2.

3. The best choice for this item is **A.** (SMR 1.1 **Algebraic Structures**)

$(i + 1)^2 = (i + 1)(i + 1)$	Equivalent forms.
$= i^2 + 2i + 1$	Multiply.
$= -1 + 2i + 1$	Simplify: $-1 + 1 = 0$.
$= 2i$	Answer.

4. The best choice for this item is **B. (SMR 1.3 Functions)**

The range of a function is the set of all the second components of the ordered pairs that make up the function. The domain of a function is the set of all the first components of the ordered pair that make up the function. In this case, we have that if the given function $g(x) = \dfrac{g^2 - 16}{g^2 + 9} = 1$, then $g^2 - 16$ must be equal to $g^2 + 9$, which is impossible because $g^2 - 16 < g^2 + 9$. This implies that 1 is not in the range of this function.

The other possible values are part of the range of the function g. You can verify this, but you do not need to verify it.

5. The best choice for this item is **C. (SMR 1.3 Functions)**

This is because finding the square root of a negative number is undefined under the set of real numbers. You will need to use complex numbers as part of the range of the function to be able to find a solution.

6. The best choice for this item is **D. (SMR 1.4 Linear Algebra)**

In order for the vectors to be perpendicular, the dot product must be zero. Examining each pair gives the following:

A. dot product $= (-5)(-3) + (-3)(-5) = 15 + 15 = 30$
B. dot product $= (5)(-3) + (-3)(5) = -15 + -15 = -30$
C. dot product $= (-5)(3) + (3)(-5) = -15 + -15 = -30$
D. dot product $= (-5)(-3) + (3)(-5) = 15 + -15 = 0$

The only solution that has a dot product of zero is Choice **D.**

7. The best choice for this item is **B. (SMR 1.1 Algebraic Structures)**

Natural numbers, rational numbers, and real numbers can all be found on a one-dimensional number line. However, to find the solution of the equation $x^2 = -9$, you need to move off the number line. The solution to this equation is a complex number, written as $3i$. By definition, the number i is one unit from 0, but off the one-dimensional number line, and a number whose square is -1: $i^2 = -1$. Complex numbers cannot be shown on the one-dimensional number line.

8. The best choice for this item is **C. (SMR 1.1 Algebra)**

$(a + bi)(a - bi) = a^2 - abi + abi - b^2 i^2$ Multiply.

$= a^2 - b^2(-1)$ Combine like terms.

$= a^2 + b^2$ Answer.

9. The best choice for this item is **B. (SMR 1.3 Functions)**

A relation is a function if and only if no vertical line can be drawn that interests the graph of the relation more than once. In this case, only graph B fails the vertical line test.

10. This best choice for this item is **A. (SMR 1.3 Functions)**

The graph of alternative **A** does not pass the vertical line test for a graph to be a function. The graph of $x = 5$ is a vertical line that passes through the ordered pairs (5, 0), (5, 1), (5, 2), and so on. Since there is more than one ordered pair whose first component is 5, this equation is not a function. All of the other alternatives pass the vertical line test and are functions.

11. The best choice for this item is **C. (SMR 1.1 Algebraic Structures)**

By definition, we know that $i = \sqrt{-1}$, so $\sqrt{-16} = \sqrt{-1} \cdot \sqrt{16}$. Remember that when the number under the radical is negative, the number is imaginary or part of the complex number system.

12. The best answer for this item is **D. (SMR 1.2 Polynomials Equations and Inequalities)**

The region that represents the solution for the system of inequalities $y - x \leq -1$ and $x + y \leq 4$ is region D.

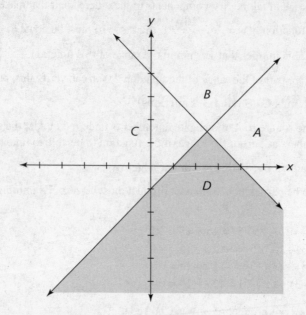

13. The best answer for this item is **A. (SMR 1.2 Polynomial Equations and Inequalities) (ENHANCED)**

You must be able to raise i to any positive integer power. The following is a list of the most frequent ones:

$i^1 = i$ — Remember that $a^1 = a$ for any number.

$i^2 = -1$ — This true by definition of imaginary numbers.

$i^3 = -i$ — $\quad i^3 = i \cdot i \cdot i = (i \cdot i) \cdot i = i^2 \cdot i = -1(i) = -i$

$i^4 = 1$ — $\quad i^4 = i \cdot i \cdot i \cdot i = (i \cdot i)(i \cdot i) = (-1)(-1) = 1$

$i^5 = i$ — $\quad i^5 = i^4 \cdot i = 1 \cdot i = i$

$i^6 = -1$ — $\quad i^6 = i^5 \cdot i = i \cdot i = i^2 = -1$

$i^7 = -i$ — $\quad i^7 = i^6 \cdot i = -1 \cdot i = -i$

$i^8 = 1$ — $\quad i^8 = i^7 \cdot i = -i \cdot i = -i^2 = -(-1) = 1$

The pattern of i form a repeating sequence in which four terms repeat: i, -1, $-i$, and 1. It repeats in this order indefinitely. This also implies that to find the value of i^n, where n is any positive integer, you can find the divide n by 4 and calculate the remainder. This gives us two situations:

- If n is a multiple of 4, $i^n = 1$.

- If n is not a multiple of 4, $i^n = i^r$, where r is the remainder when n is divided by 4.

In this item, we have that $i^2 = -1$ and $i^4 = 1$. Also, we have the following: $ai^2 = bi^4 \Rightarrow a(-1) = b(1) \Rightarrow -a = b$

Alternative I, $a = b$, could be true if a and b were each 0, but it is not always true.

Alternative II, $a = -b$, is true.

Alternative III, $|a| = |b|$, is true because $|a| = |-b| = |b|$.

So, only alternatives II and III are true for this item.

14. The best choice for this item is **B.** (**1.2 Polynomials Equations and Inequalities**) (ENHANCED)

If i^2 is -1, what is the value of $i^{27} - (-i)^{27}$?

i^{27} is equal to i^r, where r is the remainder of 27 divided by 4. In this case, we have that $27 \div 4 = 6$ with a remainder of 3, because $6 \cdot 4 + 3 = 27$. Therefore,

$i^{27} = i^3$ and $(-i)^{27}$

$\quad = (-1)^{27}(i)^{25}$

$\quad = -1(i)^3 = -i^3$.

Since $i^3 = -i$, then $-i^3 = i$, and

$i^{27} - (-i)^{27} = i^3 - (-i^3)$

$\qquad\qquad = -i - i$

$\qquad\qquad = -2i$.

15. The best choice for this item is **D.** (**SMR 1.2 Polynomials Equations and Inequalities**)

You need to solve the equation $\sqrt{2n} + 5 = 3$:

$\sqrt{2n} + 5 - 5 = 3 - 5$	Subtract 5 from both sides of the equation.
$\sqrt{2n} + 0 = -2$	$5 - 5 = 0$, and $3 - 5 = -2$
$\sqrt{2n} = -2$	Simplify.

We know that by definition a square root cannot be a negative number; this equation has no solution.

16. The best choice for this item is **C.** (**SMR 1.3 Functions**) (ENHANCED)

Given that $f(x) = x^2 - 1$, and $g(x) = x^2 + 1$, we have the following relationships.

$(f \circ g)(x) = f(g(x))$

$\qquad\qquad = f(x^2 + 1)$

$\qquad\qquad = (x^2 + 1)^2 - 1$

$\qquad\qquad = (x^4 + 2x^2 + 1) - 1$

$\qquad\qquad = x^4 + 2x^2$

$(g \circ f)(x) = g(f(x))$

$\qquad\qquad = g(x^2 - 1)$

$\qquad\qquad = (x^2 - 1)^2 + 1$

$\qquad\qquad = (x^4 - 2x^2 + 1) + 1$

$\qquad\qquad = x^4 - 2x^2 + 2$

Then we have that $(f \circ g)(x) - (g \circ f)(x) = (x^4 + 2x^2) - (x^4 - 2x^2 + 2) = 4x^2 - 2$.

17. The best choice for this item is **C.** (**SMR 1.3 Functions**)

Remember that an equation of the form $y = b_x$, with $b > 0$ and $b \neq 1$) is called an exponential function. The exponential function with base b can be written in the following manner:

$y = f(x) = b_x$

The inverse of an exponential function is called a logarithmic function and can be written in the following manner:

$f^{-1}(x) = \log_b x$

If M, N, p, and b are positive numbers and $b = 1$, then the correct form of alternative C is the following: $\log_b M^p = p \log_b M$ instead of $\log_b M^p = p \log_b N$. The other alternatives are correct logarithm properties.

18. The best choice for this item is **A. (SMR 1.3 Functions)**

In this case, we can say that $12 = 4 \cdot 3$ and that $\log_{10}12 = \log_{10}(4)(3)$.

One of the logarithm properties states that $\log_b M\,N = \log_b M + \log_b N$. Therefore, we have the following solution:

$\log_{10}12 = \log_{10}4 + \log_{10}3$

$\qquad = 0.6021 + 0.4771$

$\qquad = 1.0792$

19. The best choice for this item is **C. (SMR 1.4 Linear Algebra) (ENHANCED)**

The vector's ordered pair is determined by subtracting the coordinates of the endpoint from the corresponding coordinates of the tip. In this case, the tip of $\overrightarrow{MN}$ is the point corresponding to the second letter of the notation, which is N. The endpoint is the point corresponding to the first letter of the notation, which is M. Also, notice that the vectors involved in this problem do not lie at the origin.

First, you need to find the order pair that represents $\overrightarrow{MN}$:

$\overrightarrow{MN}$ has ordered pairs $(5, {}^-4)$ and $N = ({}^-8, 3)$.

$\overrightarrow{MN}$ vector ordered pair $= \langle {}^-8 - 5, 3 - {}^-4 \rangle = \langle {}^-13, 7 \rangle$. Remember that usually the "$\langle\ \rangle$" notation indicates vectors.

Then find the vector ordered pair that represents each of the vectors:

- $\overrightarrow{QR}$ has ordered pairs $Q = ({}^-4, 5)$ and $R = (3, {}^-8)$.

  $\overrightarrow{QR}$ vector ordered pair $= \langle 3 - {}^-4, {}^-8 - 5 \rangle = \langle 7, {}^-13 \rangle$.
- $\overrightarrow{LP}$ has ordered pairs $({}^-5, 4)$ and $P = ({}^-3, 8)$.

  $\overrightarrow{LP}$ vector ordered pair $= \langle {}^-3 - {}^-5, 8 - 4 \rangle = \langle 2, 4 \rangle$.
- $\overrightarrow{ST}$ has ordered pairs $(5, {}^-3)$ and $T = ({}^-8, 4)$.

  $\overrightarrow{ST}$ vector ordered pair $= \langle {}^-8 - 5, 4 - {}^-3 \rangle = \langle {}^-13, 7 \rangle$.

You should see that only $\overrightarrow{ST}$ is equal to $\overrightarrow{MN}$.

20. The best choice for this item is **A. (SMR 1.4 Linear Algebra) (ENHANCED)**

Given that A is a 2-by-3 matrix, and B is a 3-by-4 matrix, the resulting product AB is a 2-by-4 matrix. This means that responses **B** and **C** are not possible answers. We are left with responses **A** or **D**. AB is equal to the product of A and B:

$$AB = \begin{bmatrix} 4 & 5 & 9 \\ 0 & 5 & 2 \end{bmatrix} \begin{bmatrix} 2 & 4 & -8 & 8 \\ 1 & -7 & 5 & 7 \\ 0 & -5 & 3 & 8 \end{bmatrix}$$

$$= \begin{bmatrix} 4 \cdot 2 + 5 \cdot 1 + 9 \cdot 0 & 4 \cdot 4 + 5(-7) + 9 \cdot (-5) & 4 \cdot (-8) + 5 \cdot 5 + 9 \cdot 3 & 4 \cdot 8 + 5 \cdot 7 + 9 \cdot 8 \\ 0 \cdot 2 + 5 \cdot 1 + 2 \cdot 0 & 0 \cdot 4 + 5 \cdot (-7) + 2 \cdot (-5) & 0 \cdot (-8) + 5 \cdot 5 + 2 \cdot 3 & 0 \cdot 8 + 5 \cdot 7 + 2 \cdot 8 \end{bmatrix}$$

$$= \begin{bmatrix} 8 + 5 + 0 & 16 + {}^-35 + {}^-45 & -32 + 25 + 27 & 32 + 35 + 72 \\ 0 + 5 + 0 & 0 + {}^-35 + {}^-10 & 0 + 25 + 6 & 0 + 35 + 16 \end{bmatrix}$$

$$= \begin{bmatrix} 13 & -64 & 20 & 139 \\ 5 & -45 & 31 & 51 \end{bmatrix}$$

21. The best choice for this item is **B. (SMR 1.4 Linear Algebra)**

$0 \cdot s = 0$ instead of s. The other alternatives are correct.

22. The best choice for this item is **A.** (SMR 1.2 **Polynomials Equations and Inequalities**)

$|k + 3| < 2$ implies that $-2 < k + 3 < 2$. From this, we know that alternative II is true: $k + 3 < 2$.

Since $k + 3 < 2$, we know that $k + 3 - 3 < 2 - 3$, or $k < -1$. So, k must be a negative number, and Alternative I is also true.

Alternative III is equivalent to saying the following: $k + 3 > 2$. This is false because $k + 3 < 2$.

Alternatives I and II are true.

23. The best choice for this item is **D.** (SMR 1.4 **Linear Algebra**) (ENHANCED)

Multiply both matrices by the corresponding factor: $\begin{bmatrix} -12 & 15x \\ 3y & 12 \end{bmatrix} + \begin{bmatrix} 10 & -5y \\ 15x & 15 \end{bmatrix}$

Adding the right hand side together gives you

$$\begin{bmatrix} -12 + 10 & 15x + (-5y) \\ 3y + 15x & 12 + 15 \end{bmatrix} = \begin{bmatrix} -2 & 15x + (-5y) \\ 3y + 15x & 27 \end{bmatrix}.$$

Therefore, we can set up a system of equations $\begin{cases} 15x + (-5y) = 8 \\ 3y + 15x = 6 \end{cases}$.

We can multiply the second equation by -1 and add it to the first to eliminate the x variable. Then we have:

$\begin{cases} 15x - 5y = 8 \\ -15x - 3y = 6 \end{cases} \Rightarrow -8y = 2$

Therefore, $y = 2/8 = 1/4$. Substituting back into the original equations gives the following:

$$3y + 15x = 6$$
$$3\left(\frac{1}{4}\right) + 15x = 6$$
$$\frac{3}{4} + 15x = 6$$
$$15x = 6 - \frac{3}{4}$$
$$x = 5\frac{1}{4} \div 15$$
$$x = \frac{7}{20}$$

24. The best choice for this item is **D.** (SMR 1.4 **Linear Algebra**)

The length of a vector $\langle x, y, z \rangle$ is $\sqrt{x^2 + y^2 + z^2}$. For this vector, the length is $\sqrt{(5)^2 + (-9)^2 + (-12)^2} = \sqrt{25 + 81 + 144} = \sqrt{250}$.

Number Theory

25. The best choice for this item is **C.** (SMR 3.1 **Natural Numbers**)

The prime factors of 120 are 2, 3, and 5. The sum of these prime factors is $2 + 3 + 5 = 10$.

There are several ways to find the prime factors of 120. One of them is to use the divisibility rules, when possible using prime numbers less than 11 (the square root 120 is approximately less than 11) or 2, 3, 5, and 7:

- Since 120 is an even number, then it is divisible by 2.
- Since the sum of the digits of 120 $(1 + 2 + 0 = 3)$ is divisible by 3, then 120 is also divisible by 3.
- Since the last digit of 120 is 0, then 120 is divisible by 5.
- There is no divisibility rule for 7, but we know that 120 is not divisible by 7.

26. The best choice for this item is **A**. (**SMR 3.1 Natural Numbers**) (ENHANCED)

In this problem, you need to find the least common multiple (LCM) of 2, 3, 4, 5, 6, and 7.

This is equal to $7 \cdot 3 \cdot 5 \cdot 4 = 420$. This number is then divisible by whole numbers from 2 to 7.

The smallest number that has a reminder of 1 when it is divided by these numbers is $420 + 1 = 421$.

27. The best choice for this item is **B**. (**SMR 3.1 Natural Numbers**) (ENHANCED)

If $\left(x^a\right)\left(x^b\right) = \dfrac{x^c}{x^d}$, then we have that by definition $(x^a)(x^b) = x^{a+b}$, and $\dfrac{x^c}{x^d} = x^{c-d}$. So, $a + b = c - d$.

This implies that $a + b + d = c$, and $d = c - a - b$. This is alternative **B**.

28. The best choice for this item is **C**. (**SMR3.1 Natural Numbers**)

One way to solve this problem is by using prime factorization. Find the prime factorization of each pair of numbers and then use these prime factorizations to find the LCM. Look at the common prime factors within each pair (shown with boxes for each pair below), use the highest exponent, and include all of the other common factors.

A. $30 = 2 \cdot 3 \cdot 5$, and	$40 = 2 \cdot 2 \cdot 2 \cdot 5$	$\text{LCM} = 2 \cdot 2 \cdot 2 \cdot 3 \cdot 5 = 120$	Yes
B. $8 = 2 \cdot 2 \cdot 2$, and	$15 = 3 \cdot 5$	$\text{LCM} = 2 \cdot 2 \cdot 2 \cdot 3 \cdot 5 = 120$	Yes
C. $30 = 2 \cdot 3 \cdot 5$, and	$80 = 2 \cdot 2 \cdot 2 \cdot 2 \cdot 5$	$\text{LCM} = 2 \cdot 2 \cdot 2 \cdot 2 \cdot 3 \cdot 5 = 240 \neq 120$	No
D. $20 = 2 \cdot 2 \cdot 5$, and	$24 = 2 \cdot 2 \cdot 2 \cdot 3$	$\text{LCM} = 2 \cdot 2 \cdot 2 \cdot 3 \cdot 5 = 120$	Yes

29. The best choice for this item is **A**. (**SMR 3.1 Natural Numbers**)

In this case, you need to find the statement about operations with odd and even numbers that is false. Let $2n$ be equal to any even number and $2n + 1$ be equal to any odd number and check each one of the statements to find out if they are true of false.

A. The product of an odd number multiplied by an odd number is always an even number. This one is false because the product of two odd numbers is always equal to an odd number:

$$(2n + 1)(2n + 1) = 4n^2 + 2n + 2n + 1$$
$$= (4n^2 + 4n) + 1$$

This will always give you an even number (in parentheses) plus one more, which is an odd number by definition.

B. The sum of an even number plus an odd is always equal to an odd number. This one is always true because the sum of an odd numbers plus an even number is always equal to an odd number:

$$(2n + 1) + 2n = (4n) + 1$$

This will always give you an even number (in parentheses) plus one more, which is an odd number by definition.

C. The product of an even number multiplied by an odd number is always an even number. This one is always true because the product of an even number and an odd number is always equal to an even number:

$$(2n)(2n + 1) = 4n^2 + 2n$$

This will always give you an even number.

D. The sum of an odd number and an odd number is always equal to an even number. This one is always true because the sum of an odd number plus an odd number is always equal to an even number:

$$(2n + 1) + (2n + 1) = (4n) + 2$$

This will always give you an even number (in parentheses) plus two more (even number), which is an even number plus an even number, which is equal to an even number.

30. This best choice for this item is **D. (SMR 3.1 Natural Numbers)**

First, you need to find the factorization of each multiple:

$5abd = 5 \cdot a \cdot b \cdot d$

$45a^3b = 3 \cdot 3 \cdot 5 \cdot a \cdot a \cdot a \cdot b$

$60abd^2 = 2 \cdot 2 \cdot 3 \cdot 5 \cdot a \cdot b \cdot d \cdot d$

Select the factors that are common and not common to all three multiples, or you can select the common and uncommon factors with largest exponent.

$\text{LCM} = 2^2 \cdot 3^2 \cdot 5 \cdot a^3 \cdot b \cdot d^2$

$\text{or } 2 \cdot 2 \cdot 3 \cdot 3 \cdot 5 \cdot a \cdot a \cdot a \cdot b \cdot d \cdot d$

$= 180 \cdot a \cdot a \cdot a \cdot b \cdot d \cdot d$

$= 180a^3bd^2$

Algebra

31. Written or Constructed-Response Question. (**SMR 1.2** Polynomial Equations and Inequalities.)

In this problem, you were supposed to simplify the following mathematical expression, and show each step of your work:

$$\frac{\dfrac{1}{x-1} - \dfrac{1}{x-2}}{\dfrac{1}{x-2} - \dfrac{1}{x-3}}$$

In this case, you should start by simplifying the expression in the numerator by using the addition rule:

$$\frac{a}{b} + \frac{c}{d} = \frac{ad + bc}{bd}$$

The denominator of the resulting fraction is bd, which is the LCM or least common denominator (LCD) of the two fractions.

In the denominator of the expression, we get the following:

$$\frac{1}{x-1} - \frac{1}{x-2} = \frac{x-2-(x-1)}{(x-1)(x-2)}$$

$$= \frac{-1}{(x-1)(x-2)}$$

You need to do the same with the denominator of the expression:

$$\frac{1}{x-2} - \frac{1}{x-3} = \frac{x-2-(x-3)}{(x-2)(x-3)}$$

$$= \frac{-1}{(x-2)(x-3)}$$

Combining the result of the numerator and denominator, we get the following:

$$\frac{\dfrac{-1}{(x-1)(x-2)}}{\dfrac{-1}{(x-2)(x-3)}}$$

Inverting the fraction in the denominator in the following manner and canceling like terms can simplify this resulting expression even more. This is the same as multiplying the numerator by the reciprocal of the denominator.

$$\frac{-1}{(x-1)(x-2)} \div \frac{-1}{(x-2)(x-3)} = \frac{-1}{(x-1)(x-2)} \cdot \frac{(x-2)(x-3)}{-1}$$ Multiply by reciprocal.

$$= \frac{(-1)(x-2)(x-3)}{(-1)(x-1)(x-2)}$$ Multiply.

$$= \frac{(\cancel{-1})(\cancel{x-2})(x-3)}{(\cancel{-1})(x-1)(\cancel{x-2})}$$ Cancel out common factors.

$$= \frac{x-3}{x-1}$$ Final simplification.

32. Written or Constructed-Response Question. (**SMR 1.2 Polynomial Equations and Inequalities**)

If a, b, and c are rational numbers with $a \neq 0$, $ax^2 + bx + c = 0$, and r_1 and r_2 are two roots, then use the quadratic formula to find the following:

a. The sum of the roots:

$$r_1 + r_2 = \frac{-b + \sqrt{b^2 - 4ac}}{2a} + \frac{-b - \sqrt{b^2 - 4ac}}{2a}$$ Substitute by using the quadratic formula.

$$= \frac{-b + \sqrt{b^2 - 4ac} - b - \sqrt{b^2 - 4ac}}{2a}$$ Use the common denominator $2a$.

$$= \frac{-2b + 0}{2a}$$ Subtract.

$$= \frac{-\cancel{2}b}{\cancel{2}a}$$ Simplify the fraction.

$$= \frac{-b}{a}$$ Sum of the two roots.

b. The product of the roots:

$$r_1 \cdot r_2 = \left(\frac{-b + \sqrt{b^2 - 4ac}}{2a} \right) \left(\frac{-b - \sqrt{b^2 - 4ac}}{2a} \right)$$

$$= \frac{b^2 - (b^2 - 4ac)}{4a^2}$$ Multiply the expressions.

$$= \frac{b^2 - b^2 + 4ac}{4a^2}$$ Remove parentheses.

$$= \frac{4ac}{4a^2}$$ Subtract: $b^2 - b^2 = 0$.

$$= \frac{c}{a}$$ Simplify to get the product of the two roots.

c. A quadratic equation for which the sum of the roots is 5 and the product of the roots is 5.

Let $a = 1$ to get the following,

$$\frac{-b}{a} = 5 \Rightarrow \frac{-b}{1} = 5 \Rightarrow b = -5, \text{ and}$$

$$\frac{c}{a} = 5 \Rightarrow \frac{c}{1} = 5 \Rightarrow c = 5.$$

So the equation $ax^2 + bx + c = 0$ is $(1)x^2 + (-5)x + 5 = 0$, or $x^2 - 5x + 5$, which satisfies the given conditions.

33. Written or Constructed-Response Question. (**SMR 1.3 Functions**)

Solve the following system of equations, and use a graph to explain your answer:

$$\begin{cases} y = -x^2 + 7x - 5 \\ y - 2x = 2 \end{cases}$$

First, you need to express the equation $y - 2x = 2$ for y in terms of x:

$y - 2x + 2x = 2x + 2$ Add $2x$ on both sides of the equality.

$\quad\quad y = 2x + 2$

Second, you need to substitute this expression in the $y = -x^2 + 7x - 5$ equation:

$2x + 2 = -x^2 + 7x - 5$

This substitution yields a single equation, in terms of a single variable (x), which can be solved. You need to write this equation in standard quadratic form:

$$2x + 2 = -x^2 + 7x - 5$$
$$2x + 2 + (x^2 + 5 - 7x) = -x^2 + 7x - 5 + (x^2 - 7x + 5)$$
$$2x + 2 + (x^2 + 5 - 7x) = 0$$
$$x^2 - 5x + 7 = 0$$

Since this equation is not factorable, its roots cannot be found by using factorization. You need to evaluate the discriminant to indicate whether it has real roots. The discriminant $b^2 - 4ac$ of this equation equals $(-5)2 - 4(1)(7) = 25 - 28 = -3$. The discriminant of this equation is a negative number. This implies that this equation does not have real roots, and the system has no real solutions.

The following figure shows a possible graph to explain the answer. The line is the graph for the equation $y - 2x = 2$ or $y = 2x + 2$, and the parabola is the graph for the other equation, $-x^2 + 7x - 5$. The figure shows that the parabola and the straight line do not have a point in common.

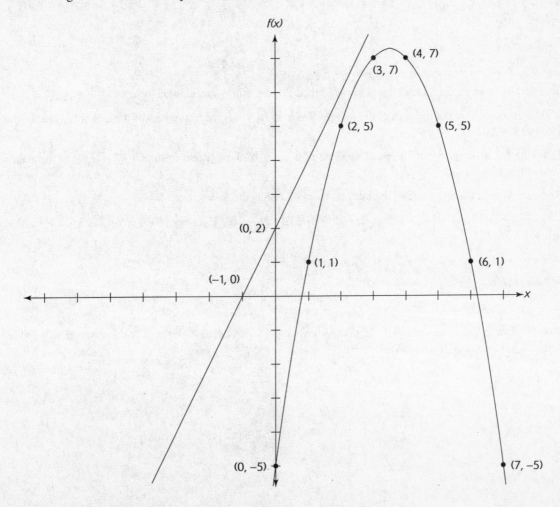

Number Theory

34. Written or Constructed-Response Question. (**SMR 3.1 Natural Numbers**)

For each of the following statements, indicate whether it is a true or false statement and explain why you think it is true or false.

A. The product of the integers from –6 to 7 is equal to the product of the integers from –7 to 6.

The integers from –6 to 7 are –6, –5, –4, –3, –2, –1, 0, 1, 2, 3, 4, 5, 6 and 7. The product of these integers is equal to zero. This is because zero is one of the integers.

The integers from –7 to 6 are –7, –6, –5, –4, –3, –2, –1, 0, 1, 2, 3, 4, 5, and 6. The product of these integers is also equal to zero because zero is one of the integers included. Since both products equal zero, the initial statement is true.

B. The sum of the integers from –6 to 7 is equal to the sum of the integers from –7 to 6.

The sum of the integers from –6 to 7 is the following:

$$-6 + -5 + -4 + -3 + -2 + -1 + 0 + 1 + 2 + 3 + 4 + 5 + 6 + 7 = (-6 + -5 + -4 + -3 + -2 + -1 + 0 + 1 + 2 + 3 + 4 + 5 + 6) + 7$$

$$= (0) + 7$$
$$= 7$$

The sum of the integers from –7 to 6 is the following:

$$-7 + -6 + -5 + -4 + -3 + -2 + -1 + 0 + 1 + 2 + 3 + 4 + 5 + 6 = -7 + (-6 + -5 + -4 + -3 + -2 + -1 + 0 + 1 + 2 + 3 + 4 + 5 + 6)$$

$$= -7 + (0)$$
$$= -7$$

The sum of these integers is not equal to each other. So, the initial statement is false.

C. The absolute value of the sum of the integers from –6 to 7 is equal to the sum of the absolute value of the integers from –7 to 6.

From the calculations above, the absolute value of the sum of the integers from –6 to 7 is equal to the absolute value of 7, which is 7.

The sum of the absolute value of the integers from –7 to 6 is the following:

$$|-7| + |-6| + |-5| + |-4| + |-3| + |-2| + |-1| + |0| + |1| + |2| + |3| + |4| + |5| + |6| = 7 + 6 + 5 + 4 + 3 + 2 + 1 + 0 + 1 + 2 + 3 + 4 + 5 + 6$$

$$= 7 + (6 + 5 + 4 + 3 + 2 + 1) + 0 + (1 + 2 + 3 + 4 + 5 + 6)$$

$$= 7 + (21) + 0 + (21)$$

$$= 49$$

The absolute value of the sum of the integers from –6 to 7 is not equal to the sum of the absolute value of the integers from –7 to 6. So, the initial statement is false.

Practice CSET: Mathematics Subset II

This Subtest involves Geometry (items 35–56 and 65–67) and Probability and Statistics (items 57–64 and 68).

Geometry

35. The best choice for this item is **B.** (**SMR 2.3 Three-Dimensional Geometry**) (ENHANCED)

The packing company can make 10 different types of boxes.

They can make the following combinations of cans:

$1 \cdot 1 \cdot 36$	$1 \cdot 4 \cdot 9$	$2 \cdot 3 \cdot 6$	$3 \cdot 1 \cdot 12$
$1 \cdot 2 \cdot 18$	$1 \cdot 6 \cdot 6$ (given)	$3 \cdot 3 \cdot 4$	
$1 \cdot 3 \cdot 12$	$2 \cdot 2 \cdot 9$	$3 \cdot 2 \cdot 6$	

36. The best choice for this item is **C.** (**SMR 2.3 Three-Dimensional Geometry**) (ENHANCED)

The formula for finding the total surface area of a circular cone is the following:

$S.A. = \frac{1}{2} \cdot (2\pi r) \cdot 1 + \cdot r^2 = \pi r l + \pi r^2$. You can use 3.14 for the approximate value for π (other values could be used as an approximation of π). For the value of the radius of the circular base of the cone, you need to divide the given diameter (6 cm) by 2 to find the radius, which gives 3 cm for the radius. The slant height is equal to 12 cm. Using these values for the formula:

$$\frac{1}{2} \cdot (2\pi r) \cdot 1 + \cdot r^2 \approx \frac{1}{2}(2)(3.14)(3)(12) + (3.14)(3^2)(12)$$
$$\approx (3.14)(3)(12) + (3.14)3^2$$
$$\approx 113.04 + 28.26$$
$$\approx 141.3 \, cm^2$$

37. The best choice for this item is **B.** (**SMR 2.3 Three-Dimensional Geometry**)

The volume formula of a pyramid is $V = \frac{1}{3}(lwh)$.

27) $\frac{1}{3}(lwh) = \frac{1}{3}(5 \cdot 5 \cdot 12.75)$

$= 106.25$ cubic centimeters

38. The best choice for this item is **A.** (**SMR 2.1 Parallelism**)

Remember that line segments are parallel if and only if the lines that contain them are parallel. If two lines form equal alternate angles with a transversal, the lines are parallel.

39. The best choice for this item is **B.** (**SMR 2.1 Parallelism**)

Remember that line segments are parallel if and only if the lines that contain them are parallel. If two lines form supplementary interior angles on the same side of a transversal, the lines are parallel.

40. The best choice for this item is **D.** (**SMR 2.1 Parallelism**)

Remember that line segments are parallel if and only if the lines that contain them are parallel. If two lines form equal corresponding angles with a transversal, the lines are parallel.

41. The best choice for this item is **A.** (**SMR 2.2 Plane Euclidean Geometry**)

Since you were given that $\overline{AB}$ and $\overline{DC}$ are parallel, angle D is congruent to angle B. So the measurement of angle y is equal to the measurement of angle B.

$m\angle B + x + 74 = 180°$. This implies that $x + y + 74° = 180°$, and $x + y = 106°$.

42. The best choice for this item is **D. (SMR 2.2   Plane Euclidean Geometry) (ENHANCED)**

Use the Pythagorean Theorem to find the measure of line segment *XZ*:

$c^2 = a^2 + b^2$

$c^2 = 9^2 + 12^2$ Substitute using the information from the figure: $a = 9$ and $b = 12$.

$c^2 = 81 + 144$ Solve: $9^2 = 81$, and $12^2 = 144$.

$c = \sqrt{81 + 144}$ Solve for *c*: $81 + 144 = 225$, and the square root of 225 is 15.

$c = 15$ The length of line segment *XN* is equal to 15 inches.

Now you have to find the length of line segment *XN*:

$m\left(\overline{XZ}\right) = m\left(\overline{XN}\right) + m\left(\overline{NZ}\right)$

$15 = m\left(\overline{XN}\right) + 5$ Substitute for the values of the respective line segments.

$15 - 5 = m\left(\overline{XN}\right) + 5 - 5$ Subtract 5 from each side of the equality.

$10 = m\left(\overline{XN}\right) + 0$ Solve: $15 - 5 = 10$, and $5 - 5 = 0$.

$10 = m\left(\overline{XN}\right)$ The length of line segment *XN* is equal to 10 inches.

43. The best choice for this item is **A. (SMR 2.2 Plane Euclidean Geometry)**

You can solve this problem by using the Pythagorean Theorem: $c^2 = a^2 + b^2$. You will need to form a right triangle and find the distance for each of the legs of this triangle as in the following figure. This yields the values for *a* and *b*: $a = 10$ units, and $b = 4$ units.

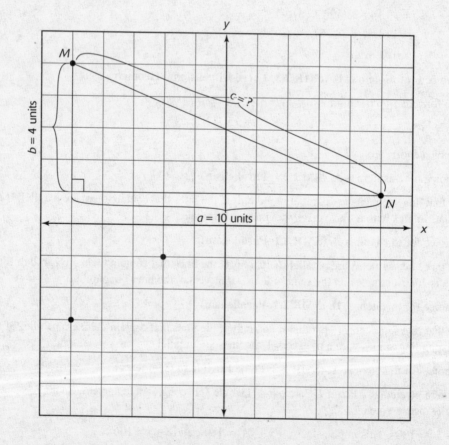

$c^2 = 10^2 + 4^2$

$c^2 = 100 + 16$

$c^2 = 116$

$c^2 = 2 \cdot 2 \cdot 29;$

$c = \sqrt{2 \cdot 2 \cdot 29}$

$= 2\sqrt{29}$ In this case you just simplify; do not solve the square root part.

Another way to solve this problem is by using the distance formula (derived from the Pythagorean Theorem):

$d^2 = (x_2 - x_1)^2 + (y_2 - y_1)^2$

$d^2 = (-5 - 5)^2 + (5 - 1)^2$ Substitute for x- and y-coordinates: $(-5, 5)$, and $(5, 1)$.

$d^2 = (-10)^2 + (4)^2$ Solve inside the parentheses first.

$d^2 = 100 + 16 = 116 = 2 \cdot 2 \cdot 29$

$d = \sqrt{2 \cdot 2 \cdot 29} = 2\sqrt{29}$ Same answer as with the other method.

44. The best choice for this item is **A**. (**SMR 2.2 Plane Euclidean Geometry**)

$\angle ACB$ and $\angle BCF$ are complementary angles. This means that the sum of their angle measures is equal to $90°$. The measure of $\angle ACB$ is equal to $30°$. Then the measure of $\angle BCF = 90° - 30° = 60°$.

45. The best choice for this item is **A**. (**SMR 2.2 Plane Euclidean Geometry**) (ENHANCED)

First, you need to find the circumference of the wheel: $C = 2\pi r$ or $C = \pi d$. If you use the $C = 2\pi r$, you need to use $r = 35/2 = 17.5$. Using $\pi = 3.14$, you have that the distance the wheel travels is equal to

120 revolution $\cdot C = 120 \cdot 2\pi(17.5)$

$= 120 \cdot 2(3.14)(17.5)$

$= 13{,}188$ inches.

You need to convert this distance to feet by dividing by 12 (number of inches in one foot): $13{,}188 \div 12 = 1{,}099$ feet.

46. The best choice for this item is **C**. (**SMR 2.3 Three-Dimensional Geometry**)

Since the ratio for the cylinders' radii is 2:3, the ratio for their volumes is $2^3:3^3$ or 8:27.

47. The best choice for this item is **D**. (**SMR 2.2 Plane Euclidean Geometry**) (ENHANCED)

You need to calculate the area of this shape. In order to do that, you may want to divide the figure in three regions as in the following figure. One of them will include the triangle in the middle with base equal 6 cm, height equal to 3 cm, and area equal to

$\frac{1}{2} bh = \frac{1}{2}(6 \cdot 3)$

$= \frac{1}{2}(18)$

$= 9 \text{ cm}^2.$

This added to the area of the other two portions ($6 \cdot 6 = 36 \text{ cm}^2$, and $3 \cdot 15 = 45 \text{ cm}^2$) makes the total area ($9 + 36 + 45 = 90 \text{ cm}^2$).

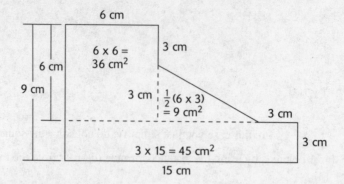

Another way to calculate the area of the figure is by dividing it in a different manner as in the following figure. One of them, as before, will include the triangle in the middle with base equal 6 cm, height equal to 3 cm, and area equal to

$$\frac{1}{2}bh = \frac{1}{2}(6 \cdot 3)$$
$$= \frac{1}{2}(18)$$
$$= 9 \text{ cm}^2.$$

This, added to the area of the other two portions ($9 \cdot 6 = 54 \text{ cm}^2$, and $3 \cdot 9 = 27 \text{ cm}^2$), makes the total area ($9 + 54 + 27 = 90 \text{ cm}^2$).

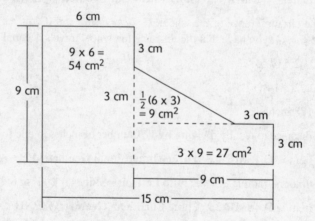

48. The best choice for this item is **C.** (**SMR 2.2 Plane Euclidean Geometry**)

You need to find the area of the room with the new dimensions added: $(30 + 5)(40 + 5)$. Then subtract the area of the room before expansions: $(30 + 5)(40 + 5) - (30)(40)$.

49. The best choice for this item is **C.** (**SMR 2.2 Plane Euclidean Geometry**)

In this context, two polygons are similar if and only if there is a correspondence between their vertices such that the corresponding sides of the polygons are proportional and the corresponding angles are equal. For example, enlargements of a picture have the same shape and are called similar.

A. All trapezoids are similar.   Not a true statement; only some trapezoids are similar.

B. All rhombi are similar.   Not a true statement; only some rhombi are similar.

C. All squares are similar.   A true statement; all squares are similar.

D. All triangles are similar.   Not true, only some triangles are similar. All equilateral triangles are similar.

50. This best choice for this item is **A. (SMR 2.3 Three-Dimensional Geometry)**

The cross section of the ball is equal to a circle. The area of the circle is equal to πr^2. Since the diameter is equal to 35 cm, the radius is equal to 17.5 cm, and $\pi \approx 3.14$. Substituting in the area formula, you have the following:

$3.14 \cdot (17.5)^2 = 961.625$

≈ 962 cm^2 (rounded to the nearest square centimeter).

51. The best choice for this item is **D. (SMR 2.3 Three-Dimensional Geometry)**

This represents the postulate stating that, if there are three noncollinear points, then there is exactly one plane that contains them. More briefly, this postulate can be stated in the following way: Three noncollinear points determine a plane. The three points are also said to be coplanar.

52. The best answer for this item is **B. (SMR 2.3 Three-Dimensional Geometry)**

You should take a look at each statement and find that only **B** describes the figure presented.

A.	Two planes that do not intersect.	False.
B.	Two planes that intersect in a line.	True.
C.	A line that contains only one plane.	False.
D.	A line that intersects a two planes in two different points.	False.

53. The best answer for this item is **B. (SMR 2.4 Transformational Geometry)**

Given that *RMDA* is the reflection image of *COEA* through line *l*, point *M* is the reflection point of point *O*.

54. The best choice for this item is **C. (SMR 2.4 Transformational Geometry)**

Given that *RMDA* is the reflection image of *COEA* through line *l*, angle *DAR* is the reflection angle of the angle *CAE*.

55. The best choice for this item is **C. (SMR 2.4 Transformational Geometry)**

Given that *IJKL* is an image of *ABCD* under certain transformation. The transformation that seems to relate *ABCD* and *IJKL* is a translation.

56. The best choice for this item is **D. (SMR 2.4 Transformational Geometry)**

Given that $\triangle P'A'L'$ is an image of $\triangle PAL$ under a certain transformation, the figure appears to preserve collinearity.

A.	It appears to be an isometry.	False. It needs to preserve distance, and it does not.
B.	It appears to preserve distance.	False.
C.	The two triangles appear to be congruent.	False.
D.	It appears to preserve collinearity.	True.

Probability and Statistics

57. The best choice for this item is **A. (SMR 4.1 Probability.) (ENHANCED)**

You need to calculate the probability for selecting a book from each box separately. There are 8 books in the first box (2 biography books + 3 children's books + 2 self-help books + 1 romance book = 8 books). Of these 8 books in this first box, 2 are biography books.

Then, the probability of randomly selecting one biography book from this first box is $\frac{2}{8}$ or $\frac{1}{4}$. There are 10 books in the second box (4 biography books + 1 children's book + 2 self-help books + 3 romance books = 10 books). Of these 10 books in this first box, 4 are biography books.

Then the probability of randomly selecting one biography book from this second box is $\frac{4}{10}$ or $\frac{2}{5}$. You need to multiply these two probabilities to obtain: $\frac{1}{4} \cdot \frac{2}{5}$, which is equal to $\frac{2}{20}$ or $\frac{1}{10}$. The probability of randomly selecting a biography book from each of the two boxes is $\frac{1}{10}$.

58. The best choice for this item is **D.** (**SMR 4.1 Probability**) (ENHANCED)

You have a total of 38 marbles (5 blue marbles + 11 red marbles + 15 green marbles + 7 yellow marbles = 38 marbles). The marbles with plastics bags are 11 red marbles + 7 yellow marbles or 18 marbles altogether. The probability for randomly selecting a marble with a plastic bag from the bowl is $\frac{18}{38}$ or $\frac{9}{19}$.

59. The best choice for this item is **C.** (**SMR 4.1 Probability**.) (ENHANCED)

You need to find the possible combinations for the two dice: $6 \cdot 6 = 36$ combinations (see table). Of these possible combinations, two involve 5 and 6 as possible outcomes: (5, 6) and (6, 5) (because order is not relevant). This is two out of 36 possible number combinations: $\frac{2}{36}$ or $\frac{1}{18}$ for the probability.

	1	*2*	*3*	*4*	*5*	*6*
1	1, 1	1, 2	1, 3	1, 4	1, 5	1, 6
2	2, 1	2, 2	2, 3	2, 4	2, 5	2, 6
3	3, 1	3, 2	3, 3	3, 4	3, 5	3, 6
4	4, 1	4, 2	4, 3	4, 4	4, 5	4, 6
5	5, 1	5, 2	5, 3	5, 4	5, 5	5, 6
6	6, 1	6, 2	6, 3	6, 4	6, 5	6, 6

60. The best choice for this item is **C.** (**SMR 4.1 Probability**)

These are two independent events. The probability of drawing a yellow marble from the first bag is $\frac{1}{5}$. The probability of drawing a purple marble from the second bag is also $\frac{1}{5}$. Then the probability of drawing a yellow from the first bag and a purple from the second bag is $\frac{1}{5} \cdot \frac{1}{5} = \frac{1}{25}$.

61. The best choice for this item is **B.** (**SMR 4.2 Statistics**.) (ENHANCED)

To find the mean of this data set, you need to add the scores and divide by 20 (number of scores):

$291 \cdot 20 = 14.55$

62. The best choice for this item is **A.** (**SMR 4.2 Statistics**)

To find the median, you need to order the data set and find the middle score.

10, 10, 10, 10, 11, 12, 12, 12, 12, 12, 13, **13, 14, 15, 15, 20, 22, 22, 23, 23**

Scores 12 and 13 are in the middle. You need average these two scores to find the median:

$(12 + 13) \div 2 = 25 \div 2 = 12.5$

63. The best choice for this item is **B.** (**SMR 4.2 Statistics**.)

The mode is the most frequent score. A frequency table should be used to organize the data.

Scores	Frequency
10	4
11	1
12	5
13	2
14	1

Scores	Frequency
15	2
20	1
22	2
23	2

64. The best choice for this item is **D. (SMR 4.2 Statistics)**

The range of the date set is the highest score minus the lowest score: $23 - 10 = 13$.

Geometry

65. Written or Constructed-Response Question. **(SMR 2.1 Parallelism)**

Possible answer:

Statements	**Reasons**
■ Lines a and b with transversal c, $\angle 1$ and $\angle 2$ are supplementary angles.	Given.
■ $\angle 2$ and $\angle 3$ are supplementary.	If two angles are a linear pair, they are supplementary.
■ $\angle 1 = \angle 3$	Supplements of the same angle are equal angles.
■ $a \parallel b$	If two lines form equal corresponding angles with a transversal, the lines are parallel.

66. Written or Constructed-Response Question. **(SMR 2.2 Euclidean Geometry)**

Following is a possible diagram for the problem.

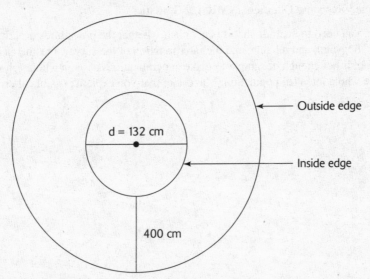

For finding the amount of fencing for the outside edge, notice that the radius of the inside circle is 132 cm $\div\ 2 = 66$ cm, and the radius of the outside circle is 400 cm $+\ 66$ cm $= 466$. Using this information, you can calculate the circumference of the outside circle: $2\pi = 2(3.14)(466) = 2926.48$ cm. Then you need to subtract 50 cm for the opening: $2926.48 - 50 = 2876.48$ cm or about 29 m.

For finding the amount of fencing for the inside edge, the circumference of the inside circle is equal to $2\pi = 2(3.14)(66) = 414.48$ cm. Assuming you will also have an opening of 50 cm, you need to subtract 50 cm from $414.48 - 50 = 364.48$ cm or about 4 m. The inside fencing is equal to 29 m – 4 m = 25 extra meters. The number of dollars per meter is equal to $\$375 \div 25$ m = \$15 per meter.

67. Written or Constructed-Response Question. (**SMR 2.3 Three-Dimensional Geometry**)

You need to find the volume of the complete solid without the indentation (rectangular prism) and then subtract the area of the indentation (triangular prism) from this number.

$V = 1 \cdot w \cdot h$ Volume of complete solid figure.

$V = 9 \cdot 8 \cdot 8 = 576 \text{ cm}^3$ Substitute values given from the figure.

You now need to find the volume of the triangular prism. You have the values for $b = 3$ cm and $w = 8$ cm, but not for the height (one of the legs) of the right triangle.

$c^2 = a^2 + b^2$ You need to calculate the height using the Pythagorean Theorem ($b = h$).

$3^2 = 1.5^2 + b^2$ Substitute for $c = 3$, and $a = 3 \div 2 = 1.5$.

$9 = 2.25 + b^2$ Solve.

$9 - 2.25 = 2.25 - 2.25 + b^2$ Subtract 2.25 from both sides of the equation.

$6.75 = b^2$ $9 - 2.25 = 6.75$

$\sqrt{6.75} = b$ Then $b = 2.6$ (square root of $6.75 = 2.6$).

The volume of the triangular prism is the following:

$V = \frac{1}{2}(bh) \cdot w$

$V = \frac{1}{2}(3 \cdot 2.5) \cdot 8$ Substitute for the values you have now.

$V \approx 30 \text{ cm}^3$ Volume for the triangular prism.

Subtract this number from the total volume of the solid figure: $576 \text{ cm}^3 - 30 \text{ cm}^3 = 546 \text{ cm}^3$

Probability and Statistics

68. Written or Constructed-Response Question. (**SMR 4.2 Statistics**)

In your explanation, you need to mention that it is not clear whether the procedures used by Carlos to develop the survey were systematic, valid, and reliable, and the interpretation of the survey's results is not correct. Asking students in one school is not enough of sample to make generalizations about a whole school county. This is not representative of the whole intended population. Make sure that you explain possible alternatives to improve the quality of the study.

Practice CSET: Mathematics Subset III

This Subtest involves Calculus (items 69 – 94 and 99 – 101) and History of Mathematics (items 95 – 98 and 102).

Calculus

69. This best choice for this item is **C**. (SMR 5.2 **Limits and Continuity**)

In order for $\lim_{x \to 4} f(x)$ to exist, the limit from the right side must equal the limit from the left side. Since the function changes at $x = 4$, look at each limit individually. First, look at $\lim_{x \to 4^-} f(x) = \lim_{x \to 4^-} 2x + 1 = 2(4) + 1 = 9$. Then, look at $\lim_{x \to 4^+} f(x) = \lim_{x \to 4^+} x^2 = (4)^2 = 16$. Since these limits are not equal, the $\lim_{x \to 4} f(x)$ does not exist.

70. The best answer for this item is **A**. (SMR 5.1 **Trigonometry**)

In order to solve $2\cos^2 x + \cos x - 1 = 0$ for x, we need to factor the left hand side of the equation. This gives $(2\cos x - 1)(\cos x + 1) = 0$. Therefore, either $2\cos x - 1 = 0$ or $\cos x + 1 = 0$. The first case gives $\cos x = \frac{1}{2}$, so $x = \frac{\pi}{3}, \frac{5\pi}{3}$. The second case gives $\cos x = -1$, so $x = \pi$. Therefore, the values for x in the given interval that satisfy the equation are $\left\{ \frac{\pi}{3}, \pi, \frac{5\pi}{3} \right\}$.

71. The best choice for this item is **A**. (SMR 5.1 **Trigonometry**)

Using 30-60-90 right triangle relationships, we know $\sin\left(\frac{\pi}{3}\right) = \frac{\sqrt{3}}{2}$. Therefore, $x + \frac{\pi}{4} = \frac{\pi}{3}$. This gives $x = \frac{\pi}{3} - \frac{\pi}{4} = \frac{\pi}{12}$. We are looking at the interval $0 \le x \le 2\pi$, so we also need to consider that $\sin\left(\frac{2\pi}{3}\right) = \frac{\sqrt{3}}{2}$. This gives $x + \frac{\pi}{4} = \frac{2\pi}{3}$, so $x = \frac{2\pi}{3} - \frac{\pi}{4} = \frac{8\pi}{12} - \frac{3\pi}{12} = \frac{5\pi}{12}$. If we consider the next possible solution, we would have $\sin\left(\frac{7\pi}{3}\right) = \frac{\sqrt{3}}{2}$. Then $x + \frac{\pi}{4} = \frac{7\pi}{3}$. Then $x = \frac{7\pi}{3} - \frac{\pi}{4} = \frac{28\pi}{12} - \frac{3\pi}{12} = \frac{25\pi}{12}$. This is outside the given interval, so there are two possible solutions in the desired interval, $\frac{\pi}{12}, \frac{5\pi}{12}$.

72. The best answer for this item is **B**. (SMR 5.3 **Derivatives and Applications**)

The slope of the tangent line is found by evaluating $f'(x)$ when $x = -2$. Taking the first derivative gives $f'(x) = 6x^2 + 2x - 5$. Substituting $x = -2$ into $f'(x)$ gives $f'(x) = 6(-2)^2 + 2(-2) - 5 = 6(4) - 4 - 5 = 24 - 4 - 5 = 15$. Therefore, the slope of the tangent line is 15.

73. The best choice for this item is **B**. (SMR 5.2 **Limits and Continuity**)

In order to be continuous, three criteria must be met. The function must be defined at every point in the interval; the limit must exist everywhere in the interval; and the limit must be the value of the function at every point in the interval. Choices **A**, **C**, and **D** are defined everywhere on the interval. Choice **B** is undefined at $x = -7$, so there is a discontinuity at that point, therefore, Choice **B** is not continuous on the given interval.

74. The best choice for this item is **A**. (SMR 5.3 **Derivatives and Applications**) (ENHANCED)

To find $\lim_{x \to 1} \frac{\ln x}{2x - 2}$, first try plugging in $x = 1$ into the function. This gives $\frac{0}{0}$. Therefore, you can use L'Hôpital's Rule. Then $\lim_{x \to 1} \frac{\ln x}{2x - 2} = \lim_{x \to 1} \frac{\frac{1}{x}}{2} = \lim_{x \to 1} \frac{1}{2x} = \frac{1}{2(1)} = \frac{1}{2}$.

75. The best choice for this item is **D**. (SMR 5.2 **Limits and Continuity**) (ENHANCED)

The Intermediate Value Theorem states that:

Suppose that f is continuous on the closed interval $[a, b]$ and let N be any number strictly between $f(a)$ and $f(b)$. Then there exists a number c in (a, b) such that $f(c) = N$.

In order to use the Intermediate Value Theorem to show there is a root in the interval $(-2, 3)$, we need to find a function in which either $f(-2) < 0$ and $f(3) > 0$ or $f(-2) > 0$ and $f(3) < 0$. So, examine the choices. Find the value of each of the functions at the endpoints of the interval. For Choice **A**, $f(-2) = (-2)^2 - 4(-2) + 5 = 4 + 8 + 5 = 17$ and $f(3) = (3)^2 - 4(3) + 5 = 9 - 12 + 5 = 2$. These are both positive, so the Intermediate Value Theorem does not tell us there is a root. The same is true for choices **B** and **C**. For Choice **D**, $f(-2) = (-2)^2 + 2(-2) - 5 = 4 - 4 - 5 - = -5$ and $f(3) = (3)^2 + 2(3) - 5 = 9 + 6 - 5 = 10$. Since $f(-2) < 0$ and $f(3) > 0$, the Intermediate Value Theorem tells us there is a root in the interval $(-2, 3)$.

76. The best choice for this item is **D**. (SMR 5.1 **Trigonometry**)

The standard form for a graph of $\sin x$ is $f(x) = A \sin(Bx + C) + D$ where A is the amplitude, D is the vertical shift, $\frac{2\pi}{B}$ is the period, and $\frac{C}{B}$ is the phase shift. In this case, the graph of $f(x) = 3\sin\left(\frac{x}{2}\right) - 1$ has an amplitude of 3 and is shifted down 1 unit from the parent graph of $f(x) = \sin x$. The period of the function is defined as $\frac{2\pi}{B} = \frac{2\pi}{\frac{1}{2}} = 4\pi$. The graph in choice A has a period of π, not 4π. The graph in Choice **B** has a parent graph of $f(x) = \cos x$. The graph in Choice **C** has a period of π and a parent graph of $f(x) = \cos x$. The graph in Choice **D** is the correct graph.

77. The best choice for this item is **A**. (SMR 5.3 **Derivatives and Applications**) (ENHANCED)

We are looking at the surface area of a sphere, so we know $A = 4\pi r^2$. We are looking for the rate at which the diameter decreases, so we need the surface area in terms of the diameter. We know $r = \frac{d}{2}$, so $A = 4\pi\left(\frac{d}{2}\right)^2 = 4\pi\left(\frac{d^2}{4}\right) = \pi d^2$. Differentiating this with respect to time gives $\frac{dA}{dt} = \pi(2d)\frac{dd}{dt}$. We know $\frac{dA}{dt} = 0.5$, and $d = 10$. Therefore, $0.5 = \pi(2(10))\frac{dd}{dt}$, so $0.5 = 20\pi\frac{dd}{dt}$. Then $\frac{dd}{dt} = \frac{1}{40\pi}$ cm/min.

78. The best choice for this item is **C**. (SMR 5.1 **Trigonometry**)

From the equation $\sin(A + B) = \sin A \cos B + \cos A \sin B$, we can make A and B equal, so we have $\sin(A + A) = \sin A \cos A + \cos A \sin A$, so $\sin 2A = 2 \sin A \cos A$. This is Choice **C**. Choices **A**, **B**, and **D** also rely on the cos $(A + B)$ identity, so they cannot be derived directly from $\sin(A + B) = \sin A \cos B + \cos A \sin B$.

79. The best choice for this item is **B**. (SMR 5.1 **Trigonometry**) (ENHANCED)

To find $\left(\frac{1}{\sqrt{2}} + \frac{1}{\sqrt{2}}i\right)^5$, we can use De Moivre's Theorem. First, we need to find a polar representation for $\left(\frac{1}{\sqrt{2}} + \frac{1}{\sqrt{2}}i\right)$. This is equivalent to $\frac{1}{\sqrt{2}}(1 + i)$. We need to find the magnitude and direction for the complex number $1 + i$. The magnitude is $r = |z| = \sqrt{1 + 1} = \sqrt{2}$. The angle is found with $\tan\theta = \frac{1}{1}$. This gives $\theta = \frac{\pi}{4}$.

So the polar form is of $1 + i$ is $\sqrt{2}\left(\cos\frac{\pi}{4} + i\sin\frac{\pi}{4}\right)$. Then we can write $\frac{1}{\sqrt{2}}(1 + i)$ as $\frac{1}{\sqrt{2}}\left(\sqrt{2}\left(\cos\frac{\pi}{4} + i\sin\frac{\pi}{4}\right)\right) = \left(\cos\frac{\pi}{4} + i\sin\frac{\pi}{4}\right)$. To find $\left(\cos\frac{\pi}{4} + i\sin\frac{\pi}{4}\right)^5$, we use De Moivre's Theorem, which states that $\left(r(\cos\theta + i\sin\theta)\right)^n = r^n(\cos n\theta + i\sin n\theta)$. So $\left(\cos\frac{\pi}{4} + i\sin\frac{\pi}{4}\right)^5 = \left(\cos\frac{5\pi}{4} + i\sin\frac{5\pi}{4}\right) = -\frac{1}{\sqrt{2}} - i\frac{1}{\sqrt{2}}$.

80. The best choice for this item is **C**. (SMR 5.3 **Derivatives and Applications**) (ENHANCED)

Since bacterial growth is proportional to its size, we can say $\frac{dy}{dt} = ky$ where $\frac{dy}{dt}$ is the rate at which the bacteria grows, k is the proportionality constant, t is the time in hours, and y is the amount of bacteria present at time t. This is a separable differential equation that is equivalent to $\frac{dy}{y} = kdt$. Integrating both sides gives $\ln y = kt + C$, so $y = e^{kt + C} = Ce^{kt}$. Using the information in the problem, when $t = 0$, $y = 500$ and when $t = 3$, $y = 2000$. This gives two equations. So, $500 = Ce^{k(0)}$. Then, $2000 = (500)(e^{k(3)})$. So, $e^{3k} = 4$. This gives $3k = \ln 4$, so $k = \frac{\ln 4}{3}$. Then, our equation becomes $y = 500e^{\left(\frac{\ln 4}{3}\right)t}$. We want to find y when $t = 6$. Then, $y = 500e^{\left(\frac{\ln 4}{3}\right)6} = 500e^{2\ln 4} = 500e^{\ln 16} = 500(16) = 8000$ bacteria.

81. The best choice for this item is **D. (SMR 5.5 Sequences and Series)**

If we define the number $n = 1.\overline{32}$. We can say that $100n = 132.\overline{32}$. If we subtract these two numbers, we get $100n - n = 132.\overline{32} - 1.\overline{32}$. This leads to $99n = 131$ so $n = \frac{131}{99} = 1\frac{32}{99}$.

82. The best choice for this item is **C. (SMR 5.3 Derivatives and Applications) (ENHANCED)**

To find the intervals for concavity, the second derivative needs to be found. For this function, the first derivative is $f'(x) = 4x^3 - 3x^2 - 18x + 12$. The second derivative is $f''(x) = 12x^2 - 6x - 18$. To find the points at which concavity changes, find the values of x that make the second derivative zero. So, $12x^2 - 6x - 18 = 0$. This gives $6(2x^2 - x - 3) = 6(2x - 3)(x + 1) = 0$. This gives $x = \frac{3}{2}$ or $x = -1$. When $x < -1$, both $2x - 3 < 0$ and $x + 1 < 0$, so $f''(x) = 6(2x - 3)(x + 1) > 0$. Therefore, the function is concave up on the interval $(-\infty, -1)$. When $-1 < x < \frac{3}{2}$, $2x - 3 < 0$ and $x + 1 > 0$, so $f''(x) = 6(2x - 3)(x + 1) < 0$. Therefore, the function is concave down on the interval $\left(-1, \frac{3}{2}\right)$. Finally, when $x > \frac{3}{2}$, $2x - 3 > 0$, and $x + 1 > 0$, so $f''(x) = 6(2x - 3)(x + 1) > 0$. Therefore, the function is concave up on the interval $\left(\frac{3}{2}, \infty\right)$. So the intervals where the function is concave up are $(-\infty, -1)$ and $\left(\frac{3}{2}, \infty\right)$.

83. The best choice for this item is **C. (SMR 5.4 Integrals and Applications) (ENHANCED)**

First, it is often helpful to graph the functions to have a picture of the region which is being rotated.

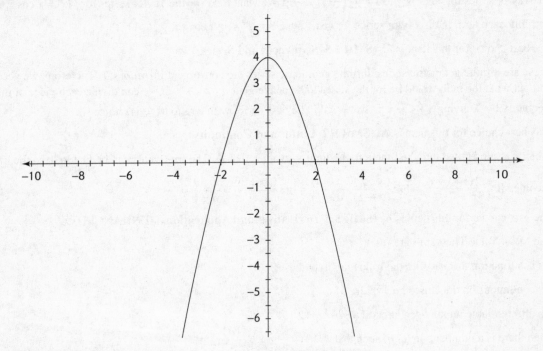

After this is determined, we need to look at a slice of the region revolved about, in this case, the y-axis. The slice, or disk, would have a radius of x, and the height of the disk would be dy. Use the volume of a cylinder formula to determine the volume of the disk. This gives $Disk = \pi r^2 h = \pi x^2 dy$. To find the volume of the entire region, we need to integrate this volume over the region. This gives $V = \int_0^4 \pi x^2 dy$. In order to find this, we need to replace x with what it is equal to from the original function. This gives

$$V = \int_0^4 \pi \left(\sqrt{4-y}\right)^2 dy = \pi \int_0^4 (4-y)\, dy = \pi \left(4y - \frac{y^2}{2}\right)\Big|_0^4 = \pi\left(\left(4(4) - \frac{(4)^2}{2}\right) - \left(4(0) - (0)^2\right)\right) = \pi\left(16 - \frac{16}{2}\right) = 8\pi.$$

84. The best choice for this item is **A. (SMR 5.4 Integrals and Applications.)**

The Fundamental Theorem of Calculus states that:

If f is continuous on $[a, b]$, then the function g defined by $g(x) = \int_a^x f(t)\,dt$ where $a \le x \le b$ is continuous on $[a, b]$ and differentiable on (a, b), and $g'(x) = f(x)$. $f(t) = 2t - 5$ is continuous and differentiable for all real numbers; however, the representation for $g(x)$ is not the same as that in the Fundamental Theorem of Calculus. To make it equivalent, we must first reverse the bounds on the integral, so $g(x) = -\int_4^x (2t - 5)\,dt = \int_4^x (-2t + 5)\,dt$.

Then, the Fundamental Theorem of Calculus can be used to find $g'(x) = f(x) = -2x + 5$.

85. The best choice for this item is **D. (SMR 5.4 Integrals and Applications)**

The Reimann Sum is the sum of the rectangles when the area under the curve is partitioned. There are 6 rectangles. If we use the left endpoint, the height of each rectangle is determined by the x-values of $-2, -1.5, -1, -0.5, 0,$ and 0.5. The width of each rectangle is 0.5. The sum of the rectangles is then

$$\frac{f(-2)}{2} + \frac{f(-1.5)}{2} + \frac{f(-1)}{2} + \frac{f(-0.5)}{2} + \frac{f(0)}{2} + \frac{f(0.5)}{2} = \frac{4}{2} + \frac{1}{2}\left(\frac{9}{4}\right) + \frac{1}{2} + \frac{1}{2}\left(\frac{1}{4}\right) + 0 + \frac{1}{2}\left(\frac{1}{4}\right) =$$

$$2 + \frac{9}{8} + \frac{1}{2} + \frac{1}{8} + 0 + \frac{1}{8} = \frac{16}{8} + \frac{9}{8} + \frac{4}{8} + \frac{1}{8} + \frac{1}{8} = \frac{31}{8}.$$

86. The best choice for this item is **A. (SMR 5.5 Sequences and Series) (ENHANCED)**

The Taylor series for $\cos x$ is $f(x) = \sum_{n=0}^{\infty} (-1)^n \frac{x^{2n}}{(2n)!}$. We want to know the Taylor series for $f(x) = x \cos x$. Multiply each term in the Taylor series for $\cos x$ by x. So, $f(x) = x \cos x = \sum_{n=0}^{\infty} (-1)^n \frac{x^{2n+1}}{(2n)!}$.

87. The best choice for this item is **C. (SMR 5.5 Sequences and Series)**

These are infinite geometric series. Infinite geometric series are convergent if $|ratio| < 1$. Therefore, we need to find out what the ratio would be for the series to be convergent if $-2 < r < 2$. We can divide each piece of this inequality by 2, giving $-1 < \frac{r}{2} < 1$, so $\left|\frac{r}{2}\right| < 1$. The only series with a ratio of $\frac{r}{2}$ is choice C.

88. This best choice for this item is **A. (SMR 5.2 Limits and Continuity)**

When 2 is substituted into the function, the limit is evaluated at $\frac{0}{0}$. The trinomials can be factored, so the limit

becomes $\lim_{x \to 2} \frac{2x^2 - x - 6}{3x^2 - 7x + 2} = \lim_{x \to 2} \frac{(x - 2)(2x + 3)}{(x - 2)(3x - 1)} = \lim_{x \to 2} \frac{(2x + 3)}{(3x - 1)} = \frac{4 + 3}{6 - 1} = \frac{7}{5}$.

89. The best choice for this item is **A. (SMR 5.3 Derivatives and Applications) (ENHANCED)**

The Mean Value Theorem states that:

If f is a function that satisfies the following hypotheses:

f is continuous on the closed interval $[a, b]$.

f is differentiable on the open interval (a, b).

Then there is a number c in (a, b) such that $f'(c) = \frac{f(b) - f(a)}{b - a}$.

For this problem, $f(x) = x^2 + 2x - 5$, $a = 0$, and $b = 2$. Since f is a polynomial, it is continuous and differentiable on $[0, 2]$. We want to find the values of c that satisfy the Mean Value Theorem. $f'(x) = 2x + 2$. So, we have

$$2c + 2 = \frac{\left((2)^2 + 2(2) - 5\right) - \left((0)^2 + 2(0) - 5\right)}{2 - 0} = \frac{3 - (-5)}{2} = \frac{8}{2} = 4.$$ Therefore, $2c + 2 = 4$. Therefore, $2c = 2$,

so $c = 1$. This is in the interval $[0, 2]$, so $c = 1$ is the only value of c that satisfies the Mean Value Theorem in the interval $[0, 2]$.

90. The best choice for this item is **B. (SMR 5.1 Trigonometry)**

We want to rewrite $1 + \sqrt{3}\,i$, which is in $a + bi$ form as $r(\cos\theta + i\sin\theta)$. We need to find r and θ. We know $r^2 = a^2 + b^2$ and $\tan\theta = \dfrac{b}{a}$. So, $r^2 = (1)^2 + \left(\sqrt{3}\right)^2 = 1 + 3 = 4$. This gives $r = 2$. Then $\tan\theta = \dfrac{\sqrt{3}}{1}$. This gives $\theta = \dfrac{\pi}{3}$. So we can write $1 + \sqrt{3}\,i$ as $2\left(\cos\left(\dfrac{\pi}{3}\right) + i\sin\left(\dfrac{\pi}{3}\right)\right)$.

91. The best choice for this item is **B. (SMR 5.3 Derivatives and Applications)**

The limit definition of a derivative can be written as $f'(x) = \lim\limits_{h \to 0} \dfrac{f(x+h) - f(x)}{h}$. We are given

$$\lim_{h \to 0} \frac{3(x+h)^2 - 3(x+h) - 3x^2 + 2x}{h} = \lim_{h \to 0} \frac{\left(3(x+h)^2 - 3(x+h)\right) - \left(3x^2 - 2x\right)}{h},\ \text{so}\ f(x) = 3x^2 - 2x.$$

92. The best choice for this item is **B. (SMR 5.5 Sequences and Series)**

The series is arithmetic. There are 11 terms. The first term is 5, the 11th term is 35. The formula for the sum of an arithmetic series is $S = \dfrac{n\left(a_1 + a_n\right)}{2} = \dfrac{11(5 + 35)}{2} = \dfrac{11(40)}{2} = 220$.

93. The best answer for this item is **C. (SMR 5.4 Integrals and Applications)**

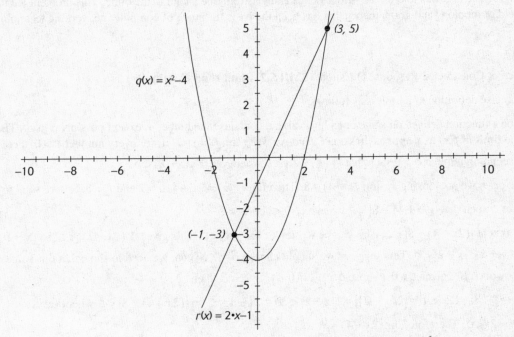

The curves intersect at the points $(-1, -3)$ and $(3, 5)$. The area between the curves is $\displaystyle\int_{-1}^{3} (2x - 1) - (x^2 - 4)\,dx$. This leads to

$$\int_{-1}^{3} (2x - 1 - x^2 + 4)\,dx = \int_{-1}^{3} (-x^2 + 2x + 3)\,dx = \left(-\frac{x^3}{3} + x^2 + 3x\right)\Bigg|_{-1}^{3} = \left(-\frac{3^3}{3} + (3)^2 + 3(3)\right) -$$

$$\left(-\frac{(-1)^3}{3} + (-1)^2 + 3(-1)\right) = -9 + 9 + 9 - \left(\frac{1}{3} + 1 - 3\right) = 9 - \frac{1}{3} + 2 = 10\frac{2}{3} = \frac{32}{3}$$

94. The best answer for this item is **A. (SMR 5.5 Sequences and Series) (ENHANCED)**

There is a common ratio of $\dfrac{1}{2}$, so this is a geometric sequence. We can write this sum as $\displaystyle\sum_{n=1}^{7} \frac{4}{3}\left(\frac{1}{2}\right)^{n-1}$. The formula for the sum of a finite geometric series is $S_n = \dfrac{a_1\left(1 - r^n\right)}{1 - r}$. We know that $a_1 = \dfrac{4}{3}$ and $r = \dfrac{1}{2}$. So, the sum of the first seven terms is $S_7 = \dfrac{\dfrac{4}{3}\left(1 - \left(\dfrac{1}{2}\right)^7\right)}{1 - \left(\dfrac{1}{2}\right)} = \dfrac{\dfrac{4}{3}\left(1 - \dfrac{1}{128}\right)}{\dfrac{1}{2}} = \dfrac{\dfrac{4}{3}\left(\dfrac{127}{128}\right)}{\dfrac{1}{2}} = \dfrac{8}{3}\left(\dfrac{127}{128}\right) = \dfrac{127}{48}$.

History of Mathematics

95. The best choice for this item is **A. (SMR 6.1 History of Mathematics)**

The Babylonians were the only of these people groups who had a numeration system involving place value. The others had systems that were simply additive and did not rely on place value.

96. The best choice for this item is **C. (SMR 6.1 History of Mathematics)**

The Sieve of Eratosthenes is used to find prime numbers. By eliminating multiples of every number, only the prime numbers remain. So, start with a chart of all numbers from 2 to 100, for example. Cross off every multiple of 2. This eliminates anything that is a composite number with a factor of 2. Then do the same for multiples of 3. Four has already been eliminated, so skip 4 and cross out all multiples of 5. Continue in this fashion, and all prime numbers between 2 and 100 will be remaining in the end.

97. The best choice for this item is **A. (SMR 6.1 History of Mathematics)**

Sofia Kovalevskaya was known for her contributions to differential equations.

98. The best choice for this item is **B. (SMR 6.1 History of Mathematics)**

The Bridges of Konigsburg was a problem examined by Leonhard Euler. The problem involved a town that had 7 bridges. The task was to cross all bridges once and get from one island to the other. This problem led to work in the field of topology and graph theory that has been the basis for much of computer networking technology.

Calculus

99. Written or Constructed-Response Question. **(SMR 5.2 Limits and Continuity)**

The precise definition of a limit is as follows:

Let f be a function defined on some open interval that contains the number a, except possibly a itself. Then we say the **limit of $f(x)$ as x approaches a is L,** and we write $\lim_{x \to a} f(x) = L$ if, for every number $\varepsilon > 0$, there is a corresponding number $\delta > 0$ such that $|f(x) - L| < \varepsilon$ whenever $0 < |x - a| < \delta$.

In this case, we are looking at $\lim_{x \to 2}(2x + 4) = 8$. Therefore, $f(x) = 2x + 4$, $a = 2$ and $L = 8$. So, we want to find a number δ such that $|(2x + 4) - 8| < \varepsilon$ whenever $0 < |x - 2| < \delta$.

Look first at $|(2x + 4) - 8| < \varepsilon$. This can be written as $|2x - 4| < \varepsilon$. This gives $|2(2x - 2)| < \varepsilon$, so $|x - 2| < \frac{\varepsilon}{2}$ whenever $x < |x - 2| < \delta$. This suggests we should choose $\delta = \frac{\varepsilon}{2}$. Then, we need to show that this value of $\delta = \frac{\varepsilon}{2}$ works. So, given $\varepsilon > 0$, choose $\delta = \frac{\varepsilon}{2}$. If $0 < |x - 2| < \delta$, then $|(2x + 4) - 8| = |2x - 4| = |2(x - 2)| = 2|x - 2| < 2\delta = 2\left(\frac{\varepsilon}{2}\right) = \varepsilon$, so $|(2x = 4) - 8| < \varepsilon$ whenever $0 < |x - 2| < \delta$. Therefore, $\lim_{x \to 2}(2x + 4) = 8$.

100. Written or Constructed-Response Question. **(SMR 5.1 Trigonometry)**

Beginning with $\sin^2 x + \cos^2 x = 1$, divide each side of this identity by $\sin^2 x$. This gives $\frac{\sin^2 x}{\sin^2 x} + \frac{\cos^2 x}{\sin^2 x} = \frac{1}{\sin^2 x}$. So $1 + \cot^2 x = \csc^2 x$.

Similarly, divide each side of the original identity by $\cos^2 x$. This gives $\frac{\sin^2 x}{\cos^2 x} + \frac{\cos^2 x}{\cos^2 x} = \frac{1}{\cos^2 x}$. So $1 + \tan^2 x = \sec^2 x$.

101. Written or Constructed-Response Question. **(SMR 5.3 Derivatives and Applications)**

The definition of the derivative states that $f'(x) = \lim_{h \to 0} \frac{f(x + h) - f(x)}{h}$.

Therefore, if $F(x) = f(x)g(x)$, then $F'(x) = \lim_{h \to 0} \frac{f(x + h)\, g(x + h) - f(x)\, g(x)}{h}$. In order to simplify this limit, we can add and subtract the same term, namely $f(x + h)g(x)$ to the numerator. This gives

$$F'(x) = \lim_{h \to 0} \frac{f(x+h)\,g(x+h) - f(x+h)\,g(x) + f(x+h)\,g(x) - f(x)\,g(x)}{h}$$

$$= \lim_{h \to 0} \frac{f(x+h)\big(g(x+h) - g(x)\big) + g(x)\big(f(x+h) - f(x)\big)}{h}$$

$$= \lim_{h \to 0} f(x+h)\left(\frac{g(x+h) - g(x)}{h}\right) + g(x)\left(\frac{f(x+h) - f(x)}{h}\right)$$

$$= \lim_{h \to 0} f(x+h) \lim_{h \to 0} \frac{g(x+h) - g(x)}{h} + \lim_{h \to 0} g(x) \lim_{h \to 0} \frac{f(x+h) - f(x)}{h}$$

$$= f(x)\,g'(x) + g(x)\,f'(x).$$

History of Mathematics

102. Written or Constructed-Response Question. (**SMR 6.1 History of Mathematics**)

Since there is no overlap and no gaps, the sum of the three triangles is equal to the area of the trapezoid. The three squares have areas of $\frac{1}{2}\,ab$, $\frac{1}{2}\,ab$, and $\frac{1}{2}\,c^2$. The trapezoid has an area of $\frac{1}{2}(a+b)(a+b)$. Therefore,

$$\frac{1}{2}(a+b)(a+b) = \frac{1}{2}\,ab + \frac{1}{2}\,ab + \frac{1}{2}\,c^2$$
$$a^2 + 2ab + b^2 = ab + ab + c^2$$
$$a^2 + 2ab + b^2 = 2ab + c^2$$
$$a^2 + b^2 = c^2.$$

Since a and b are the legs of a right triangle and c is the hypotenuse of the same right triangle, this proves the Pythagorean Theorem.

PART III

STUDY AIDS

Glossary of Important Terms

The following is a list of important mathematics terms and their definitions. Studying these terms and respective definitions will help you prepare to take the practice tests included in the book and the actual CSET: Mathematics. The glossary is intended to be a brief description of the terms included, and a quick reference as you study for the tests. Although it is not a substitute for coursework or other types of teacher preparation—or intended to represent a comprehensive listing of all potential mathematics terms—it may enhance your knowledge of the possible terms and definitions covered on the examination. Notice that some terms might appear across one or more content areas or have different meanings depending on the content area. *Note:* You are not expected to memorize all the definitions listed here. The terms are organized alphabetically and by area: algebra, number theory, geometry, probability and statistics, calculus, and trigonometry.

Algebra

Absolute value A number or its opposite, whichever is positive. The distance a number is from zero on a number line. The absolute value of -78, written $|-78|$, is 78.

Additive identity Zero is the additive identity because adding zero to a number leaves the original number unchanged.

Additive inverse The opposite of a number. The sum of a number and its additive inverse is zero. For example, -78 is the additive inverse of 78 because $78 + -78 = 0$.

Algebra A branch of mathematics in which variables are used to express numerical relationships.

Algebraic expressions A combination of variables, numbers, and at least one operation. For example, $n + 2$ is called an algebraic expression.

Arithmetic sequence A sequence in which each term is found by adding the same number to the previous term. For example, 2, 4, 6, 8, 10, 12, ...; or 1, 7, 13, 19, 25, 31, ...

Bar notation In repeating decimals, the segment, line, or bar placed over the digits that repeat. For example, $6.\overline{78}$ indicates that the digits 78 are repeated indefinitely.

Base In a power, the number used as a factor. For example, in 10^3, the base is 10. That is $10 \cdot 10 \cdot 10$. In a percent proportion, the whole quantity, or the number to which the part is being compared.

Binomial A polynomial with two terms. For example, $2x + y$ is a binomial.

Broken-line graph A statistical graph in which points are joined by straight-line segments.

Coefficient A numerical factor of a term that contains a variable. For example, 9 is the coefficient of x in the expression $9x$.

Common denominator A common multiple of the denominators of two or more fractions. For example, 24 is the common denominator for $\frac{1}{3}$, $\frac{5}{8}$, and $\frac{3}{4}$ because 24 is a common multiple of 3, 8, and 4.

Constant A term in an expression or equation that does not contain a variable.

Coordinates of a point The ordered pair that describes the position of a point on a graph in a coordinate plane.

Cross product In a proportion, a cross product is the product of the numerator of one ratio or fraction and the denominator of the other ratio or fraction.

Cubed The product in which a number is a factor three times. For example, two cubed is $2 \cdot 2 \cdot 2 = 2^3 = 8$.

Cup A customary unit of capacity equal to eight fluid ounces.

Decimal Decimal fraction in which the denominator is a power of 10, written in shortened form using a decimal point. For example, the decimal form of $\frac{34}{100}$ is 0.34.

Defining the variable Choosing a variable to represent an unknown value in a problem and using it to write an expression or equation to solve the problem.

Degree The degree of a polynomial is the highest exponent of any of its terms. For example, the degree of the polynomial $5x^3 + 4x^2 + x + 1$ is 3.

Denominator The term of a fraction that is below the fraction line and that indicates the number of equal parts into which a unit is divided.

Discount The amount by which the list price or original price is reduced.

Domain The set of input values for a function.

Empty set A set that contains no elements. Also known as the null set and written $\oslash$ or $\{\ \}$.

Equation A mathematical sentence using an equal sign to indicate that the two sides of the equation are equivalent.

Equivalent expressions Expressions that have the same value.

Equivalent fractions Fractions that have the same value. For example, $\frac{2}{3}$ and $\frac{4}{6}$ are equivalent fractions.

Equivalent ratios Two ratios that have the same value.

Evaluate To find the value of an expression.

Exponent In a power, the number that tells how many times the base is used as a factor. In 5^3, the exponent is 3. That is, $5^3 = 5 \cdot 5 \cdot 5$.

Exponential form Numbers written as bases with exponents.

Extremes The first and fourth terms of a proportion. For example, in the proportion $\frac{a}{b} = \frac{c}{d}$, a and d are the extremes.

Factorial The expression $n!$ is the product of all counting numbers beginning with n and counting backward to 1. For example, $4! = 4 \cdot 3 \cdot 2 \cdot 1 = 24$.

Formula An expression in which letters representing words are related by mathematical symbols. It shows a relationship among certain quantities.

Function A relation in which each element of the input is paired with exactly one element of the output according to a specified rule.

Function table A table used to organize the input numbers, output numbers, and the function rule.

Fundamental counting principle A principle that uses the multiplication of the number of ways each event in an experiment can occur to find the number of possible outcomes in a sample space.

Gallon A customary unit of capacity equal to four quarts.

Geometric mean The number b is the geometric mean between the numbers a and c if and only if $\frac{a}{b} = \frac{b}{c}$.

Geometric sequence A sequence in which each term can be found by multiplying the previous term by the same number. For example, 3, 6, 12, 24, 48, ...; or 1, 3, 9, 27, 81, 243, ...

Gram The basic unit of weight in the metric system equivalent to 0.001 kilogram.

Graph The process of placing a point on a number line or coordinate system at its proper location.

Greatest common factor (GCF) The largest number by which each of a given set of two or more numbers is divisible. For example, 5 is the GCF of 25 and 30. This is also written as GCF (25, 30) = 5.

Indirect measurement Finding a measurement by using similar triangles and writing a proportion.

Inequality A mathematical sentence using one or more of the following symbols: $<$, $>$, $\neq$, $\leq$, and $\geq$.

Integers The positive and negative whole numbers and zero. The whole numbers and their opposites: ..., -3. -2, -1, 0, 1, 2, 3, ...

Interest The amount paid for the use of borrowed money.

Inverse operations Operations that undo each other. Addition and subtraction are inverse operations, as well as multiplication and division.

Irrational number A number that cannot be written as a fraction. For example, π or the square root of 2.

Kilogram The base unit of mass in the metric system equivalent to 1,000 grams.

Least common denominator (LCD) The smallest counting number into which two or more denominators will be divided exactly. It is equivalent to the least common multiple.

Least common multiple (LCM) The least common multiple of two or more numbers is the smallest number that has each of the original numbers as a factor. For example, the LCM of 2, 3, and 4 is 12. This is also written as LCM (2, 3, 4) = 12.

Like fractions These fractions have the same denominator. For example, $\frac{3}{5x}$ and $\frac{8}{5x}$ have like denominators and are like fractions.

Like terms Terms that have identical variable factors. For example, $5xy$ and $3xy$ are like terms.

Linear equation An equation that contains no terms higher than the first degree and no terms with variables in the denominator. For example, $3a + 2b = 25$ is a linear equation. The graph of a linear equation is a straight line.

Liter The basic unit of liquid measure of capacity in the metric system. A liter is slightly more than a quart.

Lowest terms of a fraction A fraction is in lowest terms when the numerator and denominator have no common factors other than 1. For example, $\frac{3}{4}$ is a fraction in lowest terms.

Mathematical expression: It contains variables, numbers, and at least one operation. For example, $a + 2$, and $2a$ are mathematical expressions.

Means The second and third terms of proportion. For example, in the proportion $\frac{a}{b} = \frac{c}{d}$, b and c are the means of the proportion.

Meter The basic unit of length in the metric system. A meter is about 1.1 yards.

Metric system Measurements based on the decimal system. Each unit is $\frac{1}{10}$ of the next larger unit. It uses base units: Meter for length, gram for mass, and liter for capacity.

Monomial A polynomial of only one term. For example, 4, x, $4x$, and $6nm^2$ are monomials.

Multiplicative identity The number 1 is the multiplicative identity because the product of 1 and any number leaves the original number unchanged.

Multiplicative inverse (reciprocal) When the product of two numbers is 1, each number is called the multiplicative inverse of the other. For example, $\frac{4}{8}$ and $\frac{8}{4}$ are multiplicative inverses or reciprocals.

Negative number Any number less than zero.

Net price The price paid after a discount or reduction is made.

Nonagon A polygon having nine sides.

Numerator The term of a fraction that is above the fraction bar. For example, in the fraction $\frac{3}{10}$, 3 is the numerator.

Opposite of a number The same as the additive inverse of a number. Two numbers are opposite if they are represented on the number line by points that are the same distance from zero, but on opposite sides of zero. The sum of opposite numbers is zero.

Order of operations The sequence in which the arithmetic is done in finding the value of a numerical expression. In some cases, two or more answers are possible when calculating numerical expressions and an order of operation is not followed. A system called order of operations is needed and was developed by mathematicians. The following order of operations should be used when evaluating an expression containing more than one operation:

1. If the expression contains parentheses, work within them first.
2. Calculate all exponents (powers) in order, from left to right.
3. Do multiplications or divisions in order, from left to right.
4. Do additions or subtractions in order, from left to right.

A common abbreviation of these four steps is the expression "Please Excuse My Dear Aunt Sally" or PEMDAS (using the first letter of the words in the phrase), which corresponds to "Parenthesis, Exponents, Multiplication, Division, Addition, Subtraction."

Ounce A customary unit of weight, 16 ounces equal one pound.

Part In a percent, the number that is compared to the whole quantity.

Percent A ratio that compares a number to 100. A fraction whose denominator is 100, or a decimal in hundredths. For example, 56 % means 56 out of a hundred, and is written as $\frac{56}{100}$ or 0.56.

Percent of change A ratio that compares the change in a quantity to the original amount.

Percent of decrease A percent of change when the original quantity decreased.

Percent equation An equation that describes the relationship between the part, base, and percent: part = percent · base.

Percent of increase A percent of change when the original quantity increased.

Percent proportion Compares part of a quantity to the whole quantity using a percent: $\frac{\text{part}}{\text{base}} = \frac{\text{percent}}{100}$.

Pint A customary unit of capacity equal to two cups.

Polynomial An expression containing one or more terms. For example, $5n$ (a monomial), $a + 6$ (a binomial), and $x^3 + 4x + 7$ (a trinomial) are polynomials.

Positive number Any number greater that zero.

Pound A customary unit of weight equal to 16 ounces.

Powers Numbers expressed using exponents. The power 5^6 is read "five to the sixth power."

Precision The exactness of a measurement, which depends on the unit of measure.

Precision unit The smallest unit on a measuring tool.

Properties Statements that are true for any number of variables.

Quart A customary unit of capacity equal to two pints.

Radical An expression using the symbol $\sqrt{}$ (radical sign). For example, $\sqrt{25}$ and $\sqrt[3]{1000}$ are radicals.

Radicand The number under the radical sign.

Range The set of output values for a function.

Rate A ratio that compares two quantities with different kinds of units.

Ratio A comparison of two numbers by division. The ratio of 2 to 3 can be expressed as 2 out of 3, 2 to 3, 2 : 3, or $\frac{2}{3}$.

Rational number A number that can be expressed as the ratio of two integers, $\frac{p}{q}$, where $q \neq 0$. This includes fractions, terminating decimals, repeating decimals, and integers.

Reciprocal The multiplicative inverse of a number.

Repeating decimal A decimal whose digits repeat in groups of one or more. Examples are 0.181818...and 0.83333....

Root Of an equation, it is the solution of an equation or inequality. For example, the root of the equation $y + 7 = 10$ is $y = 3$ because $3 + 7 = 10$.

Sales tax An additional amount of money charged on items that people buy.

Scale The set of all possible values of a given measurement, including the least and greatest numbers in the set, separated by equal intervals. On a map, intervals used representing the ratio of distance on the map to the actual distance.

Scale drawing A drawing that is similar but either larger or smaller than the actual object.

Scale factor A scale written as a ratio in simplest form.

Scale model A model used to represent something that is too large or too small for an actual-size model.

Scientific notation A convenient way of writing very large numbers. A number written as a product of a number that is at least 1 but less than 10 and a power of 10. For example, 20,000,000 can be written as 2×10^7, and 687,000 as 6.87×10^5.

Sequence A list of numbers in a certain order, such as 0, 1, 2, 3; or 2, 4, 6, 8.

Significant digits All of the digits of a measurement that you know for sure, plus one estimated digit.

Simplest form A fraction is in simplest form when the GCF of the numerator and the denominator is 1.

Simultaneous equations Two or more equations with more than one variable that have a common solution. The equations $x + y = -2$, and $2x - y = 8$ are simultaneous equations because they have the solution (2, –4), or $x = 2$ and $y = -4$.

Solution A value for the variable that makes an equation true. The solution of $40 = n + 10$ is 30.

Solving an equation The process of finding a solution to an equation.

Square of a number The square of a number is the product of the number and itself. For example, the square of 3 (written 3^2) is $3 \cdot 3$ or 9.

Square root x is the square root of a number, n, if $x \cdot x = n$. For example, 5 is the square root of 25 because $5 \cdot 5 = 25$, –5 is also the square of 25 because $-5 \cdot -5 = 25$.

Term One or more numerals and variables connected by multiplication or division only. For example, 5, x, $5x$, x^2, $2x^2$, $2x^2y^3$, and $\frac{3xy^2}{2}$ are terms. Also, a term is used to define each number in a sequence.

Terminating decimal A decimal whose digits end. Every terminating decimal can be written as a fraction with a denominator of 10, 100, 1,000, and so on.

Ton A customary unit of weight equal to 2,000 pounds.

Trinomial A polynomial with three terms. For example, $12x^2 + 4x - 45$ is a trinomial.

Two-step equation An equation having two different operations.

Variable A variable takes the place of number. It represents a set of values. In algebra, an alphabet letter or literal symbol is used as a variable. For example, in $12x^2 + 4y - 45$, x and y are the variables.

Number Theory

Associative property The way in which three numbers are grouped when they are added or multiplied does not change their sum or product. For any numbers a, b, and c, $a + (b + c) = (a + b) + c$ and $a \cdot (b \cdot c) = (a \cdot b) \cdot c$ or $a(bc) = (ab)c$.

Base In a power x^y, x is the base. For example, in 5^4, 5 is the base.

Commutative property The order in which two numbers are added or multiplied does not change their sum or product. For example, $3 \cdot 4 = 4 \cdot 3$, or $a \cdot b = b \cdot a$; multiplication is commutative, so the order of the factors does not matter.

Composite numbers Whole numbers greater than 1 that have more than two factors.

Distributive property of multiplication over addition To multiply a sum by a number, multiply each addend of the sum by the number outside the parentheses. For example, $3(4 + 6) = 3(4) + 3(6)$ or $a(b + c) = a(b) + a(c)$, where a, b, and c are any number.

Even numbers Any number that is divisible by 2.

Exponent In a power x^y, y is the exponent, or in 3^4, 4 is the exponent.

Factors Two or more numbers that are multiplied together to form a product. The numbers that divide evenly into another number. Also called *divisors*. To find the divisors of a particular number.

Identity property The sum of an addend and zero is the addend. The product of a factor and one is the factor.

Multiple The product of two numbers. Also, a multiple of a number is evenly divisible by that number; for example, a multiple of 4 is divisible by 4.

Numerical expression A numerical expression is a combination of numbers and operations. The expressions $3 \cdot 5 - (4 + 6)$ is a numerical expression.

Odd numbers Any number that is not divisible by two.

Perfect square It is the product of a whole number multiplied by itself.

Power The result of x^y. For example, the power of 2^3 is 8. Many people also refer to the exponent as the power.

Prime factorization Every composite number can be written as a product of prime numbers in exactly one way. The product is called prime factorization of the number.

Prime number It is a whole number greater than 1 that has exactly two factors, 1 and itself. The first prime number is 2.

Principal The amount of money, borrowed or invested, on which interest is paid.

Principal square root The positive square root of a number.

Proportion When two ratios or rates are equivalent, they form a proportion. An equality between two ratios: $\frac{a}{b} = \frac{c}{d}$, or $a : b = c : d$ (read: *a* is to *b* as *c* is to *d*).

Rate A ratio that compares two quantities with different kinds of units.

Ratio The comparison of two numbers by division.

Rectangular array A geometric arrangement formed by a rows and columns.

Relatively prime Two or more numbers are relatively prime if their only common factor is 1. For example, 3 and 5 are relatively prime, and 4 and 12 are not relatively prime.

Unit rate When a rate is simplified so that it has a denominator of 1 unit.

Geometry

Abscissa The *x*-coordinate of an ordered pair of numbers. It is the distance from the *y*-axis (ordinate) and is the first number of the ordered pair.

Acute angle An angle whose measure is greater than 0 and less than 90°.

Acute triangle A triangle all of whose angles are acute.

Altitude of a prism Also known as height of a prism. A line segment that connects the planes of the bases of a prism and that is perpendicular to both of them.

Altitude of a pyramid Also known as height of a pyramid. A perpendicular line segment joining the vertex of the pyramid to the plane of its base.

Altitude (or height) of a quadrilateral with parallel sides A perpendicular line segment that joins a point on one of the parallel sides to the line that contains the other side.

Altitude of a triangle Also known as height of a triangle. A perpendicular line segment drawn from a vertex of the triangle to the line of the opposite side.

Angle A pair of rays that have the same endpoint. The ray and vertex are used to name the angle. For example, if you have $\overrightarrow{BA}$ and $\overrightarrow{BC}$, and vertex *B*, you can name the angles $\angle ABC$, $\angle CBA$, or $\angle B$.

Apothem of a regular polygon A perpendicular line segment from the center of the polygon to one of its sides.

Area The number of square units needed to cover a surface enclosed by a geometric figure.

Area of a circle The limit of the areas of the inscribed regular polygons.

Base The base of a parallelogram or triangle is any side of the figure. The bases of a trapezoid are the parallel sides.

Betweenness of points As illustrated in Figure 6–1, suppose that points *A*, *B*, and *C* are collinear with coordinates *a*, *b*, and *c*, respectively. Point *B* is between points *A* and *C* (written *A-B-C*) if and only if either $a < b < c$, or $a > b > c$.

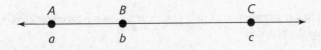

Figure 6–1

Betweenness of rays As illustrated in Figure 6–2, suppose that $\overrightarrow{OA}$, $\overrightarrow{OB}$, and $\overrightarrow{OC}$ are in a half-rotation with coordinates a, b, and c, respectively. $\overrightarrow{OB}$ is between $\overrightarrow{OA}$ and $\overrightarrow{OC}$ (written $\overrightarrow{OA} - \overrightarrow{OB} = \overrightarrow{OC}$) if and only if either $a < b < c$, or $a > b > c$.

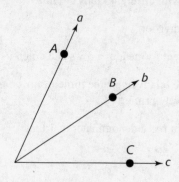

Figure 6–2

Biperpendicular quadrilateral A quadrilateral that has a pair of sides both of which are perpendicular to the third side.

Bisector of an angle A ray that is between the sides of the angle and that divides it into two equal angles.

Center The given point from which all points on a circle or sphere are the same distance.

Center of a regular polygon The center of the circumscribed or inscribed circle of the polygon.

Central angle of a circle An angle whose vertex is the center of the circle.

Central angle of a regular polygon An angle formed by radii drawn to two consecutive vertices of the polygon.

Centroid of a triangle The point in which the medians of the triangle are concurrent.

Cevian of a triangle A line segment that joins a vertex of the triangle to a point on the opposite side.

Chord of a circle A line segment that joins two points of the circle.

Circle The set of all points in a plane that are at a given distance from a given point in the plane. A closed curve in a plane such that every point is the same distance from the center.

Circumcenter of a polygon The center of the circle circumscribed about the polygon.

Circumference of a circle The limit of the perimeters of the inscribed regular polygons. It is the measure of the distance around a circle.

Circumscribed circle about a polygon The circle that contains all of the vertices of the polygon.

Collinear points Points that lie on the same line.

Complementary angles Two angles the sum of whose measures are 90°.

Complex figure A figure made of circles, rectangles, squares, and other two-dimensional figures.

Concave polygon A polygon that is not convex. A polygon in which two nonconsecutive vertices can be connected by a line segment that goes outside the polygon.

Concentric circles Circles that lie in the same plane and have the same center.

Concurrent lines Lines that contain all the same points.

Concyclic points Points that lie on the same circle.

Cone Suppose that *A* is a plane, *R* is a circular region in plane *A*, and *P* is a point not in plane *A*. The set of all segments that join *P* to a point of region *R* form a cone (see Figure 6–3).

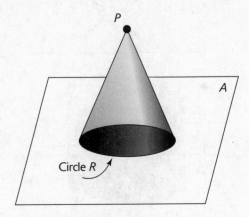

Figure 6–3

Congruent angles Angles that have the same measure.

Congruent figures Two figures for which there is an isometry such that one figure is the image of the other.

Congruent polygons Two polygons for which there is a correspondence between their vertices such that all of their corresponding sides and angles are equal.

Congruent segments Two line segments having the same length.

Contrapositive of a conditional statement The statement formed by interchanging the hypothesis and conclusion to the statement and denying or negating both.

Converse of a conditional statement The statement formed by interchanging the hypothesis and conclusion of the statement.

Convex polygon A polygon such that, for each line that contains a side of the polygon, the rest of the polygon lies on one side of the line. All diagonals are contained inside the polygon. Not concave.

Coordinate grid A plane in which a horizontal number line and vertical number line intersect at their zero points. Also called a *coordinate plane*.

Coordinate plane This is the same as coordinate grid.

Coplanar points Points that lie in the same plane.

Corollary A theorem that can be easily proved as a consequence of another theorem.

Cosine of an acute angle of a right triangle The ratio of the length of the adjacent leg to the length of the hypotenuse.

Cross section of a geometric solid The intersection of a plane and a solid.

Cube A rectangular solid all of whose dimensions are equal. It is a three-dimensional solid figure with six square faces.

Cyclic polygon A polygon for which there exists a circle that contains all of its vertices.

Cylinder A three-dimensional figure with two parallel congruent circular bases. Suppose *A* and *B* are two parallel planes, *R* is a circular region in one plane, and *m* is a line that intersects both planes but not *R*. The set of all segments parallel to line *m* that join a point of region *R* to a point of the other plane and form a cylinder (see Figure 6–4).

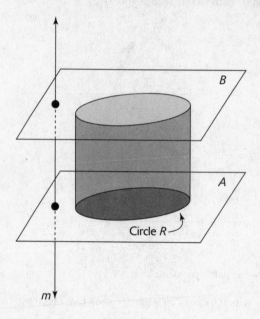

Figure 6–4

Decagon A polygon that has 10 sides.

Degrees The most common unit to measure for angles. If a circle were divided in 360° equal-sized parts, each part would have an angle measure of 1 degree (also written as 1°).

Degree measure of a major arc 360° minus the measure of the corresponding minor arc.

Degree measure of a minor arc The measure of its central angle.

Degree measure of a semicircle The degree measure of a semicircle is equal to 180°.

Diagonal of a polygon A line segment that joins any two nonconsecutive vertices of the polygon.

Diameter of a circle A chord that contains the center of the circle. A line segment whose midpoint is the center of the circle and endpoints are on the circle. It is the distance across a circle through its center.

Distance between two parallel lines It is the length of any perpendicular segment that joins one line to the other.

Distance from a point to a line The length of the perpendicular segment from the point to the line.

Dodecagon A polygon that has 12 sides.

Equiangular polygon A polygon all of whose angles are equal.

Equilateral polygon A polygon all of whose sides are equal.

Equilateral triangle A triangle having three congruent sides.

Exterior angle of a polygon An angle that forms a linear pair with one of the angles of the polygon.

Great circle of a sphere A set of points that is the intersection of the sphere and a plane containing its center.

Height The length of the segment perpendicular to the base with endpoints on opposite sides. In a triangle, it is the distance from a base to the opposite vertex.

Heptagon A polygon that has seven sides.

Hexagon A polygon that has six sides.

Hypotenuse of a right triangle The side opposite the right angle of the triangle. The longest side of a right triangle.

Incenter of a polygon The center of the inscribed circle of the polygon.

Inscribed angle of a circle An angle whose vertex is on the circle and each of whose sides intersects the circle in another point.

Inscribed circle in a polygon A circle for which each side of the polygon is tangent to the circle.

Inverse of a conditional statement The statement formed by denying or negating both the hypothesis and conclusion of the statement.

Isometry A transformation that preserves distance.

Isosceles trapezoid A trapezoid whose legs are equal.

Isosceles triangle A triangle that has at least two equal sides.

Lateral area of a prism The sum of the areas of the lateral faces of the prism.

Leg The legs of a right triangle are the two sides that form the right angle. The legs of an isosceles triangle are the two equal sides.

Length of a line segment The distance between the endpoints of the line segment.

Line segment The set of two points and all the points between them.

Line symmetry Figures that match exactly when folded in half have a line symmetry.

Line of symmetry A line that divides a figure into two halves that are reflections of each other.

Linear pair Two angles that have a common side and whose other sides are opposite rays. The sum of two angles that form a linear pair is 180°.

Median of a triangle A line segment that joins a vertex of the triangle to the midpoint of the opposite side.

Midpoint of a line segment A point between the endpoints of the line segment that divides it into two equal segments.

Midsegment of a triangle A line segment that joins the midpoints of two sides of the triangle.

Nonagon A polygon that has nine sides.

Noncollinear points Points that do not lie on the same line.

Oblique line and plane (or two planes) A line and plane (or two planes) that are neither parallel nor perpendicular. They intersect at non-right angles.

Obtuse angle An angle whose measure is more than 90° but less than 180°.

Obtuse triangle A triangle that has an obtuse angle.

Octagon A polygon that has eight sides.

Opposite rays $\overrightarrow{AB}$ and $\overrightarrow{AC}$ are opposite rays if and only if $B\text{-}A\text{-}C$. Opposite rays form a straight line.

Ordered pair A pair of numbers (x, y) in which the order is considered, so that (x, y) is different from (y, x). Each ordered pair of numbers corresponds to a point in a coordinate plane and vice versa.

Ordinate The *y*-coordinate of an ordered pair of numbers. It is the second number of the ordered pair. It is the distance from the *x*-axis.

Origin The point (0, 0) or the intersection of the *x*-axis and *y*-axis in a coordinate plane.

Orthocenter of a triangle The point in which the lines containing the attitudes of the triangle are concurrent.

Parallel lines Lines that lie in the same plane and do not intersect.

Parallel planes Planes that do not intersect.

Parallelogram A quadrilateral (four-sided plane figure) in which both pairs of opposite sides are parallel.

Pentagon A polygon that has five sides.

Perimeter of a polygon The sum of the lengths of the sides of a polygon. It is the measure of the distance around a polygon.

Perpendicular bisector of a line segment The line that is perpendicular to the line segment and that divides it into two equal parts.

Perpendicular line and plane A line and plane that intersect such that the line is perpendicular to every line in the plane that passes through the point of intersection.

Perpendicular lines Intersecting lines that form right angles.

Perpendicular planes Planes such that one plane contains a line that is perpendicular to the other plane.

Polar points The points of intersection of a line through the center of the sphere with the sphere.

Polygon A closed plane figure whose sides are three or more line segments. Let *A*, *B*, ..., *C* be a set of at least three points in a plane such that no three consecutive points are collinear. If line segments P_1P_2, P_2P_3, ..., P_nP_1 intersect only at their endpoints, they form a polygon (see Figure 6–5).

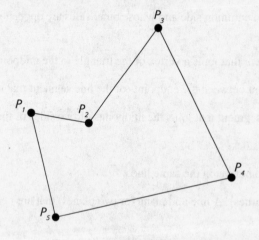

Figure 6–5

Polygonal region The union of a finite number of nonoverlapping triangular regions in a plane.

Polyhedron A solid bounded by parts of intersecting planes.

Postulate A statement that is assumed to be true without proof.

Prism A three-dimensional figure in which two faces are congruent and parallel and all the other faces are parallelograms (see Figure 6–6).

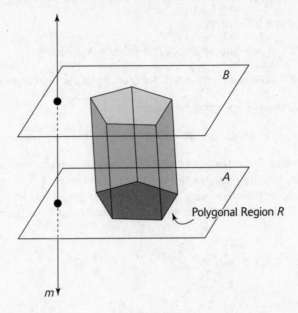

Figure 6–6

Pyramid A three-dimensional figure in which there is one base and all other faces are triangles that meet at a point not on the base plane (see Figure 6–7).

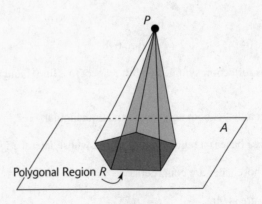

Figure 6–7

Pythagorean relationship In any right triangle, the square of the hypotenuse equals the sum of the squares of the other two sides. If a and b represent the legs of a right triangle and c represents the hypotenuse, then $a^2 + b^2 = c^2$.

Pythagorean triple A set of three integers that can be the lengths of the sides of a right triangle.

Quadrant One of the four regions into which the two perpendicular lines of the coordinate plane separate the plane. There are four possible quadrants combining different ordered pairs (x, y) for the x-axis and y-axis: Quadrant I (x is positive, y is positive), Quadrant II (x is negative, y is positive), Quadrant III (x is negative, y is negative), and Quadrant IV (x is positive, y is negative).

Quadrilateral A polygon with four sides.

Radius of a circle A line segment that joins the center of the circle to any point on the circle.

Radius of a regular polygon A line segment that joins the center of the polygon to any vertex of the regular polygon.

Ratio The ratio of the numbers a to b is the number $\frac{a}{b}$.

Ray $\overrightarrow{AB}$ is the set of points A, B, and all points of X such that either A-X-B or A-B-X.

Rectangle A parallelogram all of whose angles are equal. All four angles are right angles.

Rectangular solid A polyhedron that has six rectangular faces.

Reflection A type of transformation in which a figure is flipped over a line of symmetry.

Reflection of a point through a line The reflection of point P through line m is point P itself if P is on m or the point P' such that m is the perpendicular bisector of line segment PP' if P is not on m. For example, in Figure 6–8, the reflection of point X through line m is point X itself or point X' since point X is not on line m, and the reflection of point Y is Y' such that line m is the perpendicular bisector of line segment YY' since point Y is not on line m.

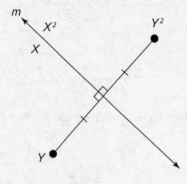

Figure 6–8

Reflection symmetry A figure has reflection symmetry with respect to a line if and only if it coincides with its reflection image through the line.

Regular polygon A convex polygon that is both equilateral and equiangular.

Regular pyramid A pyramid whose base is a regular polygon and whose lateral edges are equal.

Rhombus A quadrilateral all of whose sides are congruent.

Right angle An angle whose measure is 90°.

Right triangle A triangle that has a right angle.

Rotation A transformation that is the composite of two successive reflections through intersecting lines. A turn.

Rotation symmetry A figure has rotation symmetry with respect to a point if and only if it coincides with its rotation image about the point.

Sachcheri quadrilateral A biperpendicular quadrilateral whose legs are equal.

Scalene triangle A triangle that has no equal sides.

Secant A line that intersects a circle in two points.

Secant angle An angle whose sides are contained in two secants of a circle so that each side intersects the circle in at least one point other than the angle's vertex.

Secant segment A segment that intersects a circle in two points, exactly one of which is an endpoint of the segment.

Sector of a circle A region bounded by an arc of the circle and the two radii to the endpoints of the arc.

Semiperimeter of a triangle The number that is half the perimeter of the triangle.

Similar polygons Two polygons for which there is a correspondence between their vertices such that the corresponding sides of the polygons are proportional and the corresponding angles are equal. Figures have the same shape but not necessarily the same size.

Sine of an acute angle of a right triangle The ratio of the length of the opposite leg to the length of the hypotenuse.

Slope The slope of a line in a coordinate plane refers to the steepness of the line. The slope of a horizontal line is zero. The slope of a vertical line is undefined. The slope of a line is determined from two points on the line: (difference of y-coordinate)/(difference of x-coordinate). The slope m of a nonvertical line that contains the points $P_1(x_1, y_1)$ and $P_2(x_2, y_2)$ is $m = \dfrac{y_2 - y_1}{x_2 - x_1}$.

Solid It is a three-dimensional figure. Prisms, pyramids, cones, and cylinders are examples of solids.

Sphere The set of all points in space that are at a given distance from a given point.

Square A quadrilateral that is both equilateral and equiangular.

Straight angle An angle whose measure is $180°$.

Supplementary angles Two angles the sum of whose measures is $180°$.

Surface area The sum of areas of all the surfaces (faces) of a three-dimensional figure.

Tangent A line in the plane of a circle that intersects the circle in exactly one point.

Tangent of an acute angle of a right triangle The ratio of the length of the opposite leg to the length of the adjacent leg.

Tangent segment Any segment of a tangent line to a circle that has the point of tangency as one of its endpoints.

Tessellation A repetitive pattern of polygons that fit together with no holes or gaps.

Theorem A statement that is proved by reasoning deductively from already accepted statements.

Transformations A one-to-one correspondence between two sets of points. It is a movement of a geometric figure.

Translation A transformation that is the composite of two successive reflections through parallel lines. The figure is slid horizontally, vertically, or both.

Transversal A line that intersects two or more lines that lie in the same plane in different points.

Trapezoid A quadrilateral that has exactly one pair of parallel sides.

Triangle A polygon that has three sides.

Triangular region The union of a triangle and its interior.

Vertex The point where two sides of an angle meet.

Vertical angles Two angles such that the sides of one angle are opposite rays to the sides of the other angle.

Volume The measure of the amount of space occupied by a figure in three dimensions.

x-axis The horizontal line in a coordinate plane.

x-coordinate The x-coordinate, or *abscissa,* of an ordered pair of numbers is the first number in the pair. For example, in (4, –9), 4 is the x-coordinate.

y-axis The vertical number line in a coordinate plane.

y-coordinate The y-coordinate, or ordinate, of an ordered pair of numbers is the second number in the pair. For example, in (4, –9), –9 is the y-coordinate.

y-intercept The y-intercept of a line in a coordinate plane is the y-coordinate of the point of intersection of the line with the y-axis. For example, in the equation of a line, $y = mx + b$, b is the y-intercept.

Probability and Statistics

Average The sum of a set of quantities divided by the total number of quantities. Also known as *mean.*

Bar graph A statistical graph used to compare quantities. It may be made up of all vertical bars or all horizontal bars. This type of graph is used mainly for purposes of comparison.

Box-and-whisker plot A diagram that summarizes data using the median, the upper and lower quartiles, and the extreme values. A box is drawn around the quartile values, and whiskers extend from each quartile to the extreme data points.

Circle graph A type of statistical graph used to compare parts of a whole.

Cluster Data that are grouped closely together.

Combination An arrangement, or listing, of objects in which order is not important.

Complementary events The events of one outcome happening and that outcome not happening are complementary events. The sum of the probabilities of complementary events is equal to 1.

Compound event An event consisting of two or more simple events.

Dependent events Two or more events in which the outcome of one event affects the outcome of the other event.

Experimental probability An estimated probability based on the relative frequency of positive outcomes occurring during an experiment.

Fair game A game in which players of equal skill have an equal chance of winning.

Frequency For a collection of data, the number of items in a given category.

Frequency table A table for organizing a set of data that shows the number of pieces of data that fall within given intervals or categories.

Histogram A bar graph of a frequency distribution. The bars are used to represent the frequency of the numerical data that have been organized in intervals.

Independent events Two or more events in which the outcome of one event does not affect the outcome of the other event(s).

Interquartile range The range of the middle half of a set of numbers: UQ–LQ.

Interval On a scale, the difference between the greatest and least values in each category.

Leaf The second greatest place value of data in a stem-and-leaf plot.

Line graph A type of statistical graph using lines to show how values change over time.

Line plot A graph that uses an × above a number on a number line each time that number occurs in a set of data.

Lower extreme The least number of a set of data.

Lower quartile The median of the lower half of a set of numbers, indicated by LQ.

Mean The sum of a set of quantities divided by the total number of quantities. Also known as *average*.

Measures of central tendency Numbers that are used to describe the center of a set of data. These measures include the mean, median, and mode.

Median The middle score of a set of scores when arranged according to size (or numerical order); for an even number of scores or quantities, the median is the average of the middle two scores.

Mode The number that occurs with the greatest frequency in a set of scores. There may be one or more modes or no mode.

Outcome One possible result of a probability event. For example, 3 is an outcome when a number cube is rolled.

Outlier A piece of data that is quite separated from the rest of the data. In a box-and-whisker plot, data that are more than 1.5 times the interquartile range from the quartiles.

Permutation An arrangement, or listing, of objects in which order is important.

Population The entire group of items or individuals from which the samples under consideration are taken.

Probability The probability of an event occurring is the ratio of the number of favorable outcomes to the total number of possible outcomes.

Random Outcomes occur at random if each outcome is equally likely to occur.

Random sample A sample is called random if the members of the sample are selected purely on the basis of chance.

Range The range of a set of scores or quantities is the difference between the highest score and lowest score in the data set.

Sample space The set of all possible outcomes of a probability experiment.

Scatter plot In a scatter plot, two sets of related data are plotted as ordered pair on the same graph.

Simple event One outcome or a collection of outcomes.

Survey A question or set of questions designed to collect data about a specific group of people.

Theoretical probability The ratio of the number of ways an event can occur to the number of possible outcomes.

Upper extreme The greatest number of a set of data.

Upper quartile The median of the upper half of a set of numbers, indicated by UQ.

Calculus

Arithmetic series A series in which the difference between subsequent terms is constant. The nth term of an arithmetic series can be defined as $a_n = a_1 + d(n - 1)$ where a_n is the nth term, a_1 is the first term, d is the difference between any two subsequent terms, and n is the number of terms.

Composite function If f is a function from X to Y and g is a function from Y to Z, then the composite function $g \circ f$ is the function from X to Z defined by $(g \circ f) = g(f(x))$.

Concavity The bend of a graph. Concave up bends below. Concave down bends above. If the graph of a function lies above all of its tangents, then it is concave upward. If the graph of a function lies below all of its tangents, then it is concave downward. If the slope of the tangent line is increasing, the graph is concave up; if slope of the tangent line is decreasing, the graph is concave down. Concavity is determined by examining the second derivative.

Continuity of an interval A function f is continuous on an interval if f is continuous at every number in the interval.

Continuous A function f is continuous at a number a if $\lim_{x \to a} f(x) = f(a)$. Continuity requires three things: $f(a)$ is defined; $\lim_{x \to a} f(x)$ exists; and $\lim_{x \to a} f(x) = f(a)$.

Convergent A sequence is convergent if $\lim a_n$ exists and is finite. A series is convergent if the corresponding sequence is convergent and the $\lim_{n \to \infty} s_n = s$ where s_n is a partial sum of the first n terms and s is a real number.

Derivative If a function f is defined on an open interval containing a, then the derivative $f'(a)$ of f at a is given by
$$f'(a) = \lim_{h \to 0} \frac{f(a+h) - f(a)}{h}$$ provided the limit exists.

Differential If $y = f(x)$, where f is differentiable, and if Δx is an increment of x, then (a) the differential dy of the dependent variable y is given by $dy = f'(x) \Delta x$; (b) the differential dx of the independent variable x is given by $dx = \Delta x$.

Divergent Not convergent. A sequence or series which does not approach a single value. For example, the sequence 2, 4, 6, 8, ... is divergent because it does not approach a single value.

Domain The set of possible values for x is called the domain of the function.

Extrema Maximum or minimum points of a function f.

Function A function f is a correspondence that associates with each element x a unique element of y. The element y is called the image of x under f and is denoted $f(x)$. *Alternative definition:* A function from a set X to a set Y is a subset W of $X \times Y$ such that for each x in X there is exactly one ordered pair (x, y) in W having x as its first element. A function is a relation in which every x value is paired with a unique y value.

Fundamental theorem of calculus This theorem includes the following two parts:

Part One: If f is continuous on $[a, b]$, then the function g defined by $g(x) = \int_a^x f(t)\,dt$ where $a \leq x \leq b$ is continuous on $[a, b]$ and differentiable on (a, b), and $g'(x) = f(x)$.

Part Two: If f is continuous on $[a, b]$, then $\int_a^b f(x)\,dx = F(b) - F(a)$ where F is any antiderivative of f, that is $F' = f$.

Geometric series A series in which the ratio of a term and the subsequent term is constant. An infinite geometric series has a sum (converges) if $|y| < 1$ where r is the ratio of one term to the previous term. If $|y| \geq 1$, the geometric series diverges.

Integral The area under a curve. The inverse of the derivative.

Intermediate value theorem Suppose that f is continuous on the closed interval $[a, b]$, and let N be any number strictly between $f(a)$ and $f(b)$. Then there exists a number c in (a, b) such that $f(c) = N$.

Inverse function If f is a one-to-one function with domain X and range Y, then a function g with domain Y and range X is called the inverse function of f if $f(g(x)) = x$, for every x in Y; and $g(f(x)) = x$, for every x in X.

L'Hôpital's rule Suppose f and g are differentiable and $g'(x) \neq 0$ on an open interval I that contains a (except possible at a). Suppose that $\lim_{x \to a} f(x) = 0$ and $\lim_{x \to a} g(x) = 0$ or $\lim_{x \to a} f(x) = \pm \infty$ and $\lim_{x \to a} g(x) = \pm \infty$.

Then $\lim_{x \to a} \dfrac{f(x)}{g(x)} = \lim_{x \to a} \dfrac{f'(x)}{g'(x)}$ if the limit on the right side exists or is ∞ or $-\infty$.

Limit of a function If a function is defined throughout an open interval containing a, except possibly at a itself, then the limit of $f(x)$ as x approaches a is L, written $\lim_{x \to a} f(x) = L$, if for every $\varepsilon > 0$ there corresponds a $\delta > 0$ such that $|f(x) - L| < \varepsilon$ whenever $0 < |x - a| < \delta$. The value that the function f approaches as x approaches a given number a.

Maximum The point at which a graph changes from increasing to decreasing. The largest value of $f(x)$ within a given interval. Absolute maximum is the largest value of $f(x)$ for the entire function.

Mean value theorem Let f be a function that satisfies the following hypotheses:

1. f is continuous on the closed interval $[a, b]$.
2. f is differentiable on the open interval (a, b).

Then there is a number c in (a, b) such that $f'(c) = \dfrac{f(b) - f(a)}{b - a}$, or equivalently $f(b) - f(a) = f'(c)(b - a)$.

Minimum The point at which a graph changes from decreasing to increasing. The smallest value of $f(x)$ within a given interval. Absolute minimum is the smallest value of $f(x)$ for the entire function.

Point of inflection The point at which a graph changes from concave upward to concave downward or vice versa.

Range The range of the function is the set of all images of elements of X.

Riemann sum When finding the area under a curve, the integral can be approximated with a Riemann Sum which is given as $\sum_{i=1}^{n} f\left(x_i^*\right) \Delta x_i$, where x_i^* are points in the interval, Δx_i are the widths of each partition, and n is the number of partition points. In essence, the Riemann Sum is the sum of the rectangles approximated by partition points.

Rolle's theorem Let f be a function that satisfies the following three hypotheses:

1. f is continuous on the closed interval $[a, b]$.
2. f is differentiable on the open interval (a, b).
3. $f(a) = f(b)$.

Then there is a number c in (a, b) such that $f'(c) = 0$.

Sequence A list of terms written in a definite order. Sequences are often either arithmetic or geometric.

Series The sum of the terms in a sequence. Series are often either arithmetic or geometric.

Statistics The mathematics of collecting, organizing, analyzing, and interpreting numerical information.

Taylor series The Taylor series of a function f at a is given by

$$f(x) = \sum_{n=0}^{\infty} \frac{f^{(n)}(a)}{n!} (x - a)^n = f(a) + \frac{f'(a)}{1!}(x - a) + \frac{f''(a)}{2!}(x - a)^2 + \frac{f'''(a)}{3!}(x - a)^3 + \dots.$$

Trigonometry

Amplitude One-half the distance between the minimum and maximum value of a periodic function. The amplitude of the periodic sine function $f(x) = A \sin x$ is A.

Cosecant Abbreviated as csc. The reciprocal of sine: $\csc A = \dfrac{1}{\sin A}$.

Cosine Abbreviated as cos. The cosine of an acute angle in a right triangle is the ratio of the length of the leg adjacent to the angle to the length of the hypotenuse of the triangle: $\cos A = \dfrac{(\text{adjacent leg})}{\text{hypotenuse}}$.

Cotangent Abbreviated as cot. The reciprocal of tangent: $\cot A = \dfrac{1}{\tan A}$.

Degree A unit of measure for angles. One degree is equal to $\frac{1}{360}$ of a full rotation around a circle.

Graph A drawing of the coordinate plane with points plotted on it.

Periodic A periodic function is one that keeps repeating the same pattern of values.

Phase shift The constant by which functions are horizontally shifted from one another.

Shift The vertical or horizontal movement of the graph of a function without changing the shape of the graph.

Secant Abbreviated as sec. The reciprocal of cosine: $\sec A = \frac{1}{\cos A}$.

Sine Abbreviated as sin. The sine of an acute angle in a right triangle is the ratio of the length of the side opposite the angle to the length of the hypotenuse of the triangle: $\sin A = \frac{(\text{opposite leg})}{\text{hypotenuse}}$.

Stretch The vertical or horizontal changing of the graph of a function such that its shape changes, but its orientation does not—for a function f, $f(0, 0)$ remains the same.

Tangent Abbreviated as tan. The tangent of an acute angle in a right triangle is the ratio of the length of the side opposite the angle to the length of the side adjacent to the angle: $\tan A = \frac{(\text{opposite leg})}{(\text{adjacent leg})}$.

Vertical line test A method to determine whether a given plotted line on a graph is a function. If a vertical line can be placed somewhere in the coordinate plane such that it intersects with the graph twice, the graph is not a function. Two intersections with a vertical line signify that for a given value of x, there are two possible values of $f(x)$, which by definition is impossible for a function.

Description of Important Formulas

The following is a list of important mathematics formulas and properties. Studying these formulas will help you prepare to take the practice tests in this book, and the actual CSET: Mathematics. This list is not intended to represent a comprehensive listing of all the formulas necessary for the test. You are not expected to memorize all these formulas, but should familiarize yourself with all of them. The formulas are organized by area: algebra, geometry, trigonometry, differentiation rules, and table of integrals.

Algebra

Arithmetic Operations:

$$a(b + c) = ab + ac$$

$$\frac{a}{b} + \frac{c}{d} = \frac{ad + bc}{bd}$$

$$\frac{a + c}{b} = \frac{a}{b} + \frac{c}{b}$$

$$\frac{\frac{a}{b}}{\frac{c}{d}} = \frac{a}{b} \cdot \frac{d}{c} = \frac{ad}{bc}$$

Exponents and Radicals:

$$x^m x^n$$

$$(x^m)^n = x^{mn}$$

$$x^{1/n} = \sqrt[n]{x}$$

$$x^{m/n} = \sqrt[n]{x^m} = \left(\sqrt[n]{x}\right)^m$$

$$= x^{m+n}$$

$$x^{-n} = \frac{1}{x^n}$$

$$\left(\frac{x}{y}\right)^n = \frac{x^n}{y^n}$$

$$\sqrt[m]{\sqrt[n]{x}} = \sqrt[n]{\sqrt[m]{x}} = \sqrt[mn]{x}$$

$$\frac{x^m}{x^n} = x^{m-n}$$

$$(xy)^n = x^n y^n$$

$$\sqrt[n]{xy} = \sqrt[n]{x}\sqrt[n]{y}$$

$$\sqrt[n]{\frac{x}{y}} = \frac{\sqrt[n]{x}}{\sqrt[n]{y}}$$

Factoring Special Polynomials:

$$x^2 - y^2 = (x + y)(x - y)$$

$$x^3 + y^3 = (x + y)(x^2 - xy + y^2)$$

$$x^3 - y^3 = (x - y)(x^2 + xy + y^2)$$

Binomial Theorem:

$$(x + y)^2 = x^2 + 2xy + y^2$$

$$(x - y)^2 = x^2 - 2xy + y^2$$

$$(x + y)^3 = x^3 + 3x^2y + 3xy^2 + y^3$$

$$(x - y)^3 = x^3 - 3x^2y + 3xy^2 - y^3$$

$$\left(x + y\right)^n = x^n + nx^{n-1} + \frac{n(n-1)}{2}x^{n-2}y^2 + \ldots + \binom{n}{k}x^{n-k}y^k + \ldots + nxy^{n-1} + y^n, \text{ where } \binom{n}{k} = \frac{n(n-1)\ldots(n-k+1)}{1 \cdot 2 \cdot 3 \cdot \ldots \cdot k}$$

Quadratic Formula:

If $ax^2 + bx + c = 0$, then $x = \dfrac{-b \pm \sqrt{b^2 - 4ac}}{2a}$

Inequalities and Absolute Value:

If $a < b$ and $b < c$, then $a < c$.

If $a < b$, then $a + c < b + c$

If $a > 0$, then

If $a < b$ and $c > 0$, then $ca < cb$.

If $a < b$ and $c < 0$, then $ca > cb$

$|x| = a$ means $x = a$ or $x = -a$; $|x| < a$ means $-a < x < a$; $|x| > a$ means $x > a$ or $x < -a$.

Conversions:

Length:

1 yard = 3 feet = 36 inches

1 mile = 1,760 yards = 5,280 feet

1 acre = 43,560 square feet

1 meter = 100 centimeters = 1000 millimeters

1 kilometer = 1000 meters

Time:

1 hour = 60 minutes

1 minute = 60 seconds

Capacity:

1 cup = 8 fluid ounces

1 pint = 2 cups

1 quart = 2 pints

1 gallon = 4 quarts

1 liter = 1000 milliliters = 1000 cubic centimeters

Mass/Weight:

1 gram = 1000 milligrams

1 pound = 16 ounces

1 kilogram = 1000 grams

1 ton = 2,000 pounds

Other Formulas:

Distance, rate, time formula: $d = rt$, where d = distance, r = rate, t = time.

Simple interest formula: $I = prt$, where p = principal, r = rate, t = time.

Geometry

Geometry Formulas:

Formulas for area A, circumference C, and volume V:

Triangle

$A = \frac{1}{2}bh$

$\quad = \frac{1}{2}bh\sin\theta$

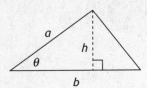

Circle

$A = \pi r^2$

$C = 2\pi r$

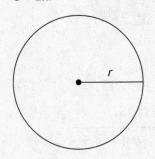

Sector of a Circle

$A = \frac{1}{2}r^2\theta$

$s = r\theta$

(θ in radians)

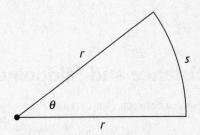

Rectangle

$A = lw = bh$

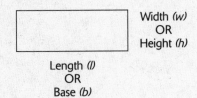

Width (w)
OR
Height (h)

Length (l)
OR
Base (b)

Parallelogram

$A = bh$

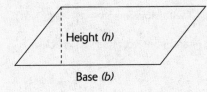

Height (h)

Base (b)

Trapezoid

$A = \frac{1}{2}h\left(b_1 + b_2\right)$

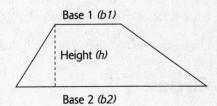

Base 1 $(b1)$

Height (h)

Base 2 $(b2)$

Prism

$V = Bh$

Where B is the area of the base

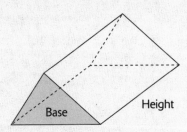

Base

Height

Pyramid

$V = \frac{1}{3}Bh$

Where B is the area of the base

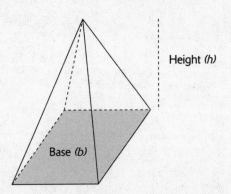

Height (h)

Base (b)

225

Sphere

$$V = \frac{4}{3}\pi r^3$$

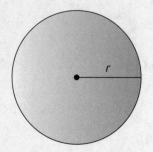

Cylinder

$$V = \pi r^2 h$$

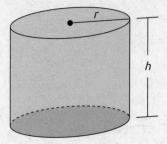

Cone

$$V = \frac{1}{3}\pi r^2 h$$

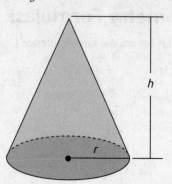

Distance and Midpoint Formulas:

Distance between $P_1(x_1, y_1)$ and $P_2(x_2, y_2)$: $d = \sqrt{\left(x_2 - x_1\right)^2 + \left(y_2 - y_1\right)^2}$

Midpoint of $\overline{P_1 P_2}$: $\left(\dfrac{x_1 + x_2}{2}, \dfrac{y_1 + y_2}{2}\right)$

Lines:

Slope of line through $P_1(x_1, y_1)$ and $P_2(x_2, y_2)$: $m = \dfrac{y_2 - y_1}{x_2 - x_1}$

Point-slope equation of line through $P_1(x_1, y_1)$ with slope m: $y - y_1 = m(x - x_1)$

Slope-intercept equation of line with slope m and y-intercept b: $y = mx + b$

Circles:

Equation of circle with center (h, k) and radius r: $(x - h)^2 + (y - k)^2 = r^2$

Trigonometry

Angle Measurement:

π radians $= 180°$ 　　　 $1° = \dfrac{\pi}{180}$ rad 　　　 1 rad $= \dfrac{180°}{\pi}$ 　　　 $s = r\theta$ (θ in radians)

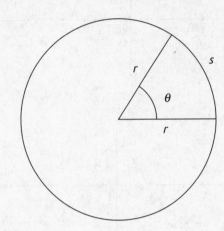

Right Angle Trigonometry:

$\sin\theta = \dfrac{\text{opp}}{\text{hyp}}$ 　　　 $\csc\theta = \dfrac{\text{hyp}}{\text{opp}}$ 　　　 $\cos\theta = \dfrac{\text{adj}}{\text{hyp}}$

$\sec\theta = \dfrac{\text{hyp}}{\text{adj}}$ 　　　 $\tan\theta = \dfrac{\text{opp}}{\text{adj}}$ 　　　 $\cot\theta = \dfrac{\text{adj}}{\text{opp}}$

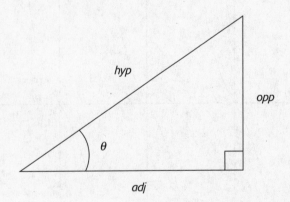

Graphs of the Trigonometric Functions:

$y = \sin x$

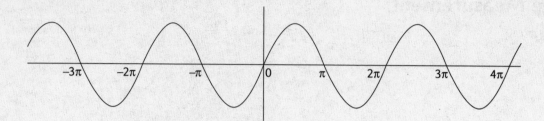

$y = \cos x$

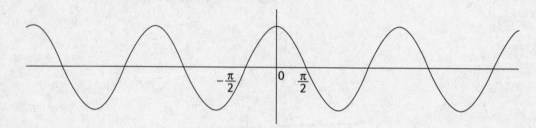

$y = \tan x$

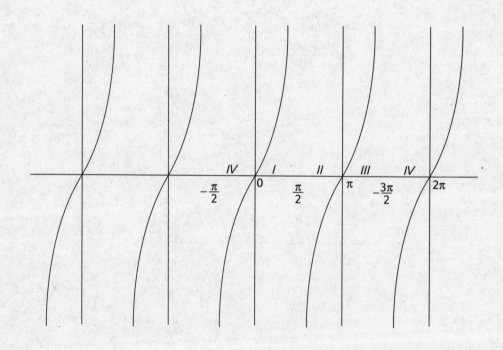

$y = \sec x$

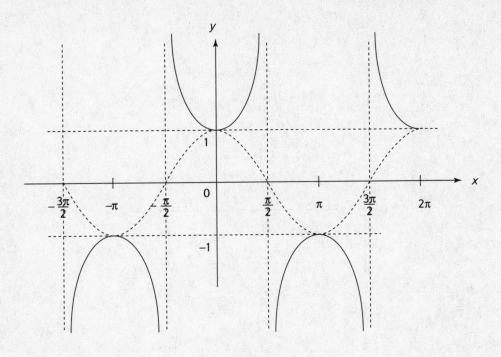

$y = \cot x$

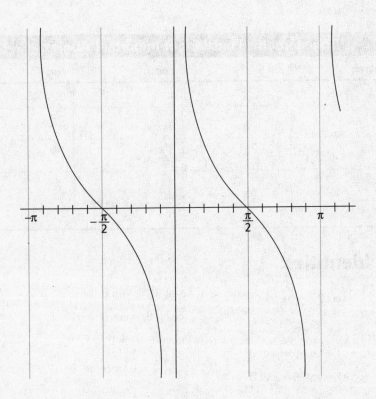

$y = \csc x$

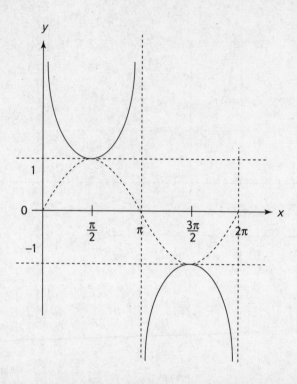

Trigonometric Functions of Important Angles:				
θ	*radians*	*sin* θ	*cos* θ	*tan* θ
0°	0	0	1	0
30°	$\frac{\pi}{6}$	$\frac{1}{2}$	$\frac{\sqrt{3}}{2}$	$\frac{\sqrt{3}}{3}$
45°	$\frac{\pi}{4}$	$\frac{\sqrt{2}}{2}$	$\frac{\sqrt{2}}{2}$	1
60°	$\frac{\pi}{3}$	$\frac{\sqrt{3}}{2}$	$\frac{1}{2}$	$\sqrt{3}$
90°	$\frac{\pi}{2}$	1	0	–

Fundamental Identities:

$\csc\theta = \dfrac{1}{\sin\theta}$

$\sec\theta = \dfrac{1}{\cos\theta}$

$\tan\theta = \dfrac{\sin\theta}{\cos\theta}$

$\cot\theta = \dfrac{\cos\theta}{\sin\theta}$

$\cot\theta = \dfrac{1}{\tan\theta}$

$\sin^2\theta + \cos^2\theta = 1$

$1 + \tan^2\theta = \sec^2\theta$

$1 + \cot^2\theta = \csc^2\theta$

$\sin(-\theta) = -\sin\theta$

$\cos(-\theta) = \cos\theta$

$\tan(-\theta = \tan\theta$

$\sin\left(\dfrac{\pi}{2} - \theta\right) = \cos\theta$

$\cos\left(\dfrac{\pi}{2} - \theta\right) = \sin\theta$

$\tan\left(\dfrac{\pi}{2} - \theta\right) = \cot\theta$

The Law of Sines:

$$\frac{\sin A}{a} = \frac{\sin B}{b} = \frac{\sin C}{c}$$

The Law of Cosines:

$$a^2 = b^2 + c^2 - 2bc \cos A$$

$$b^2 = a^2 + c^2 - 2ac \cos B$$

$$c^2 = a^2 + b^2 - 2ab \cos C$$

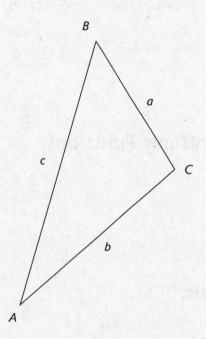

Addition and Subtraction Formulas:

$$\sin (x + y) = \sin x \cos y + \cos x \sin y$$

$$\cos (x + y) = \cos x \cos y - \sin x \sin y$$

$$\tan (x + y) = \frac{\tan x + \tan y}{1 - \tan x \tan y}$$

$$\sin (x - y) = \sin x \cos y - \cos x \sin y$$

$$\cos (x - y) = \cos x \cos y + \sin x \sin y$$

$$\tan (x - y) = \frac{\tan x - \tan y}{1 + \tan x \tan y}$$

Double-Angle Formulas:

$$\sin 2x = 2 \sin x \cos x \qquad \cos 2x = \cos^2 x - \sin^2 x = 2 \cos^2 x - 1 = 1 - 2 \sin^2 x \qquad \tan 2 = \frac{2 \tan x}{1 - \tan^2 x}$$

Half-Angle Formulas:

$$\sin^2 x = \frac{1 - \cos 2x}{2} \qquad\qquad \cos^2 x = \frac{1 + \cos 2x}{2}$$

Calculus

General Formulas:

$$\frac{d}{dx}(c) = 0$$

$$\frac{d}{dx}\left[c\,f(x)\right] = c\,f'(x)$$

$$\frac{d}{dx}\left[f(x) + g(x)\right] = f'(x) + g'(x)$$

$$\frac{d}{dx}\left[f(x) + g(x)\right] = f'(x) + g'(x)$$

$$\frac{d}{dx}\left[f(x)g(x)\right] = f(x)g'(x) + g(x)f'(x) \quad \text{(Product rule)}$$

$$\frac{d}{dx}f\big(g(x)\big) = f'\big(g(x)\big)g'(x) \quad \text{(Chain rule)}$$

$$\frac{d}{dx}\left[\frac{f(x)}{g(x)}\right] = \frac{g(x)f'(x) - f(x)g'(x)}{\left[g(x)\right]^2} \quad \text{(Quotient rule)}$$

$$\frac{d}{dx}(x^n) = nx^{n-1} \quad \text{(Power rule)}$$

$$\int u\,dv = uv - \int v\,du \quad \text{(Integration by parts)}$$

Exponential and Logarithmic Functions:

$$\frac{d}{dx}(e^x) = e^x$$

$$\frac{d}{dx}(a^x) = a^x \ln a$$

$$\frac{d}{dx}\ln|x| = \frac{1}{x}$$

$$\frac{d}{dx}(\log_a x) = \frac{1}{x \ln a}$$

$$\int \ln u\,du = u\ln u - u + C$$

Trigonometric Functions:

$$\frac{d}{dx}(\sin x) = \cos x$$

$$\frac{d}{dx}(\cos x) = -\sin x$$

$$\frac{d}{dx}(\tan x) = \sec^2 x$$

$$\frac{d}{dx}(\csc x) = -\csc x \cot x$$

$$\frac{d}{dx}(\sec x) = \sec x \tan x$$

$$\frac{d}{dx}(\cot x) = -\csc^2 x$$

$$\int \sin u\,du = -\cos u + C$$

$$\int \cos u\,du = \sin u + C \quad \int \tan u\,du = \ln|\sec u| + C$$

Inverse Trigonometric Functions:

$$\frac{d}{dx}(\sin^{-1} x) = \frac{1}{\sqrt{1 - x^2}}$$

$$\frac{d}{dx}(\cos^{-1} x) = \frac{1}{\sqrt{1 - x^2}}$$

$$\frac{d}{dx}(\tan^{-1} x) = \frac{1}{1 - x^2}$$

$$\frac{d}{dx}(\csc^{-1} x) = -\frac{1}{x\sqrt{x^2 - 1}}$$

$$\frac{d}{dx}(\sec^{-1}) = \frac{1}{x\sqrt{x^2 - 1}}$$

$$\frac{d}{dx}(\cot^{-1} x) = -\frac{1}{1 + x^2}$$

Inverse Hyperbolic Functions:

$$\frac{d}{dx}(\sinh^{-1} x) = \frac{1}{\sqrt{1 + x^2}}$$

$$\frac{d}{dx}(\cosh^{-1} x) = \frac{1}{\sqrt{x^2 - 1}}$$

$$\frac{d}{dx}(\tanh^{-1} x) = \frac{1}{1 - x^2}$$

$$\frac{d}{dx}(\operatorname{csch}^{-1} x) = -\frac{1}{|x|\sqrt{x^2 + 1}}$$

$$\frac{d}{dx}(\operatorname{sech}^{-1} x) = -\frac{1}{x\sqrt{1 - x^2}}$$

$$\frac{d}{dx}(\coth^{-1} x) = \frac{1}{1 - x^2}$$

Resources

This list identifies some resources that may help you as you study and prepare to take CSET: Mathematics. They are not a substitute for coursework or other types of teacher preparation, but may enhance your knowledge of the content covered on the examination. The references listed, moreover, are not intended to represent a comprehensive listing of all potential resources. You are not expected to read all of the materials listed here, and passage of the examination will not require familiarity with these specific resources. Resources are organized alphabetically and by content domain in the CSET: Mathematics subtest order.

Books

Algebra

Bramson, Morris. *Algebra: An Introductory Course: One-Volume Edition.* New York: Amsco School Publishing, Inc., 1987.

Jacobs, Harold R. *Elementary Algebra.* NY: W. H. Freeman and Company, 1979.

Lay, David C. *Linear Algebra and Its Applications.* 3rd ed. Boston, MA: Addison-Wesley, 2002.

Martin-Gay, K. Elayn. *Intermediate Algebra.* 3rd ed. Upper Saddle River, NJ: Prentice Hall, 2001.

Pinter, Charles C. *A Book of Abstract Algebra.* Boston, MA: McGraw-Hill Higher Education, 1990.

Usiskin, Zalman, project director. *Advanced Algebra: The University of Chicago School Mathematics Project.* 2nd ed. Glenview, IL: Scott, Foresman and Company, 2002.

———. *Algebra: The University of Chicago School Mathematics Project.* 2nd ed. Glenview, IL: Scott, Foresman and Company, 2002.

———. "First Year Algebra via Applications Development Project." Pt. I of *Algebra through Applications with Probability and Statistics.* 2nd ed. Reston, VA: National Council of Teachers of Mathematics, 1979.

———. "First Year Algebra via Applications Development Project." Pt. II of *Algebra through Applications with Probability and Statistics.* 2nd ed. Reston, VA: National Council of Teachers of Mathematics, 1979.

Wah, Anita, and Henri Picciotto. *Algebra: Themes, Concepts, and Tools.* Mountain View, CA: Creative Publication, 1994.

Number Theory

Rosen, Kenneth H. *Elementary Number Theory and Its Applications.* 3rd ed. Murray Hill, NJ: AT&T Bell Laboratories, 1993.

Geometry

Chakerian, G. D., Calvin D. Crabill and Sherman K. Stein. *Geometry: A Guided Inquiry.* Pleasantville, NY: Sunburst Communications, Inc., 1987.

Greenberg, Marvin J. *Euclidean and Non-Euclidean Geometries: Development and History.* 3rd ed. New York: W. H. Freeman and Company, 1993.

Herzog, David A. *CliffsStudySolver Geometry*. Hoboken, NJ: Wiley Publishing, Inc., 2004.

Holme, Audun. *Geometry: Our Cultural Heritage*. New York: Springer-Verlag, 2000.

Jacobs, Harold R. *Geometry*. 2nd ed. NY: W. H. Freeman and Company, 1979.

Usiskin, Zalman, project director. *Geometry: The University of Chicago School Mathematics Project*. 2nd ed. Glenview, IL: Scott, Foresman and Company, 2002.

Wallace, Edward C., and Stephen F. West. *Roads to Geometry*. 2nd ed. Upper Saddle River, NJ: Prentice Hall, 1998.

Probability and Statistics

Newmark, Joseph. *Statistics and Probability in Modern Life*. 6th ed. Philadelphia, PA: Saunders College Publishing, 1997.

Calculus

Anton, Howard. *Calculus: A New Horizon*. 6th ed. New York: John Wiley & Sons, 1998.

Goldstein, Larry J., David C. Lay and David I. Schneider. *Calculus and Its Applications*. Englewood, NJ: Prentice Hall, Inc., 1977.

Herzog, David A. *CliffsStudySolver Trigonometry*. Hoboken, NJ: Wiley Publishing, Inc., 2005.

Stein, Sherman K. *Calculus and Analytic Geometry*. NY: McGraw-Hill Book Company, 1973.

Stewart, James. *Calculus*. 5th ed. Pacific Grove, CA: Brooks Cole Publishing, 2002.

Swokowski, Earl W. *Calculus with Analytic Geometry*. Boston, MA: Prindle, Weber, and Schmidt, Incorporated, 1975.

Thomas, George B., Ross L. Finney, Maurice D. Weir, and Frank Giordano. *Thomas' Calculus*. 10th ed. Boston, MA: Addison-Wesley, 2000.

Usiskin, Zalman, project director. *Function, Statistics, and Trigonometry: The University of Chicago School Mathematics Project*. 2nd ed. Glenview, IL: Scott, Foresman, and Company, 2002.

History of Mathematics

Boyer, Carl B. *A History of Mathematics*. 2nd ed. Revised by Uta C. Merzbach. New York: John Wiley & Sons, 1991.

Courant, Richard, and Herbert Robbins. *What Is Mathematics? An Elementary Approach to Ideas and Methods*. Oxford: Oxford University Press, 1978.

Eves, Howard. *An Introduction to the History of Mathematics*. 6th ed. Pacific Grove, CA: Brooks Cole, 1990.

Suzuki, Jeff. *A History of Mathematics*. Upper Saddle River, NJ: Prentice Hall, 2002.

Web References

The Algebra Helper
www.softmath.com/ah/ah.htm

Algebrahelp.com
www.algebrahelp.com/

Ask Dr. Math®
www.mathforum.org/dr.math/

Coolmath's online graphing calculator
www.coolmath.com/calculators/index.html

e–z Geometry
www.e-zgeometry.com/

Stewart Calculus online
www.stewartcalculus.com/_

Tutorials for the Calculus Phobe
www.calculus-help.com/funstuff/phobe.html

Visual Calculus
archives.math.utk.edu/visual.calculus/

Other Resources of Interest

Brumbaugh, Douglas K., and David Rock. *Teaching Secondary Mathematics.* Mahwah, NJ: Lawrence Erlbaum Associates, Inc., 2006.

Burger, Edward B., and Michael Starbird. *The Heart of Mathematics: An Invitation to Effective Thinking.* Emeryville, CA: Key College Publishing, 2000.

Cangelosi, James S. *Teaching Mathematics in Secondary and Middle School: An Interactive Approach.* NJ: Merrill, 2003.

Lial, Margaret L., and Charles D. Miller. *Trigonometry.* 2nd ed. Glenview, IL: Scott, Foresman and Company, 1983.

Mathematics Content Standards for California Public Schools, Kindergarten through Grade Twelve. Sacramento, CA: California Department of Education, 1998.

Mathematics Framework for California Public Schools, Kindergarten through Grade Twelve. Sacramento, CA: California Department of Education, 2000.

Posamentier, Alfred S., and Jay Stepelman. *Teaching Secondary Mathematics: Techniques and Enrichment Units.* NJ: Merrill, 2002.

Rotman, Joseph J. *Journey into Mathematics: An Introduction to Proofs.* Upper Saddle River, NJ: Prentice Hall, 1997.

Stillwell, John, and F. W. Gehring. *Numbers and Geometry.* New York: Springer-Verlag, 1997.